The *New* Consecrated Cocoon

Emerging from Intimate Isolation with Power and Purpose!

Written by

Ann Thomas

SIMPLYIDEAL Publishing

ANN THOMAS

Copyright © 2015 by Ann Thomas

The NEW Consecrated Cocoon

Emerging from Intimate Isolation with Power and Purpose!

By Ann Thomas

Printed in the United States of America

ISBN 13: 978-1517483364

All rights reserved solely by the author. The author guarantees all contents are original and do not infringe upon the legal rights of any other person or work. No part of this book may be reproduced in any form without the permission of the author. The views expressed in this book are not necessarily those of the publisher.

Unless otherwise indicated, Bible quotations are taken from The Holy Bible, New Living Translation. Copyright © 1996, 2004, 2007 by Tyndale House Foundation. Used by permission; The Message. Copyright © 1993, 1994, 1995, 1996, 2000, 2001, 2002 by NavPress Publishing Group. Used by permission; The New King James Version. Copyright © 1982 by Thomas Nelson, Inc. Used by permission; The NEW AMERICAN STANDARD BIBLE®. Copyright © 1960, 1962, 1963, 1968, 1971, 1972, 1973, 1975, 1977, 1995 by The Lockman Foundation. Used by permission; The HOLY BIBLE, NEW INTERNATIONAL VERSION®. NIV®. Copyright ©1973, 1978, 1984 by International Bible Society. Used by permission of Zondervan.

www.simplyidealpublishing.com

Table of Contents

Foreword 5
What Others Say About This Book 6
Dedication 10
Acknowledgements 11
Introduction 15
Dying for a Change 35
Created on Purpose for a Purpose 46
Training to Reign 56
Metamorphosis – The Great Exchange 70
CREATION 77
   Born Identity 78
   Eve – Bad Apple or the Apple of God's Eye? 97
   Created to Be Blessed - Not Cursed 116
PREPARATION 132
   Parents – Set Up or Set Back 133
   Leaving and Cleaving 163
CONSECRATION 176
   Set Up to Be Set Apart 177
   I Surrender All 189
   God's Power Versus Ours 205
   Intimacy with God – It's Personal 229
TRANSFORMATION 239
   I'm Coming Out 241
   Wave-Walking Power 247
   Possessing the Promise 254
   Divine Positioning 261
Going All the Way 263

Please Pray With Me	266
About the Author	268
A Message from Ann to You	269
Other Books	270

Foreword

Willie L. Benton III, Author

WARNING! This book was written with the assistance of the Holy Spirit, and has the power to radically transform your way of thinking and dramatically change your life.

Ladies, this is a MUST READ book that details your common struggle and vividly describes the remarkable end result - victory in Christ Jesus!

Gentlemen, this is a MUST READ book that offers incredible insight into what a woman goes through to become a queen. The woman of God she was created to be. Empowered to do what she was created to do.

It is very seldom that we look to nature to understand and explain what transpires within us and in our lives, yet Ann does an incredible job of doing just that. Brilliant and Spirit-filled, she masterfully chronicles and compares the metamorphosis of a caterpillar to the life-transforming changes undertaken by the woman of God. In nature, this process yields a beautiful butterfly ready to soar. In life, this process yields a powerful and confident queen ready to claim her crown. A queen ready to inherit her throne. A queen ready to pursue her God-given destiny. Her purpose.

Not only is Ann immensely intelligent, gifted, and witty; but she is also unbelievably transparent as she candidly shares from her personal struggles. She will have you crying, laughing, and shaking your head in disbelief at the same time. She keeps it so real you can't help but to relate. You can't help but see yourself, your mother, your sister, or your friends in her situations.

You have been WARNED! Now sit back, relax, and allow the Holy Spirit to have His way as you devour this thought-provoking work. Be open to receive. Be fed. Be blessed.

ANN THOMAS

What Others Say About This Book

Below are some of the comments posted to Amazon by men and women who read the first edition of "The Consecrated Cocoon" published in 2012.

"I have read and re-read Ann Thomas' book at least three times now, and I have to say I glean something new that I've missed during the first two times! I'm sure I'll be reading it again! This book takes you right to the heart of seasons in life what they could mean, how to effectively deal with each season through the grace of God. This speaks to my situation in my life on so many levels. The metaphor of the life cycle of a butterfly is perfectly in synchronization with the anointed and inspired writing of this book. I was and still am, blessed by the help and understanding this book achieves. I recommend it for anyone and everyone going through a solitude or isolating season in their life." ~ Laura

---

"Wow! Really just scratching the surface of this GOD appointed book and this book will not stay out of my hands. I feel like the contents of this book are powerful enough for a man, but aimed at a woman. As I read, it was so easy for me to connect with everything that was going on. For every three ladies that read this book, one man should be enlightened as well. Gotta go more to read!" ~ Cleo

---

"I have been reading this book since it came out. Not because it's hard to get through, but because I've been using it as a life study! Ms. Thomas takes us on a journey unlike any other. You will laugh and cry! A book that can be enjoyed by men and women! Buckle your seat belts tho! You're in for the ride of your life!" ~ Maria

"This book is a true enhancement to my literary collection. It is the kind of book that you can read and re-read and get spiritual rejuvenation every time! Ann so eloquently parallels the personal relationship one goes through with God as it relates to the process of a caterpillar's metamorphosis to a butterfly. Just as Mother Nature designed the caterpillar to go through stages of change, God does the same by strategically refining and molding us to expose our true beauty and destiny. Thank you Ann for providing a resource for women to better understand the level of intimacy required by our father in order to live to our fullest potential." ~ Maalikah

---

"This book is truly a masterpiece that touches the dynamics of womanhood. The spiritual content as well as the real life experience is sure to connect every reader with a need for a profound and deeper relationship with the Lord. Ms. Thomas is a gifted minister and it shows in her writing. This book is a must-have for both women and men. I'm giving this book 10 stars!" ~ Anonymous

---

"Often we wonder why our lives go in the direction they do. Sometimes we think God may have even forgotten about us on this journey we call life. The truth is we must be stripped and reborn. Ann Thomas has shared her story of rebirth and allowed us to join in on her journey. I for one am honored and blessed. It's a book you can read over again and gain even more insight. This was everyone's present this past Christmas. Worth every penny and every moment it took to read it." ~ Ebony

---

"I have a huge library of many top speakers and writers. I came across Ann's Facebook page out of nowhere. I have to say this woman is one of the most amazing souls I have ever come across. I was in the midst of the storm and this book changed my world! Not only is she true to who she is by following her on Facebook but this book will touch your soul and you will never be the same! Ann is at the top of my list and

I so can't wait for the next book. A mighty warrior and amazing things are going to happen for this amazing woman!" ~ Pennie

----

"I highly recommend this incredible book!! I personally am not one to like reading books... I'd rather watch the movie! Lol. But when I picked it up it captivated me and I couldn't put it down! It was passed midnight before I had to force myself to stop reading it because I had to get up early for work! I laughed, I cried and I truly was touched and changed by her words of wisdom!!! It encouraged me be a stronger woman!!

Thank you Ann for being so transparent." ~ Nicole

"I must confess, I am not a "reader," but I could not put this book down! It has changed my life in so many ways, and the Lord put on my heart, friends that I needed to bless with this amazing book as well. Read it...share it...watch your life transform." ~ Patricia

----

"I do not have enough space to write all that the Consecrated Cocoon did for me. This book came to me at a time when I was definitely in my cocoon, but didn't know what was happening. I found myself relating to the Author in so many ways, and what peace and comfort it brought to know, that what I was going through was a process, and that on the other side of it, what was to come, would make the process So worth it. Although this book is geared to women, it is certainly not limited to women, I personally know men who have read this book and found themselves not wanting to put it down because they too were in the process of the cocoon." ~ Debra

----

"This book has a lot to chew on. I can't tell you how many times I go back and re-read a chapter because it captured a particular situation I was going through. It helped me understand the "whys" and the "why nots" of God's perfect timing. Perfect for teaching, devotionals or just sharing with others. It is definitely a must read! Thank you Ann, for sharing your story." ~ Nancy

---

"Ms. Ann Thomas is very transparent in this book. God really used her to talk to me and cause me to self-reflect and reevaluate my priorities. Ms. Ann, thank you for sharing your truth and continue to do what you are anointed to do because it is helping young women like myself step out of fear and shame and showing us that just because something is hard doesn't mean it is impossible. Faith in God, perseverance, and the ability to hear God's voice and being obedient to it will change lives." ~ Kesha

---

"I found this book to be a great read for all. Ms. Thomas did an excellent job in being transparent and allowing God to use her to minister to her needs as well as the needs of many others. In her transparency she allowed you to know her intimately and share in her pain, disappointments, happiness, and the love and peace she found as she evolved into the person God created her to be. I believe all can benefit from reading this captivating book!" ~ Philiece

---

"This book has truly helped me over the past month or so of reading it. It seems as if Ms. Ann Thomas prayed over this book and asked God to let it be a revelation to every individual's life. I am in an area of growth in my cocoon and this book has helped me have a better understanding of what I am going through. The bible and The Consecrated Cocoon has been my go-to; if I am not reading the bible, then I am reading this book. This book applies to anyone's life who is TRULY seeking God's face, answers, direction, and His will. This is a must read. God bless you Ms. Ann Thomas!" ~ Arnesjah

Dedication

This book is dedicated to my Lord and Savior Jesus. I don't say that to sound cliché. I say it because it's true.

I am grateful for Jesus my Savior, who saved me from hell when I was eleven years old. And He continues to save me daily. He saves me from myself and from the wicked schemes of the enemy.

I am grateful for His Lordship. I desire to be obedient and live a life that pleases Him. On many days I don't get it right, but I thank God He loves me for who I am (His), not what I do.

I love Jesus with all of my heart. #SoldOutforChrist

Acknowledgements

I would like to thank all (family and friends) who have supported and believed in the gifts God has placed in me. I am grateful for your unconditional love.

Your prayers, words of encouragement, and spiritual counsel continues to be a needed and priceless gift in my life.

May I continue to make my Jesus proud as I endeavor to make HIS name great and advance His Kingdom!

ANN THOMAS

YOU WERE CREATED TO SOAR

ANN THOMAS

THE NEW CONSECRATED COCOON

Introduction

Life has a way of throwing painful, unexpected, and unwanted curve balls at us. Sometimes we are able to see it coming and brace ourselves for the impact. But most times, a curve ball appears out of nowhere and knocks us off our feet. Like a category five hurricane it rummages through the belongings of our hearts and leaves us devastated.

We may be able to salvage some things, but life as we knew it ceases to exist.

Unfortunately, I entered into my first serious relationship at sixteen years old (as serious as sixteen gets), and it lasted three painstaking years. During this time, I experienced a lot of losses: virginity, dignity, innocence, self-respect, and self-worth. This wasn't that young man's fault, or even my own. At sixteen years old you just don't know what you don't know. And therefore we often learn some lessons the hard way.

Once that relationship ended, I found myself attracted to a certain type of guy and my standards for what would be considered a healthy relationship were very low. From there, additional relationships simply reinforced my lack of self-worth and lowered the bar of expectation on what I believed I deserved.

In December of 1988, I met a young man who broke that vicious cycle. And through that relationship, I had my first true to life curve ball experience. He was my knight in shining armor. When we first met, we were instantly attracted to each other. However, as I got to know him, he was more than a gorgeous smile; he respected me. He had good home training. He made me feel very special. He was in the military and was trying to make a life for himself. We had a lot of fun together.

At that time, I had my own apartment, so we'd spend a lot of time together on the weekends. It's amazing that when young, we enjoy each day as it comes without bothering with the full picture. When we are young, we have such a false sense of being invincible. We tend to think that we have our whole life to correct things and figure things out. In the short time we knew each other, we did discuss the future. We talked about getting married. He wanted me to meet his family that lived in another state. But for now, we enjoyed each day as it came.

During the month of April, I brought up the subject of church. We shared our feelings about God, Christians in general, and our salvation experiences. I was eleven years old when I asked Jesus into my heart, but since then had not attended a church regularly or consistently. As I reflect back, it is clear to me that the tugging at my heart was God trying to get my attention. He wanted to reconnect with me. Though I didn't understand it at the time, I did have a desire to find a church and attend with my boyfriend. He was also a Christian, and therefore wasn't opposed to the idea of going to church. But he shared that due to his military lifestyle, his wardrobe was very limited. Other than his uniform, his closet was filled with jeans, shorts, and athletic wear. And for us at that time, none of these were acceptable church wear. Of course times have changed; and I mean changed!

So we tabled the conversation. But two weeks later, I'm standing in a nightclub on the military base waiting for him to arrive. It was a Friday evening and we were unwinding from a long and busy week. And to my surprise, he walked in wearing a nice pair of slacks and a button down shirt. He looked good! He was so incredibly handsome. Tall, great physique, dreamy eyes, and a killer smile. I was so proud as I watched him walk across the dance floor. He took my hand and asked me to dance. While dancing we talked about his new wardrobe. I encouraged him to dress that way more often. Deep down, I was excited because I knew, though he never said it, that we would soon be heading to church.

A couple of weeks later, on a Tuesday I made a special trip on my lunch hour to eat with him at a Burger King on the military base. I picked him up from the dorm and en route to

THE NEW CONSECRATED COCOON

our lunch spot we saw a minor fender bender. If you are familiar with military bases, you know that the speed limit is typically between 25-30 miles per hour and the military police will pull you over in a heartbeat. And therefore, accidents were far and few. So few that he commented, "In the couple of years I've been stationed here, that's the first accident I've seen."

We arrived at our destination, ordered our food and sat across from each other, smiling and talking. I was laughing so much I could hardly eat. He had a way of cracking me up. I don't remember much of our conversation; I simply remember heading back to work smiling and thinking, "That was one of the best times we've spent with each other. Ever!"

Memorial Day was approaching, which meant a nice long weekend. And this also meant he would spend it with me. I couldn't wait. Thursday afternoon he called my apartment before I arrived home and left a message on my answering machine. He and his buddy were getting fresh haircuts for the weekend. I listened to the message, smiled, and didn't mind because I knew we would be together later that evening. Around 7pm, he called to say he was invited by a few friends to go to a nightclub off base. I was upset. I had my heart set on seeing him that evening. Instead I would now see him the next day. I pouted over the phone. I wanted him to know I was unhappy.

Being sensitive to my feelings he asked, "Baby, when I have free time, who do I spend it with?" I reluctantly answered, "Me."

He continued, "And how often do I ask you to hang out with the fellas?"

Again, with reluctance I responded, "Hardly ever." How could I say no? He did spend a lot of time with me. So with that, we said our good-byes, but because of my disappointment and immaturity, I did not say my usual "I love you."

That evening, I visited an old friend. We had fun. We laughed and caught up. But I couldn't wait to get back home and speak with my honey. I arrived home at 11pm and checked my messages. No new messages. Only the one he had left earlier about the haircuts. He typically called from a pay phone to let me know he was thinking of me. But he didn't that night. That didn't stop me from sleeping like a baby because I looked forward to our long weekend together.

The next morning, my mom woke me with a phone call at a little after 5am. I answered and she engaged me in a little small talk. She asked how I was doing and whether my boyfriend was with me. She knew he was due to come over the night before. I told her he didn't make it, but I would see him later that day. She paused. Then I asked what was wrong. She had been watching the news and they reported that a terrible accident had happened on the base. She said it was so bad, they were withholding the names of the ones involved and it appeared there had been fatalities. She just wanted to ensure my boyfriend was safe. I quickly reassured her that everything was fine. We hung up and I forced myself to go back to sleep for another half hour or so.

I arrived at work a little before 9am, and the red light indicating I had a voice mail message was lit on my work phone. This was odd. I didn't typically receive work-related calls or messages that early. I listened to the voice message, and it was a former co-worker and friend. Oddly enough, she said she was calling to see how I was doing and to call her back. I erased the voicemail and started getting myself together to start the day. Then my phone rang.

I answered and heard what sounded like the phone being shuffled around from person to person. Then another dear friend of mine who works with the one who left the voice message spoke up.

I later learned that I threw everyone for a loop when I answered the phone (hence the shuffling around of the phone) because that meant I was unaware of what they needed to share.

She asked how I was doing, and I said fine. Then she asked when the last time I spoke with my boyfriend was. Okay, now I was becoming concerned. I told her that I'd spoken to him the previous day before he went to the club. Why?

Apparently, another co-worker's husband worked in the same squadron as my boyfriend and he contacted his wife when the names of those involved in the accident were released.

While waiting for a response, I reached for my purse and my car keys. "OK, so he was in the accident? How bad is he? He's in the hospital on the base, right?" She didn't respond, so I continued. "I gotta go. I need to call someone so they can vouch for me to get on the base." I finally paused and asked, "How bad is he?"

The phone went silent and then I heard the phone shuffle hands again. At this point another friend took the phone and said hello.

I asked again. "How bad is he?" She said, "Ann, he's dead."

I forgot I was at work. I screamed at the top of my lungs, "No!" I hung up on her and called the dormitory. There was a hall phone that I knew someone would answer. It rang several times and then one of the guys answered. I knew the guy who picked up the phone. I asked to speak with my boyfriend.

He replied, "He's not in."

I said, "Please tell me the truth. Was he in that accident?"

He broke into tears. I hung up. Suddenly, some sort of shock took over my system. My thoughts immediately became scrambled and I experienced an adrenaline rush like never before. My co-workers later told me that I began screaming, then snatched my purse and keys and headed for the elevator. They apparently tried to stop me from leaving, but said I fought them off and pushed my way into the elevator. Honestly, I don't remember anything that happened between hanging up the phone and finding myself on the interstate driving like a mad woman.

About ten minutes after I left my job, my mom and sister arrived. They had learned an hour earlier that it was in fact my boyfriend and two other guys involved in the deadly accident. My boyfriend and another dear friend of ours were passengers. Without getting too much into the details, the person driving, someone I had never met before apparently missed a crucial turn. They were all but two minutes from the dorm. The street leading to the dorm had a sharp curve that required slowing down. And rather than mash the brakes, the driver mashed the gas instead. This wasn't a fender bender like we had seen earlier that week. It was the worst accident that military base had experienced to date.

When I left my job, I remember screaming the entire way. I was heading home. To this day I don't know why I chose home. I was just heading home. I was on the interstate dangerously exceeding the speed limit and screaming at the top of my lungs the entire time. I made it home. Ran into my apartment. Dropped my keys and purse and fell to my knees. Honestly, I was beside myself. I didn't know what to do. I called my mom. No answer. Then something told me to call my job and let them know I was home. They informed me my mom and sister had come looking for me and were headed to my place. I hung up the phone, opened my front door, and walked outside. In the distance I saw my mom and sister walking toward me at a hurried pace. And the look on their faces confirmed my worst nightmare. I ran into my mother's arms and bawled.

Life's curveball – I didn't see it coming.

I laid on my parents' couch the remainder of Friday and all day Saturday. I didn't eat and hardly spoke. When I opened my mouth it was to cry. I curled up in a fetal position. I wanted to go to sleep hoping I would wake up and learn it was all a cruel nightmare. But I couldn't sleep due to the hundreds of thoughts running through my mind. Why didn't I say I love you when we last spoke? I wonder if we would have made it to church whether this would have happened. Why didn't I insist

THE NEW CONSECRATED COCOON

that he come to my place Thursday night instead of letting him to go to the nightclub? Who was this driver and how could he come into the picture to bring this type of pain? How in the world could the sun possibly rise and the birds sing outside?

Everything in the world needs to just stop; life can't possibly move forward. Did God allow this? Is this my punishment for not getting to church sooner? I finally found someone who loves me and respects me and I lose him this way? I never met his family; how could I possibly go to his funeral? They live in another state and don't even know me. Before now, I never wanted to die. But now I don't care if I do.

By God's amazing grace and tremendous love for me, one of my girlfriends called that Saturday evening, and I agreed to speak with her. I rejected all other calls that weekend. I didn't want to speak to anyone. I didn't want to hear someone acknowledge the loss because it would make it real. I still wanted to deny it happened. After all, I didn't see it happen with my own eyes. I never saw his body. I had his clothes hanging in my closet and some of his belongings in my apartment. I had the last voice mail message he left, where he was alive and perfectly fine. I was not ready to accept this and I didn't want to speak with anyone who would try to convince me otherwise. But for some reason I accepted this particular friend's call. And she invited me to her church.

This was a Saturday night. And although everything in me wanted to decline, I felt like I had reached the depths of despair. I didn't believe it could get any worse. There *had* to be a way for me to find hope. There had to be hope. Even though at that time I sensed none, I accepted the invitation. It had to be better than lying on the couch for another day. That was the only plan I had.

When I arrived at church the next day, the God I met was not at all who I thought He was. He wasn't the God of rules or punishment. He didn't remind me that I had started a relationship with Him almost thirteen years earlier and had walked away. He didn't lecture me about not being at church more often. He didn't bring up all the bad things I did to guilt me into wanting more of Him. Instead I met a God who is full of love and compassion.

A forgiving God. A God whose arms had been wide open waiting for the day I would return to Him. There was a special spot in His heart for me that He guarded and protected while He waited.

I met a God whose love I had yearned and searched for for twenty three years. That Sunday, I returned home. Home wasn't the church, though that was the vehicle God used; home was my special spot in God's heart. I took my rightful place in His heart and began the difficult but rewarding work of allowing Him to take His rightful place in my heart as Lord, lover, friend, and Father.

For all of my precious sisters reading this book, I stopped by today to let you know that God has a special place in His heart for you. Maybe you've occupied it once before and like me, walked away. Or maybe you've never claimed it. Either way, God doesn't put someone else in our spot. He preserves it. He cherishes it. He watches over it. He saturates it with love awaiting our return. Unfortunately, it often takes a tragedy or hardship to remind us of the place that is designed uniquely for us. If only more women would realize that in this special place, God wants to show, teach, and reveal life-altering and mind-blowing truths.

Some of you reading this book are smack dab in the middle of a curve ball. You didn't ask for it. You didn't encourage it, but you are there nonetheless.

Or maybe you are coming out of a difficult situation and are snuggling into your renewed faith and trust in God. Or some of you might be fortunate enough to have not experienced a life-changing curve ball in a while. And if that's you – praise God! But I hate to be the bearer of bad news – it truly is just a matter of time. No one is exempt from hard times.

Life is full of both mountaintop and valley experiences. We can't remain on the mountain forever; nor can we remain in the low, despairing valley forever.

THE NEW CONSECRATED COCOON

No matter where you are in the curve ball spectrum, I want to encourage you that it's not over until God says it is. There is always an extra inning. There is always overtime. There is always another quarter. So don't be so eager to quit. Don't be so quick to wave your white flag of surrender and don't prematurely embrace an attitude of defeat. Don't let hopelessness rob you of the future God has for you. There is always purpose in your pain. A message in your mess. A testimony in your test. But even more, there is great praise that will come forth from your pressure.

God is with you. He will never leave you. But your enemy, Satan wants you to believe that you are alone. He wants to convince you that no one else knows what you are experiencing. He is deceitful. He wants to tempt you to seek your own way of escape, but his exit signs always lead to a trap with greater negative repercussions. Everything Satan says is a lie. There is only one way to expose a lie – by revealing the truth.

In this book, you and I will uncover the lies of the devil and explore God's wonderful truths. His truths are packed with promises; promises that you and I can stand on. We can take them to the bank, cash them in, and enjoy returns that exceed our wildest imaginations. As we stand on God's promises, we are able to stand in the face of adversity.

Adversity is a part of life. But when surrendered to God, it is intended to refine us. It's intended to consecrate us. The word consecrate means to set apart, separate, sanctify, or make holy. God wants to set you and me apart for something wonderful. He has a purpose for us that require us to be much more than average or mediocre. Consecration is a time of preparation and it's a process. At times a very painful process, but one that's well worth it. We will discuss consecration in more detail later in this book.

Adversity serves two purposes: To draw us closer to God and allow Him to cultivate or develop Christ-like character in each of us. When we cooperate with the process, God is able to mold us into Jesus' image. He is able to reshape our thinking.

He renews our hope. He restores our joy and removes those things that hinder our ability to be more like Jesus. As God does this often painful yet wonderful work in our lives, we have to surrender our will to His. We can't be led by the desires of our natural eyes because what we see is very limited. We must allow God to lead us because He sees eternity. He sees more than just today. He sees you a year from now after the initial sting of devastation has subsided. He sees the promise beyond your pain.

When you go through hard times, both God and Satan pursue you. They pursue you because of your potential. God created you and therefore He knows what you are capable of. And so He comes after you with the desire to use your pain as a launching pad toward the wonderful things He has for you. Satan, on the other hand, also knows your potential, and he's intimidated. He realizes that you will be a force he can't reckon with when you walk in your God-given power and authority. So he uses your pain to subdue you, to keep you bound and to abort God's plans for you.

God passionately pursues you because He loves you. However, Satan is hunting you down because he hates you. He hates Jesus and if you have Christ in you, you are also his enemy. Satan is persistent and pushy in his pursuit because he is after one thing – your destiny. Satan is not more powerful than God. He doesn't have the ability to steal anything that God says is yours. But he can cause you to forfeit your God-given inheritance by placing doubt in your mind regarding God's love for you. He uses distractions, discouragement, and disappointments. When doubt sets in, trust leaves because they cannot co-exist in the same heart.

What happens when we lose trust and belief? We lose hope. If Satan can convince you to give up all hope in a better future, then he has succeeded in stealing the plans God has specifically for you. As I lay on the couch that dreaded weekend in 1989, I felt hopeless. I questioned whether I wanted to live. What if Satan had convinced me to do something drastic? I wouldn't have given birth to my wonderful sons. I wouldn't be writing this book. I wouldn't be making a difference in the lives of women who God has so graciously allowed me to touch.

Did I see all of this while lying on the couch? Of course not! I couldn't see past my pain. And that's what the enemy wants – to blind us with hopelessness. Do you ever wonder how a person arrives at the decision to take his or her own life? They do so because they are convinced that there is no hope. They can't see beyond their current circumstance. Hopelessness causes people to make permanent decisions to fix a temporary problem. How awful is that?

Losing hope in our future is essentially the same as losing hope in God. Satan tries to convince us that God has forgotten about us or that He doesn't care and has given up on us. Losing hope in the one and true living God ushers in the desire to seek other gods – created gods. I'm talking about gods such as, money, titles, ministry, and relationships that we are dependent upon to define who we are. And unfortunately, during times of great adversity, these false gods reveal their inability to heal our pain. Their ineffectiveness becomes glaringly obvious. And when we choose a false god over the one and only God, He leaves us to our so-called gods to experience the reality of their powerlessness.

In our seasons of adversity, God desires to bring us closer to Him. Closer than ever before. It's a time of deep intimacy. And at times, this intimacy with God can feel very lonely. At times it can feel as if God and everyone around you has forgotten about you, overlooked you, or cast you aside. But nothing could be further from the truth. When you enter into deeper intimacy with God, every other distraction must be removed. He must have your undivided attention so it's just you and Him.

Complete intimacy with God can be difficult, unfamiliar, and uncomfortable. Yet the time you spend with God is priceless. If you allow Him to do what He needs, you will experience His love like never before and emerge from that time of intimacy with a renewed outlook on life and an unquenchable trust in Him. If you were hopeless going in, you come out convinced that God's plan for you is never to harm you, but to give you a future and a hope (Jeremiah 29:11).

As I shared earlier, life is full of peaks and valleys or seasons. And just like nature, we also experience spiritual winters, spring times, summers, and falls. God does something different in each season and is always preparing you for the next one. Therefore, it's important to have an idea of which season you are in so you can cooperate with and not hinder the process.

During your spiritual winter season, everything feels like it's at a standstill. It's a time of dormancy that will lead you to question whether God has forgotten you. You can't see any activity with your natural eye. However, activity is in fact occurring, and you must trust God's heart when you don't know what His hand is doing. This season requires you to dig your spiritual roots even deeper through increased intimacy with God.

The spring season is your time to sow and invest. What are you sowing? Whatever you desire to reap. You will find yourself fighting against Satan's attempts to discourage or distract you from achieving specific assignments. The summer season is a time of reaping and great favor. During this time you must vigilantly guard your blessings and press forward because Satan is out to place doubt in your mind and will use others to come against you. The fall season is a tough one because God has blessed you in the previous season, and now He is looking for a sacrifice. He's asking you to give back what He gave you so He can do even greater things with it. If you are willing to give it all back to Him, He will multiply what you gave Him. But you must be willing to lose in order to gain.

There is a tendency to want to hurry through a season we don't like, but that defeats the purpose of what God is doing. We often want to avoid the challenges and get to the good part – the reward. We look forward to the payoff. But as we meet, greet, and defeat the challenges for each season, our resolve is strengthened, and we develop a fighting spirit that refuses to let the devil keep us from what is rightfully ours.

THE NEW CONSECRATED COCOON

How do you know when you are ready to go to the next season? When God releases you. God's release is accompanied by opened doors of opportunity and closed doors of completion. He will allow certain activities to cease and new activities to begin. In each season God has something for you that's needed for your next one. So you must never exit a season prematurely to escape something you don't want to deal with or to obtain something that isn't yours to have yet. Prematurely exiting a season can abort God's plans and cause you to enter into your next season before your time like a premature birth.

A preemie is a baby that is born before her organs are developed enough to survive outside the mother's womb. Premature births put babies at a great risk for complications, to include disabilities and obstacles to their growth and mental development. In other words, when you exit a season where God is still preparing you and prematurely enter into a new season, you will not function at your full capacity. Your spiritual organs are not fully developed. Therefore you will be disabled or limited in the things of God and will experience complications due to your underdeveloped spiritual character.

When you are in a season that feels unbearable, know that God is closer than ever before. Yes, it will feel like you are being squeezed, but God needs to empty you of yourself so He can fill you with more of Him. I've heard it said, "If you want to know what a man [woman] is made of, squeeze him (her)." Settle it now – as a Christian you will be squeezed. You will encounter hardship and adversity. But rest assured that God will see you through. Psalm 34:19 says the righteous will have many afflictions, but God promises to deliver us from all of them. So let him squeeze you.

So what will you discover about yourself when squeezed? Will faith or doubt ooze from your inner being? Will you be tempted to seek relief by erecting a false god to rescue you? Spiritual squeezing reveals what's really there, not what we want others to think is there.

Let's face it. At some point in life, we all learned how to manage our appearance. We've mastered the ability to hide what's really going on inside with an "I've got it all together" demeanor. We flash fake smiles, lift unholy hands, and sing songs from our minds rather than our hearts – because we are not being real with God. You might be able to fool some of the people all of the time, and maybe even yourself most of the time, but you can't fool God any of the time. God already knows what's in each of us. The squeezing is for us to come face to face with reality so we can choose (desire) God's healing power in our lives.

The squeezing is a time of refinement – similar to the process of a silversmith who refines impure silver into a pure metal. He begins by holding the impure silver over a fire and allows the fire to heat it. He holds the silver in the middle of the fire where the flames are the hottest. This is done to burn the impurities away. The silversmith is patient and remains with the silver the entire time. He doesn't set it down and check back on it from time to time because he knows that if left in the fire for too long, the silver will be completely destroyed. So he waits and watches.

What is he watching for? A sign that the silver is free of all impurities and is ready to be removed from the fire. How does he know the silver is ready? Because he sees his reflection in the silver. How does God know when we are ready to be released from that time of squeezing? He sees His reflection in us. The Bible says that God knows where we are headed, so when He tests us, we will come out as pure gold [Job 23:10]. God doesn't test us for the purpose of failure or defeat. His tests are to strengthen us and show us that we have the victory.

The fire is not to consume us. It's to empower us. Refining fire is "friendly fire," designed to remove impurities such as lust, rebellion, pride, jealousy, envy, idolatry, self-sufficiency, unforgiveness, resentment, offense, gossip, and self-pity. And the list goes on.

Before wrapping up this chapter, I must share how God placed the seed that gave birth to this book into my heart.

THE NEW CONSECRATED COCOON

Believe it or not, the concept for this book was given to me before I knew how profoundly personal it would become.

Almost a year ago, God literally dropped a curiosity in my mind about the caterpillar metamorphosis process. Like many people, I seldom thought of the caterpillar because the butterfly represents such beauty. The butterfly represents a freedom we are all inspired by. But this day, God put the caterpillar on my heart. One afternoon I grabbed my laptop and conducted a search on the caterpillar metamorphosis process. Hundreds of pictures were readily available at my fingertips.

I saw pictures of mama butterflies laying their eggs. Pictures of hatching eggs from which baby caterpillars that resembled worms emerged. There were intriguing pictures of the caterpillar growing and shedding its skin. And then... the caterpillar went into its cocoon for a season of isolation and transformation. From that emerged a beautiful butterfly. I saw the end result, but wanted to know exactly what that caterpillar went through in that secret place to prepare for such a beautiful ending. So I searched some more.

I found a video that showed the actual process of the transformation. I watched in amazement at God's creativity and attention to marvelous details. I was floored. The changes the caterpillar experienced were radical. Then I witnessed the slow but sure emergence of the butterfly; and I was almost brought to tears. Then God spoke to me. He shared that the transformation process I witnessed is similar to that of a Christian. God instantly showed me the correlations, and I was totally inspired to write this book.

Writing has always been a passion of mine. Since the tender age of eight, when I wrote my first book, I knew I was destined to be a writer. I remember presenting the finished book to my mom. It was handwritten, held together by scotch tape, and the cover was beautifully designed with good old Crayola crayons. I was proud. In my mind I was published. From then on, I wrote poems, songs, and short stories. I loved to write. My favorite subject in elementary, high school, and college was writing. If I could write an essay for math, science, and history, I totally would. From eight years old until now, I enjoy writing as a form of expression and encouragement. And the more I draw closer to God and the more wonderful things He does in my life, I desire to share about it through writing.

Although I was pretty excited about the new revelations I received regarding the metamorphosis process, I had to be sure whether this was in fact what God wanted me to write about. So I prayed about it. And I prayed about it. As charged up as I was about this entire concept, God didn't immediately answer me. And I knew I could not get in front of God. I had to wait for His timing and His release.

That week while at my scheduled hair appointment, I shared what God had shown me with my stylist Nikki. Not knowing the details of the metamorphosis process, she was intrigued. Then, I shared the correlation between that process and the trials and triumphs of a Christian; and like me she was taken aback. She was moved. Okay, that was part of the confirmation I needed. I wasn't crazy after all. There was something there to further explore and share. Her response made me even more excited about the possibility of sharing this message with other women. The more I shared, the more we both got goose bumps and I knew then that God and I were on to something.

Interestingly enough, a week earlier, my husband (now my ex-husband) told me he wanted a divorce. And among other things I shared with Nikki, I mentioned that as well. I wasn't depressed, crying, or even worried because my marriage had seen its share of problems, but we managed to work them out. I made up my mind to trust God. I wanted God's will and not mine. I did not want a divorce. My prayer was for healing and restoration in my marriage. After listening to me talk for quite some time, Nikki stopped styling my hair, swung my chair around, looked me in the face, and said, "Ann, you are the butterfly."

I wish I could tell you that I had a profoundly deep and spiritual answer to this wonderful revelation God had given her. But that was not the case. With all of the Scriptures I'd memorized and the Christian lingo I had picked up over the years, I simply looked at her and said, "OK." If any of you have ever watched "The Fresh Prince of Bel Air," it was a Hillary response. "Ayykay."

Little did I know that the next ten months would literally be my metamorphosis process. To date, it has been the single most difficult time of my life. Anything attached to me that could be tested was tested. Where my faith was weak, the process exposed it. Where my identity was misplaced, God pointed it out. Where my ability to totally surrender to and trust God completely was lacking, the process uncovered it.

I recently shared this story with a dear friend of mine and I said, "I wonder if Nikki would have said, 'Ann, you are the caterpillar,' if I would have realized my cocoon season was coming."

My girlfriend replied, "God gave your hairstylist a picture of the end result. He didn't give her a picture of the process you would endure."

Then it dawned on me. When I finally realized what was happening to me, Nikki's words came back to me as clearly as the day she spoke them. As I remembered her words, it gave me a hope. It encouraged me to remain faithful in my transformation process because I knew the end result. That's powerful, ladies.

My main desire for sharing this book with you is to encourage you about your end result. If you trust God and faithfully persevere (with God) through your hard time - you too will soar higher than you could ever imagine and experience a freedom you didn't know was possible.

A couple of weeks after our initial conversation, I went back to Nikki's and we talked some more. I shared that I had been toying with the idea of stepping out in faith and securing a publishing company for my book. I did some checking around and it was not cheap. Then I shared that God was placing it in my heart that I was to take a step forward in faith and that He would do the rest. She agreed with me. And even more, she encouraged me. I prayed about it. I did my research. And I prayed about it some more. God gave me a peace to move forward. By the next time I went to get my hair done, I had signed a publishing contract and we rejoiced together.

At first, I kept the writing of my book sacredly close. In the beginning, Nikki was the only one who knew because I trusted her. Trusting Nikki is no light feat – she earned it. To date, Nikki has been my one and only hairstylist since the mid to late 80's and I have not entrusted the care of my hair to anyone else. Nikki is a mighty woman of God. She has been faithful in the gifts God has given her and she goes out of her way to bless others. Therefore, I drive an hour each way to get my hair done and to spend time with her. She is a good stylist, but that's not why I drive that far. I go because she loves the Lord and she is not just concerned with my hair; she is concerned about me as a whole.

When I arrive at her salon, we have church – just she and I. Sometimes other stylists or customers are within ear shot and they get a dose of what we're talking about. We laugh, cry, and often give God the glory for His goodness. We encourage each other and when with her, not only is my hair renewed but so is my spirit. She encouraged me during a time that I needed someone to believe in me. I thank God for placing Nikki in my life. I've tried explaining to her how God used her mightily, and I'm not sure she understands the full magnitude. But whether she does or doesn't, she always gives God the credit.

So here I am, writing a book about a transformation process that was being played out in real-life while I was attempting to write. I wanted to ask God, "Are you serious?" But I didn't have the guts. I must be honest. It has been a tough journey. Knowing that I was going through a spiritual metamorphosis process did help a lot because at least I knew what was happening. Knowing what was going on gave me the resolve not to quit and the hope of what would be the end result. During times of great isolation, detachment, and feelings of helplessness, knowing that I was the butterfly strengthened my resolve to one day emerge from that dark place soaring. Knowing didn't minimize my pain, but it fortified my tenacity.

I would be remiss to end this chapter without speaking to the beauty of the last ten months of my life. Isolation isn't a bad thing when you are with God. My times of weakness allowed God to show Himself strong. In my times of doubt, God showed Himself faithful. In my times of need, God made a way each and every time. During my times of loneliness, God comforted me, wrapped His arms around me, and assured me of His love for me. And during my times of wanting to quit, God reminded me of the plans and the future He had set aside just for me. I experienced a level of intimacy with God that I'd never known before and for that – it was worth it all!

Beloved, God desires to deepen His intimacy with you, too. And no matter what you are facing, there is no situation that is too hard for Him. God simply needs you to take one step toward Him and He will do the rest. I cannot promise you a smooth ride. It will get bumpy at times. But I can promise you that when it's all said and done, you will finally be able to boldly step into all God has for you. And the more you surrender your will to God, the greater the power and authority to influence the lives of countless others He will give you – for His glory! Get ready. Your life will never be the same.

Before you continue reading, please pray with me.

Prayer

"Dear God, as I read this book, give me wisdom and insight. Reveal those areas you want to heal. Give me the courage to surrender everything to you. Transform me by changing the way I see myself and the way I see you. Let me see myself the way you see me. I want to understand and accept your love for me. Give me the courage to face the difficult things I may discover and the grace to allow you to heal them.

I want Your perfect will to be done in and through my life...in Jesus' name. Amen!"

It is my prayer that you will make this book yours. Write in it. Highlight what stands out to you. And be sure to take time to answer the 'Reflection' questions posed at the end of each section.

Consider keeping a notebook or journal close by to write the answers to your reflection questions. As the Holy Spirit reveals things to you, it will be important to capture it for times of meditation and/or prayer.

I suggest that you pray before reading each section. Ask God to open your heart to receive. And pray after reading each section. Ask God to reveal, heal, and seal all He shows you.

I am excited for you! I am believing for a renewed mind, which will lead to a radically transformed life.

Your sister in Christ, Ann

THE NEW CONSECRATED COCOON

Dying for a Change

During the last ten months, I became intimately involved with the word "change." Prior to this time, I had experienced a few run-ins with change, but not to this degree.

Change became both my worst enemy and my best friend. For many, the word change instills fear and more often than not provokes a variety of emotions. There are just some things in life that we can bank on and one of them is change. It's inevitable and in the life of a Christian – it is necessary.

The most difficult changes to accept or deal with are those that are unexpected or those that require us to step out of a long-standing comfort zone. You know the comfort zones I am referring to: the ones that your friends and family know exactly where to find you when your cage is rattled. Unlike a decision to change an outfit or change the message on your voice mail, changes in your attitude, actions, character, thoughts, and view-points are very difficult. Interestingly enough, many of us seem to possess the uncanny gift of identifying an area of needed change in others. How is it we are willing to place others under a microscope but want them to look at us through a telescope? We are so quick to point out flaws in others; but are less willing and even defensive when it comes to acknowledging our own areas needing change (Luke 6:42). Have you ever prayed this super spiritual prayer?

"God please change so and so." You can fill in the blanks.

In case you don't know, we serve a very patient God. For years I prayed and asked him to change my ex-husband. And it wasn't until years later I realized I was praying the wrong prayer. God was waiting for me to say, "Change me, God; change me." I can't tell you the number of times that I cried out to God to change a situation, and he changed my heart instead. I know this because the situation was the same the following day, but I had a peace from God in the midst of it.

Most of us understand that true change often requires a sacrifice. It comes with a price. But what most of us don't understand is that price has already been paid by Jesus. He died on the cross so that we could have the power to overcome those things that would keep us from becoming the women he created us to be. When you asked Jesus into your life, you gave him permission to begin the work to make you more like him.

2 Corinthians 5:17 says when we are in Christ (and Christ is in us) we are a new creation. The old things are gone and the new things are here. Well...the old stuff doesn't just up and disappear. We must work to get rid of those things that are no longer a part of our new identity and embrace those things that are. The old must go to make room for the new – they can't co-exist; one will ultimately dominate the other.

Change is hard and for the most part uncomfortable. It shakes up our comfort zone. It removes those things with which we have become familiar. The dictionary defines the word "change" as "To make radically different." It's so radical that others around you will notice there is something different. True change that begins on the inside cannot be contained for long. It's only a matter of time before others notice.

Sometimes we must bury unhealthy relationships, pride, certain dreams and personal ambitions, destructive behaviors, and self-sufficiency. Why? Because where God is taking you requires you to travel light. No unnecessary or non-productive luggage allowed. And behaviors and thoughts that are rooted in sin is excess luggage.

Based on the definition of change, I certainly have undergone several changes in the last ten months. Actually, as I think about it, God started some of the changes almost five years ago. Some were initiated by me. And then there were those unexpected ones that hit me between the eyes and turned my world as I knew it upside down. During these tough times of change, I had to accept the death of things as I knew and wanted them to be. I had to let go of certain dreams and seek God for new ones.

THE NEW CONSECRATED COCOON

When true change occurs, others around you notice – they see a difference in you. Women around me saw the difference. Some things I didn't mind them seeing and others, I would have preferred to shrink away and struggle to embrace the change in private. But it doesn't always work that way. Sometimes, God will make our time of change very public to develop our testimony so He can get the praise.

Sometimes we are aware that change is needed, yet we put it off. But, there comes a time when change becomes necessary and no matter what, we can't put it off any longer. And the change will occur whether we cooperate with it or not. It's very easy to become complacent in situations that are not healthy but dangerously familiar. So we remain. When we avoid a necessary change, we make matters worse. There are times when we bury our head in the sand, choosing to remain in denial about a situation. And this behavior literally forces God to allow or do something to grab our attention. Change requires courage. And sometimes we don't have what it takes within ourselves, but with God, all things are possible (Matthew 19:26).

Changes we don't ask for and sometimes don't deserve are difficult to embrace. And forget the ones that are unexpected. They can throw us into an emotional whirlwind. I am recently divorced, and those who are close to me can testify to the draining emotional process I endured. Some walked closely with me, while others saw the peaks and valleys of my journey from a distance.

Some days I made it to church riding on faith fumes. To be totally honest, sometimes I didn't want to be there. I know that might shock the socks off of some of you super spiritual wonder women of God. But, I promised God I would keep it real in this book. So, there you have it. Contrary to what we think about God, He actually can handle our honesty.

On some days, the last place I wanted to be was around God's people. Why? Because He would use them to encourage me out of my spiritual funk and Satan didn't want that. So he tried to keep me isolated. I thank God that most days I pushed past all feelings and went anyhow. And, ladies, that's what you must also do when in your dark and challenging places – take control of your emotions by speaking God's Word to our feelings.

There were days when I arrived at church totally broken, and before the praise team even took the stage, I was already in tears. Then, I had my days where again I pushed past my emotions and praised God with everything I had, even though I felt like I had nothing left. Did I fake it? No, I "faithed" it! And then there were days when I was able to look past my current situation and see things from God's perspective. On these days, my situation was the same or worse, but I jumped higher and praised louder than those around me. Regardless to how I showed up, God always met me right where I was.

We all deal with trials differently. Some women lose weight during a difficult time. Not me, I tend to blow up like a house. It's hard to feel good about yourself when you can't zip up the same pair of pants you comfortably wore two weeks earlier. I lost my desire to exercise. I turned to food for comfort. I wasn't getting the sleep I needed. And even more disturbing, I began to lose my hair.

Ladies, most of you will agree that our hair is like a crown. Our beauty is associated with our hair. Almost seven years ago, the health of my hair began to suffer. After conversations with a couple of specialists, I decided to go natural and rid my hair of all harmful chemicals. I wore braids for five years. When I removed them, my hair was healthy and quite long. I was so grateful to God because my hair had not been that length since my teenage years.

After learning of my husband's intent to file for divorce, I began to fight several spiritual battles. I fought against feelings of bitterness, anger, rejection, and unforgiveness. I fought to not allow unkind words come out of my mouth. I strived to continue to honor him as he was still my husband. I fought to keep my peace and joy, and to remember God's promises to me.

THE NEW CONSECRATED COCOON

Then, one day while brushing my hair, I realized there was an unusual amount of hair on the bathroom floor. At first, I wanted to deny what I thought was happening. But more and more, the floor was covered with my hair. I spoke with Nikki and we came up with a game plan. We changed hair products, and I washed my hair more often. I even changed my diet, stopped eating fast food and started drinking more water. I prayed over my hair. I laid hands on my own head and spoke God's Word. And yet, my hair was still falling out. It became painfully obvious that my hair loss was due to stress. This was no longer an emotional and spiritual battle; this had also become a physical one.

I had both good and bad days. Some days I could feel the stress even though I prayed. That's real life. And then there were days when I know I gave my worries to the Lord and felt emotionally and mentally at peace. Yet, my body was still going through its own recovery process. Ladies, stress doesn't affect just our emotions – it also affects our health. I cannot emphasize the importance of eating healthy, and getting the proper amount of sleep and exercise during times of stress. This is needed to give your body a fighting chance.

There were nights I would cry myself to sleep looking at pictures of my hair just months earlier. The difference was night and day. I experimented with different hair styles in an effort to hide what was happening, but soon it became obvious. So, I decided to grab the bull by the horns and not wait for it to run me over. Or as the world says, "I made lemonade from lemons."

I cut my hair into a short, hip style. Most people loved it. Many asked why, and my response was simply, "I decided to do something different." I did have a handful of women who commented, "I can't believe you cut off that beautiful hair." I would simply smile and keep the conversation moving. I wasn't offended by their genuine question. They didn't know. But deep down I was hurting and not wanting to give a voice to that pain.

Sisters, sometimes we can't control the things that happen to us; but we can control how we respond. I chose to rise above my situation and not allow the enemy to use my hair as a point of defeat. I figured if God loves me and cares enough about me to know the number of hairs on my head (Luke 12:7), then surely He cares about my sadness and will not allow me to experience more than I can bear.

I can hear some of you saying, "All of this because of a divorce." Well, I have two answers to that: yes and no. Yes, the possibility of divorce crushed me because marriage is very sacred in God's eyes and therefore is very serious to me. And no, because I had other life situations happening simultaneously. The devil kept trying to kick me while I was already down.

Going back to the importance of my marriage, contrary to popular belief, marriage is *not* a contract. Marriage is a covenant and there is a difference. A contract is a legally binding agreement that is only valid when both or all parties keep their commitment. When one breaks the contract, it becomes null and void. Contracts are entered into with an expected return.

When we enter into a marriage with a contract mentality, we are willing to remain only if our spouse keeps his end of the deal. As soon as we stop receiving what we believe we deserve or what we signed up for, we're ready to drop that zero and find a new hero. Sadly, way too many people have a disgustingly casual attitude toward marriage today and it breaks God's heart.

Covenant, on the other hand, is also an agreement, but it's a three-way agreement between you, your husband, and God. Legalities are not what makes this contract binding – the love of Christ does. It's not about what you can get from your marriage; it's about what you are willing to give. Your covenant is like the three-fold cord the Bible speaks of. "Though one may be over-powered, two can defend themselves. A cord of three strands is not quickly broken." (Ecclesiastes 4:12, NIV.) When you said "I do," before friends, family, and God, you were basically grabbing a hold of one strand, giving the other strand to your husband, and then placing the third strand in God's hands. And in agreement, you all said you would do whatever it takes to protect that marriage. There will be trials in a marriage. Some days you will be too weak to stand, so in comes your husband to stand by your side. Other days, you are both exhausted and you need someone to have your back – that's where God comes in. As long as you keep God in the center of your marriage, the devil cannot defeat your three-fold cord.

Giving up on a marriage literally leaves God holding that third cord all by Himself. And I was not about to leave God hanging. God believes in marriage; He created it. He knows we are not perfect. And sometimes quite frankly, we don't always make the best choices in our mates, but it doesn't matter how we enter into the marriage if God is placed and kept at the center. God will and can take any mess of a marriage and turn it into something beautiful if we are willing to give it all to Him.

I viewed my marriage as a covenant. So, I wanted to fight for it. After 15 years, I finally understood that my battle was not against flesh and blood (Ephesians 6:12). My battle was not against my husband. I was battling against the devil's plans to steal, kill, and destroy my marriage. So, I waged war on my knees. A covenant doesn't only affect you and your husband; it also affects your children, other family members, and friends. Divorce is a vicious cycle that we should be vigilant in not starting or repeating. We should be seeking to pass on a legacy or heritage of long marriage to our children.

However, let me say this. There are times when fight as you may, your spouse wants out, and there is nothing you can do about it. I don't mean nothing in a casual manner, as in standing by and watching the tragedy unfold. I mean, you've done *all* you could possibly do. You've sought Godly counsel, and with God's grace you have worked hard to allow God to make the changes needed in you. You've humbled and yielded yourself to the process and didn't hold anything back from God. When you have done all that is humanly possible by placing the outcome of your marriage in God's hands – pray for

God's grace. If your spouse changes his heart and decides to work on the marriage, you will need God's grace for the road of healing ahead. If he chooses to leave, you will need God's grace for the road of healing ahead.

That's what I did. I prayed for God's grace.

So as I struggled with the weight gain and loss of hair and sleep over an impending divorce, there were other things happening in my life.

Satan is never satisfied with hitting us with one punch!

He always looks for ways to kick us while we are down. I was also raising two wonderful sons who were going through the normal things that an 18 and 14 year-old experienced. And guess what? They needed me. I could not put them on hold. And even more, I had to constantly seek God so I would not inappropriately project my hurt, disappointment, and frustration onto them. I wish I could say that I was able to successfully accomplish that each day, but there were times that things were easily blown out of proportion because I felt like I was drowning. Have you ever felt that way? So consumed that even the simplest things become incredibly monumental? I am so thankful for God's mercy and grace, and for sons who easily forgave.

Can you relate to what I'm sharing? When it rained, it absolutely poured. While all of this was happening, I had one home in foreclosure and was forced to put my primary residence up for sale. Oh, and how could I forget my full-time job? Some days I wanted God to stop the world so I could get off. Forget my luggage and belongings; I just wanted to run. Far, far away. Deep down I knew I couldn't run. So I would collect myself, put on my spiritual gloves, turn around, and engage the fight. However, there were days when I became battle weary. And we all can get that way when the battle seems to intensify or we are fighting in the flesh.

Ladies, your battle is not against flesh and blood. My enemy was not my ex-husband. Your enemy is not your husband, kids, parents, or best friend. Your fight is against rulers and authorities in dark places (Ephesians 6:12). You are fighting a spiritual war and your enemy is Satan. God has equipped you with weapons to fight this type of war and your weapons are not of the flesh (2 Corinthians 10:4). But when you fight in the flesh, you are fighting on Satan's turf and will lose every time. He is the ruler over the flesh realm. It's like watching a fourteen year-old fight a two year-old. The two year-old has no chance of winning and neither do we. It's a fixed match. There are also times when we are steadily fighting, and God wants us to take a back seat because the battle is His not ours.

I was in a battle. And like that impure silver, I was being held over the fire. Unlike the metal that had no choice but to remain, I did have a choice. I could run from God and not allow Him to do the necessary work in my heart or I could remain, knowing I would come out refined and ready to do great things for God. Sisters, when the enemy is wreaking havoc in your camp that is not the time to abandon ship. That's not the time to throw in your towel. It's not the time to give up on God. That's the time to hold on to Him for dear life.

John 10:29 says we are secured in our Heavenly Father's hand and no one can snatch or pluck us out of His hand. However, we can choose to not remain in His hand, and sadly, some do walk away. God doesn't want prisoners. He wants us to desire to remain in His grip. To do so, we must understand there is purpose in our pain. Pain always presents an opportunity to reveal where our trust truly lies.

To serve and love God with our whole heart, our faith in Him must be unshakable. Notice I said our faith in Him. Too many of us place our faith in people and things. As long as our lives are hunky-dory, we take the credit for it and keep stepping. We develop a false sense of self-sufficiency by pointing to our good deeds or accomplishments. Oh, but when things start to unravel and we exhaust all human efforts, we then consider looking to God. God is seeking daughters whose trust is founded in what cannot be shaken – His kingdom. What does His kingdom entail? Eternal salvation, security, power, authority, victory, wisdom, unconditional love, joy, peace, and anything else you need.

Hebrews 12:28-29 says we are receiving a kingdom that cannot be shaken and therefore we should be thankful and worship God with reverence and awe. Then it goes on to say that our God is a consuming fire. What does that mean that God is a consuming fire? It means that God is holy. His holiness is a fire that burns up anything that is sinful or not holy. If we say we desire to be more like Him, then we must draw closer to Him. We must draw closer to His holy fire. When you get close to a fire, you begin to feel the heat and then if you keep getting closer, you eventually feel the flames. If we say that we desire to be holy, then the closer we get to God we will be burned – in a good way. God doesn't associate with sin. And where sin is present, God's holy fire will burn away the impurities.

Though the fire is painful, there is purpose in your pain.

God's purpose is to make you more like Him, and more usable for His kingdom. The process never feels good, but on the other side of the pain is a new assignment with your name written all over it. It's not enough to change. We must die. For the butterfly to come forth, the caterpillar has to die. Caterpillar legs, caterpillar eyes, and a caterpillar body don't match the butterfly wings that are coming.

Like the caterpillar, you must allow God to put to death any and everything that is not needed or required for the new woman He is preparing you to become. You can't have a new perspective with the same old thoughts. You can't use your lips to bless people if your mouth still proclaims defeat and dishonor. You can't stand on God's promises if you are still focusing on the pressure. God must remove those things that can be shaken so He can strengthen what remains; while making room for what's to come. It's a good time to die for your change!

God can't fill your hands with new stuff if they are already preoccupied with the old.

Reflection

1. Are you holding on to something or someone that God has told you to let go of?
2. Change comes with a cost. Is there a price you have not been willing to pay?
3. Have you developed a *false* sense of self-sufficiency or self-dependency in an area of your life?
4. How do you respond to unwanted change?
5. Are you currently fighting a spiritual battle with natural weapons?

"Investigate my life, O God, find out everything about me; Cross-examine and test me, get a clear picture of what I'm about; See for yourself whether I've done anything wrong - then guide me on the road to eternal life." Psalm 139: 23-24 [The Message]

ANN THOMAS

Created on Purpose for a Purpose

Everyone walking around on the face of the earth has a God-given purpose. We all have a primary reason for being here. There are no accidents or mistakes with God. Your birth may have been a surprise to your parents, but it wasn't a surprise to God. He was expecting you. Some of you were conceived in the worst of scenarios. But that doesn't matter because God already had a plan for your life. His plan was in place even before you were born. In fact, all of the days of your life were already written in His book (Psalm 139:16). He created you. Everything about you is deliberately unique, so get used to being you. From your squinty eyes, rough demeanor, and skin color, to your naturally blonde hair - you were marvelously and wonderfully made (Psalm 139:14). No one can be a better you than you. You make a terrible imitation of someone else.

Imitation is limitation.

We all struggle with something about ourselves that we don't like or wish we could change. Before "buy now – pay later" cosmetic surgery became popular, most women just found a way to accept that attribute we didn't quite like. If you were flat-chested, you might buy a push-up bra, but breast implants were the furthest thing from your mind. If you didn't like your wrinkles, you used Oil of Olay; rather than having shots injected in your face.

Today, as long as we can afford it (and many of us can't), getting a new nose or fake breasts is socially acceptable and even encouraged. We now have teenagers receiving boob jobs as graduation gifts, and guess who's paying for it? You've got it, the parents. What type of message are we sending to our precious young ladies? "Ah, sweetie...your brains got you through high school, but these will help you get ahead in life." Are we serious? Why are we as a society spending so much money trying to look like someone else? What does that say about our self-image?

THE NEW CONSECRATED COCOON

There's a story about a woman who died young and went to Heaven. Feeling like she was robbed of the opportunity to live her life to the fullest, she pleaded with God to give her more time on earth. He agreed and sent her back. Upon her return, she immediately got a facelift and breast implants, liposuction, and dyed her hair. A couple of weeks later she was crossing the street and a cab driver accidentally struck and killed her. When she arrived in Heaven she asked God why He allowed her to be killed again. God apologized and said, "I'm sorry but I didn't recognize you."

The truth is, God obviously would still recognize her because He created her. But I do wonder how God feels when He sees his daughter, created in His image, striving so hard to reject who He created her to be. We women tend to struggle a lot with our physical appearance, as society places so much emphasis on body shape, body size, height, hair length, hair color, and other physical attributes.

We're often tempted to compare ourselves to Hollywood models and actresses, who are habitually starving themselves, working out five hours a day, have personal trainers and chefs, and are being airbrushed in photos to look even more perfect. We can't compete with that and we shouldn't try to. The media paints pictures of women who appear flawless on the outside, but what about who they are on the inside? Many famous women today have exchanged their femininity for their sexuality. And when men look at them, they are viewed as objects, not as people. Who they are as a woman with feelings matters very little or not at all. The Bible says that man judges people by their outer appearance, but God looks at the heart (1 Samuel 16:7).

God is more concerned about your character. He's concerned with *who* you are.

It doesn't matter how much money you have. Money can't buy integrity. God desires for you to be a woman who loves unconditionally, freely forgives, keeps your word, and is filled with compassion to help others. These inner attributes are a result of Jesus living inside of you. Not what lies in your bank account. Amen?

Ladies, I am not using the "inner beauty" thing as a way to excuse your outer appearance. You're still responsible for how you maintain yourself physically. Your goal is not to be skinny. Your goal is to be healthy. Your goal isn't to look as beautiful as another woman. However, you should strive to keep your hair nicely styled. Try to keep your nails groomed and dress femininely. Your goal is to be the best looking you that you can possibly be. God perfectly joined together your inner and outer attributes into a beautiful and unique package called [insert your name here].

A beautiful African American sister of mine is very dark skinned, and while in school together, our classmates (including other African Americans) regularly made fun of her. They called her cruel names and hurled ugly insults disguised as tasteless jokes. Sometimes, she would laugh along with everyone trying to stifle the hurt deep inside. Though I sometimes stuck up for her, it wasn't enough. She needed to know that she was precious in God's sight. She needed to know that everything about her was unique, including her skin color. I was not a Christian back then and therefore was ill-equipped to point her to the one who created her. As I reflect back on those times, I wish someone would have reached out to her and told her how beautiful she was in God's eyes.

Ephesians 2:10 says we are God's handiwork, created in Christ Jesus. What does handiwork mean? It means we are God's creative masterpiece. We are His wonderful work of art. When someone creates a masterpiece, the mold is broken. A masterpiece is extraordinary, created in excellence, and done with the utmost precision. There may be earthly attempts to duplicate it, but a masterpiece is a one of a kind. That's you.

You are God's masterpiece.

God made all of the delicate, inner pieces of your body. He joined every part of you together in your mother's womb (Psalm 139:13). That means He knows how every part of your

THE NEW CONSECRATED COCOON

being functions. He knows what makes you tick. He knows what's good for you and what's not. He knows when you are running at maximum potential or below it. If a part of you breaks down, He knows exactly what it takes to fix it.

Why is it when we purchase something of great value and it breaks we trip over ourselves to get it back to the manufacturer to have it fixed? I recently upgraded my phone and am enjoying the talk to text feature. So much so, that if the day comes that I talk and it doesn't respond, I will not hesitate to contact my mobile carrier. Why? Because they are familiar with the inner workings of the phone and can more than likely fix it. Why is it that we are not like that with God? When something goes wrong in our lives, we often attempt to fix it ourselves or seek others to make it right; and seldom go back to the one who created us.

If you purchased a Mercedes Benz and all of a sudden it stopped running, would you take it to a Hyundai or Ford dealership to have it looked over? Hopefully, your answer is a resounding "no." You'd take it back to the Mercedes dealership. The one who created it. The creator intimately knows its creation. When your car breaks down, do you ask it to tell you what's wrong? Of course not. As silly as that sounds, we often try to find what's wrong with ourselves from ourselves. If you had all the answers, you wouldn't need God.

Like a vehicle, we need regular maintenance. We need a spiritual oil change, tune-up, and a new air filter. Air filters are an important part of a car's intake system. The engine breathes through the air filter. The filter keeps out dirt and prevents other unfamiliar particles in the air from entering the system, which could damage the engine. When the foreign particles of life get caught in our spiritual filter, such as confusion, unforgiveness, low self-esteem, depression, or resentment, only God can change our filter. We can't do it ourselves.

Ephesians 2:10 goes on to say you are created in Christ Jesus, which means you are created in His image Christ lives in you. As Christians, we should be transforming daily to be more like Jesus. That's what it means to be in Him. Your character becomes more like Him. Your value and self-worth is found in Him.

What He has, you now have.

The Scripture didn't say you were created in your mom and dad. Nor did it say you were created in your kids, job, or even ministry. Your significance comes from the one in whose image you were created – Jesus. He's the only one you should consult about your worth.

Women often tend to associate our value with our roles as mothers, wives, sisters, and friends. And then, when our husband, child, or sibling isn't pleased or are non-appreciative; we interpret that as being unworthy. This must stop. Your identity and self-worth is in Christ alone. Not any person or thing.

Not only did God create each of us in a unique and special way; He also created us for a unique and special purpose. God's purpose for your life is the reason why you will face adversities in life. I've heard it said that knowledge is the key. The key to what? To understanding. First comes knowledge, and then comes understanding. It isn't enough to know the "what" of a situation; you must also understand the "why" and "how." Understanding is the strategic arrangement and application of the knowledge you receive.

In an earlier chapter, I provided a little bit of knowledge about two pursuits that are happening simultaneously. God is pursuing you because he knows your potential; and Satan's is pursuing you because he also knows your potential. That's the "what." Now comes the "why." Why are they both pursuing you? Because God has a purpose for your life and He wants to help you fulfill it. Satan knows your purpose and he wants you to forfeit it.

God created each and every one of us with a purpose and destiny. What exactly does it mean to have a purpose and destiny? It means you were created for a greater cause. Destiny is the root word of destination, which implies there is a goal, an objective, a premeditated, and pre-designated end. Your destiny is in the future. Your purpose on the other hand is the journey that gets you there. It's the here and now. It's the daily steps you take, the decisions you make, and the roles you assume that may change from time to time. When your purpose changes, your new purpose should still move you toward fulfilling your destiny.

Once God reveals your purpose, you'll begin to embrace and appreciate all of your attributes. You will realize that everything about you was uniquely created to fit into the grand scheme of things. God isn't an "after the fact" God. He plans ahead. Therefore, everything that's needed to fulfill your destiny you already have. God's simply waiting for you to figure it out and give yourself to Him completely, so he can get this destiny show on the road.

When we read about the Apostle Paul in the Bible, once God revealed His purpose, his life was never the same. His original name was Saul. Saul zealously and uncompromisingly persecuted Christians. You heard right. He killed Christians believing he was doing the will of God. Saul was a staunch Jew who lived according to the law. He believed in Yaweh (God) but didn't believe that Jesus was the son of God. He persecuted those who believed in Jesus, thinking he was obeying God. Then one day, while on the road to Damascus (Acts 9:3-6), Saul had a personal encounter with God.

That encounter resulted in a name change and a lifestyle change, but God didn't change Paul's personality. He simply used Paul's zeal, conviction, loyalty, and uncompromising character to fulfill His purpose in and through him. Paul was radically against Jesus and now he radically served Him.

My sister, you are strong-willed for a reason. Your gift of dance will open doors for God to minister to many. There's a greater purpose in your ability to speak three languages. You are strategically placed in your small and overcrowded neighborhood. God wants to use everything about your life to fulfill His purpose and destiny in you, but you must be willing to give Him all of you. You must be willing to surrender the good, bad, and the ugly. The challenges we face in life are directly related to the pursuit. When trials come, we either run away from God's promises or run toward the enemy's propaganda. Running from God displays our doubt. Running toward Satan displays our deception. Satan is a liar and a deceiver and is full of empty promises.

Don't get caught up in anything Satan promises you. He can't take away what God says is yours; and he can't give you what only God has for you. Did you get that? Satan can only pretend to offer you an imitation of what God has already set aside for you. Obviously, Satan's offers will be wrapped in eye-catching and flesh pleasing packages, but his offers almost always require a level of compromise. His promises are rooted in lies that are topped off with a little bit of truth. A little bit of truth is still a lie.

I'll give you an example of a lie that is packaged with small hints of truth. You meet a very nice man. He is handsome, well-educated, very attentive and loving, and makes you feel special. He likes you a lot and wants to spend time with you. You learn he is married, but he insists that they are separated and wants to continue the relationship with you. What's the truth? He may sincerely like you. What's the lie? That you can continue seeing him and not face repercussions. He is not yours. He is married to his wife. If you remain with him, you are having an adulterous affair. What's the lie? Your sinful relationship is okay with God. What's the truth? This man doesn't value the covenant of marriage and is a man who dishonors his wife and sins against God. You are contributing to an already painful situation. What's the lie? She was a bad wife. He will change and not do the same to you.

Ladies, let's be careful to not justify lies or explain away our sin. Justifications are simply excuses to continue doing what you know is wrong. Everything Satan offers is a temporary imitation of what God has for you and is designed to derail your purpose. Once you understand Satan's agenda, you should not be caught off guard when hard times come. Don't be surprised when you are tempted. It's during those times of adversity and temptations that your identity in Jesus is re-established and strengthened, and your purpose becomes even clearer.

I am not a mind reader, but I hear you asking, "What's God purpose and destiny for me? How will I know?" The simplest answer to that question is to identify what you're absolutely passionate about. Your purpose is rooted in your passion. What gets you totally pumped up and on fire? What would you do all day every day without getting paid one dime for it? What grieves or upsets you that if you could change it to enhance the lives of others, you would? Don't know where to begin? Start with your overall purpose: Get closer to God, develop the gifts He has given you, and tell others about His goodness.

As you pursue God, He will affirm the direction you need to go and make your specific purposes clearer. He will help you get on the right path. For God to reveal and confirm His plans for you, you must have the proper mindset. You must develop an intimate relationship with Him so your thinking becomes like His – kingdom minded. Romans 12:2 says, "Don't copy the behavior and customs of this world, but let God transform you into a new person by changing the way you think. Then you will learn to know God's will (purpose) for you, which is good and pleasing and perfect." (NLT)

How did Saul come to know God's plan and purpose for his life? His thought life had to change. He could not behave like the rest of the legalistic Jews. He could no longer think it was okay to persecute people who believed in Christ. He had to allow God to change his stinking thinking. What's stinking thinking? All thoughts we entertain that do not align with God's Word, character, and promises. Why in the world would God reveal His glorious plan to someone who isn't ready to receive it? I will let you in on a secret. He won't.

Many people believe that a change in someone's behavior causes them to have a change of heart or mind. That's not true. Our behavior follows our thoughts. That's why the Bible says we must change our thoughts first and then the

ANN THOMAS

Training to Reign

Many Christian women have a difficult time understanding and accepting their identity or worth in Christ.

If God were to physically sit with you, have a cup of coffee (or your favorite drink), and download all He has created you to be and do; it would absolutely blow your mind!

As I said earlier, we women often take our cues from our roles as wives, mothers, sisters, daughters, and friends regarding our value. As important as these roles are, they are often filled with limitations from others and ourselves.

However, we serve a God of no limits.

As daughters of the King who owns everything, we have access to everything that belongs to Him. When we truly come to the place of allowing our mind and hearts to receive this, we will walk in the power and authority we were created to have.

As God's princesses, we are created to reign with kingdom power. The word reign means a time of influence – Godly influence. That time of influence is not for Heaven, it's for here and now. It's for earth.

Reigning isn't about superiority. It's about humility.

You were created to impact the lives of many with great humility for God's glory. Some of us strive really hard to influence our immediate family and pay little attention to those we come in contact with every day, whereas others strive to influence those at our jobs, school, church, and community; with little regard to our influence at home. God calls you to have a positive influence everywhere you go and upon everyone with whom you come in contact.

Make no mistake about it that your ability to influence others does and should begin at home. By the way, influence is not control. Influence is about example, control is about emotions.

THE NEW CONSECRATED COCOON

Mark 8:36 says, "What good is it for a man to gain the whole world, yet forfeit his soul." So I ask the question, "What good is it for a woman to gain the approval and affirmation of the world, yet forfeit the love, respect, and honor of her home?

I know that your husband, children, parents, siblings, and extended family members can be the most difficult ones to minister to. Let me say that again. I realize that those closest to us can be the hardest and most challenging ones to help steer in the right direction.

The Bible says that even Jesus wasn't respected in his community and among people he knew. They were offended by his teachings (Mark 6:3). It won't be any different for you and me. Why? Because they're familiar with us. They know our junk. They know our past. They know our weaknesses. They know our imperfections. Again, they did the same thing with Jesus. As He walked about healing and doing the work of the Lord, they asked, "Isn't this Jesus, the son of Joseph?" (John 6:42). In other words, we knew Him as a little boy doing carpenter work with his father and now...

That's what those closest to you will say when you finally begin to live for God rather than live for the devil. "Isn't this Ann... who used to hang out at...?" And when they do, sister, don't go getting all super spiritual on them. One of the wonderful blessings of God is to remember what He saved us from. Our past isn't something we pretend didn't happen. Our past allows us to relate to those who are still lost; and rejoice in the fact that if God can do it for us, He can do it for them. Hallelujah!

Sometimes it's easy to see ourselves as powerless or lacking influence based on what others say about us or what we think of ourselves. But God doesn't take his cues about our worth or purpose from our defeats and mistakes. When He looks at us, He sees us completed in Him. It's like a puzzle. We see each piece, but God sees the full picture. Seeing one piece at a time often makes it difficult to embrace the end result. But that's where our trust in God must enter in.

We have to trust that each piece is significant to completing the puzzle. All pieces are needed. Those pieces that represent pain, those that represent joy, those that represent correction, and those that represent victory; all come together to make you who you are.

I love the story of King David in the Bible. God called David a "Man after God's own heart" (Acts 13:22). What made David a man after God's heart? Was he perfect? Absolutely not. Was he born with a silver spoon in his mouth? No. David's father, Jesse, wasn't even a king. So what made God say David was a man after His own heart? Because David was willing to do everything God wanted him to do. Is it that simple? Yes.

Want to be a woman after God's heart – be willing to do what He asks. Will God's request always feel good? No. Will you do it perfectly each time? Definitely not. But your obedience pleases God and lets Him know you love Him.

David's destiny was to become the King of Israel and Judah. Before becoming king, David had to fulfill several purposes along the way. There were several puzzle pieces that had to be put in place. David had to undergo a time of training before he could reign.

Like David, all of the days of your life were written in God's book before you lived one. The day you were conceived is written, the day you were born, the day you died, and every day in between are all in God's book. Your purpose and destiny are written in His book.

At some point in your life God will reveal your purpose and destiny, if He already hasn't. For some, it's revealed at an early age and others discover it later in life. God knows each of us and He knows the right time to reveal it.

As for David, God revealed and confirmed his destiny when he was 17 years old. And from the time it was revealed to the time of fulfillment, David experienced many trials and hardships before he could reign. The trials and hardships were the pieces of the puzzle coming together to fulfill God's perfect will in David's life.

THE NEW CONSECRATED COCOON

David was destined to be king, but his life didn't start out that way.

He lived in Bethlehem with his father Jesse and seven brothers. David was the youngest, a shepherd boy who regularly tended his father's sheep. You might say, how could he go from tending sheep to being a king? Stick with me. I am about to explain just how on purpose and intentional God's plans truly are.

God was displeased with the current reigning king named Saul. So He removed His favor from Saul's life. With a successor already in mind, God sent Samuel the prophet to Bethlehem to find the new king. He told Samuel to go to Jesse's house where he would choose the next king from one of Jesse's sons. But God didn't tell Samuel which son.

In complete obedience, Samuel arrived at Jesse's and explained that one of his sons would be the new king. As you can imagine, Jesse was totally excited. I'm sure he had all of his sons go comb their hair, put on their best outfits, and lots of deodorant. And then Jesse paraded each son in front of Samuel, with the exception of David.

David was out tending the sheep, oblivious to all that was going on. After Samuel had seen all of Jesse's sons, God told him that none of them were His chosen king. So Samuel asked Jesse if he had any other sons (1 Samuel 16:11). Jesse replied that he had one more son who was tending the sheep. Samuel told Jesse to send for him. The minute Samuel laid eyes on David, God confirmed that he was the one. So Samuel anointed David, affirming his destiny. In fact, the Bible says in 1 Samuel 16:13 that when David was anointed, God's Spirit of power came upon David from that day on.

From that day, David had access to the power of God needed to fulfill his purpose and destiny. He didn't look like a king, dress like a king, or live like a king. But God said he was a king.

We Christians possess that same power needed to fulfill our destiny. As I write this book I am not yet a published author. My book is not yet available on Amazon or any other bookstore. Yet God has already ordained this book to radically transform the lives of those who read it. To be honest, if just one life is forever changed, I will be eternally grateful. But I have a sneaking suspicion that God will use all I share to touch more than one life – for His glory!

Satan is intimidated by just one Christian who realizes her purpose and destiny in Christ.

His goal is to do everything possible to prevent you from stepping into all God has for you. You already have the power to become the mighty warrior God created you to be. Just like David, God has anointed and appointed you to do great things. But you must accept this high calling in order to walk boldly in your destiny and kick the enemy to the curb.

Satan can't stop you. You have overcoming power!

Before we continue with David's story I am led to pause and encourage you about being in the right place when God comes to promote you. Jesse did not consider his son David for the role of king. He probably deemed David's age, height, or stature as disqualifying factors. However, when God chooses His people for special purposes, He doesn't look at the outward appearance; He looks at the heart (1 Samuel 16:7). God's purpose for you has nothing to do with your weight, wardrobe, financial status, or anything else that gains man's approval. God could care less about your perceived limitations.

When God comes to find you, He is interested in only one thing: a heart that's willing to obey and trust Him. When your heart is set toward pleasing God and not man, God's favor will find you wherever you are; even if you are out back tending the sheep. So, dear sister, don't feel like you have to promote yourself. You don't have to be in the spotlight or be in a place of great exposure for God to find you. When God comes looking, let Him find you being faithful right where He has you and not where you think you need to be.

When Samuel sent for David, where was David? He was found exactly where he was supposed to be – tending the sheep. Don't worry about whether people notice the things you do and who appreciates or doesn't appreciate you. Faithfully serve God where He currently has you. And when it's time for Him to promote you or give you a new assignment, let Him find you being faithful to Him in that place where you are supposed to be.

Rest assured that God doesn't lose sight of where you are. He knows exactly where to find you.

Beloved, you will encounter several Jesses in life who don't believe you are qualified for this and that. Remember, it is God who chose you and anointed you with the power to reign. Not man. So stop trying to please man. Your promotion and recognition comes from God. Amen!

OK. Let's get back to David.

After Samuel anointed him, he didn't leave with Samuel to go sit on the throne. He went back to tending the sheep, awaiting further instructions from God. It's all about God's timing. Trust me, you can know what God wants you to do; but if done outside of His timing; it's done outside of His will.

God's timing is perfect. Anything done before or after His timing is outside of His plans for you. So David returned to his training in anticipation of his reign.

Our time of training consists of more than one purpose or assignment. As we walk in obedience each assignment is designed to get us closer to our destiny. David's first purpose was to be a loyal shepherd boy. As a shepherd he developed an intimate relationship with God. While tending the sheep he spent time talking to God and drawing strength from Him. He also played the harp while watching over the sheep. And there were times when he had to protect the sheep from a vicious animal that sought to kill them. Little did David know that his courage and harp playing skills would prove to be crucial for the next assignment God had for him. He was in training to reign.

It's the same with you. Every single event in your life prepares you for where you are heading. Each hurt, victory, and challenge is designed to prepare and strengthen you as you get closer to fulfilling your destiny. There will be times when your purpose feels a little mundane and not as exciting – but it's preparing you for the next level.

The Bible says that God causes all things (tragedy and victories) to work together for the good of those who love Him and are called according to His purpose (Romans 8:28). That's you and me. We have a God-given purpose and we love Him. Therefore, God will work everything out on our behalf for His glory. It's a promise! You are in training to reign.

After Samuel anointed David, he was ready for his next purpose – becoming King Saul's armor bearer. King Saul had disobeyed God, and as a result of his disobedience, was being tormented day and night. He had no peace of mind. Concerned about his agony, Saul's servants suggested he find someone to play the harp. They believed the music would soothe his soul. One of the servants heard David playing while tending the sheep and recommended him to King Saul. They sent for David and when he played, Saul felt great relief. So he asked Jesse to allow David to remain with him. David found favor in Saul's eyes and became his armor bearer, which was a close and trusted servant.

Becoming an armor bearer then positioned David for his next purpose – killing the giant Goliath. Goliath had been terrorizing the Israelites for forty days. Everyone was afraid to engage him, but not David. David asked King Saul's permission to take on Goliath, and the king granted his request. What made this 17 year-old believe he could defeat a giant that everyone else was afraid of? His time of training. He had spent time in God's presence and he understood the power and authority he possessed as God's chosen and anointed one. He'd come face-to-face with vicious animals and had taken them down. He believed that with Christ he could do all things (Philippians 4:13).

THE NEW CONSECRATED COCOON

David had already seen God in action. He experienced God's faithfulness in the past and knew God would be faithful again. So he took on the giant with a sling shot, a stone, and the God who was greater in him than the god of Goliath. The giant was soundly defeated! Beloved, we all have giants in our lives (disease, divorce, death, financial crisis, rebellious loved ones, etc.). And when we have an intimate relationship with God, like David, God uses every purpose as preparation for our victory over life's giants.

After defeating the giant, you might think David was ready to become the king of Israel. But he had yet another purpose to fulfill. His victory over Goliath won him great popularity with the Israelites, but he lost favor with King Saul.

Saul became jealous of David. During this time, David developed an intimate relationship with King Saul's son Jonathan. Jonathan and David loved each other so much that when King Saul plotted to kill David, Jonathan warned David so he could flee.

David and his men were on the run for eight long years; and so much transpired during this time. Eventually, Saul and his son Jonathan were killed in battle and at thirty years old, David was crowned the King of Israel and Judah. For those of you who don't feel like doing the calculation in your head, that's thirteen years. Thirteen years after Samuel anointed David he finally became king. And to think some of us whine about God not answering a prayer within thirteen days.

David fulfilled several purposes on his way to fulfilling his God-given destiny as king. Each of his purposes brought tremendous challenges designed to strengthen him and bring him one step closer to his destiny.

Like David, you also have a God-assigned destiny. And right now you are living out the daily purposes needed to fulfill it. There will be times when you'll feel like your current assignment has no significance. Maybe you had a Jesse or two in your life who overlooked you. Maybe you had a few King Sauls in your life who were jealous and tried to crucify your self-worth and steal your hope. Or maybe you feel like no one notices or appreciates your efforts.

Even when you cannot see or sense it, God is divinely positioning you for your next assignment. At times you will experience great exposure and will receive the praise of man. But don't get it confused. Never work for man's approval. Always seek to please God.

In each of your assignments you will face adversity. Adversity is an important part of your training. Adversity or suffering produces perseverance, perseverance produces character, and character produces hope (Romans 5:3-4). Why is it important to have character? To show yourself worthy of the great and wonderful plan God has for you to fulfill. You must be a woman who unlike the swine can be trusted with the valuable pearls of God's Kingdom.

Character is built in the trenches. It is cultivated in the heart of your training. So you cannot quit when things get difficult. Why is it important to have hope? Because hope helps you to look beyond your current circumstance. It reinforces and affirms that you have power and authority to overcome each adversity and fulfill each purpose. Hope encourages you and reminds you that you are already equipped with everything needed to reach your destiny. With God, you can do all things; nothing is impossible (Luke 1:37).

Michelle

Michelle grew up in a home with an alcoholic mother, and at sixteen years old had an abortion. She got married at twenty-four, tried to get pregnant at twenty-six, and miscarried. Now at twenty-eight, she is pregnant again and working as a waitress at a popular restaurant. A hard worker and someone who has struggled through many trials, Michelle never expected God to use her own experiences to help a total stranger – but God did. That divine encounter was already written in God's book.

THE NEW CONSECRATED COCOON

One evening as her shift came to an end, Michelle received a call from her husband stating he was running late. Frustrated but unable to change the circumstance Michelle hung up and finished cleaning the stations. Her feet were swollen, and her back hurt. She was more than ready to go home. After saying goodnight to her co-workers, she stepped outside to wait for her husband. She noticed a young lady who couldn't have been any older than fifteen or sixteen sitting on the bench smoking a cigarette. And to Michelle's surprise the girl was pregnant.

Bothered by the smoke, Michelle was about to sit on a bench on the other side of the building when she realized the girl was sobbing. "Are you okay?" Michelle asked.

"What's it to you?" the girl snapped back.

Shocked by the young girl's angry tone, Michelle thought to herself, "Lord, I am not in the mood for this." The girl stood up and attempted to walk away when Michelle said, "Hey, smoking is bad for your baby."

The girl sarcastically responded, "Tell me something I don't know. Who are you, God?"

Pausing for a second, Michelle realized she had one of two choices; allow this total stranger with a rebellious attitude to walk away or continue to engage her in conversation with the hopes of helping. To be quite honest, Michelle was exhausted and wanted to choose the first option merely out of convenience. However, she recognized the so called tough demeanor the girl displayed. Michelle knew it all too well. This girl wasn't tough, she was scared.

Attempting to prevent the girl from walking away, Michelle asked, "So, how far along are you?"

After what seemed like a long pause, the girl responded, "A little over four months."

"Wow, what do you want, a boy or girl?" "I don't want either."

Moving slowly and cautiously toward her, Michelle continued. "Can you feel the baby moving around yet?" "I don't' know...I haven't felt much of anything other than sick."

"Yeah, they do that to you sometimes." Now standing next to her, Michelle asked why she was crying. The young girl stared at the ground and then up at the sky as tears rolled down her cheeks. Michelle grabbed a tissue from her purse and handed it to her. She simply waited. She didn't push.

Finally, the girl threw the cigarette to the ground, stepped on it and replied without looking at Michelle. "My boyfriend and I were eating at your restaurant. We got into an argument and he ended the relationship. He gave me money, got in his car and told me to get rid of the baby. He said he never wanted to see me again." With those words, she covered her face with her hands and sobbed loudly.

Instinctively and without thinking Michelle reached out and hugged her. At first the girl did not reciprocate. Hands dropped at her sides, she cried even louder.

The longer Michelle hugged her, the more her body relaxed in Michelle's arms and then she laid her head on Michelle's shoulder. Slowly leading her to the bench, Michelle sat her down and began to share her heart with the girl. She shared about her own abortion at age sixteen. She spoke about how scared she was to tell her parents, and how it devastated her parents when they later learned of all Michelle went through alone.

Michelle shared about the guilt and shame she carried for many years. And then when she got married, the guilt and shame turned into unworthiness and lack of self-esteem, which caused her to be guarded, suspicious, distrustful, and insecure in her marriage. Then, when she had the miscarriage, she thought God was punishing her for the abortion.

Michelle and her husband had been going to church for one year. They gave their lives to Christ and sought Christian counseling. Everything wasn't perfect in their lives, but they were going through a healing process both as individuals and as a couple. Michelle had the girl's undivided attention. Then, a very special moment came. Michelle took the girl's hand and placed it on her tummy. "See," she said to the girl, "God is all about second chances. Like you, I am pregnant and look forward to loving my little boy or girl the way God loves me."

Surprised by it all, the girl smiled at Michelle and then asked, "Can God love me even though I wanted to get rid of my baby?"

Michelle answered with tears streaming down her face, "He already does." That night, Michelle and her husband drove the girl home. They exchanged numbers and the girl stepped out of their car with a new hope. She began attending church with Michelle and her husband and making friends. Then two months later, while the girl shared her incredible testimony with the youth group, Michelle learned even more about God's purposes and His goodness. The girl shared that the night Michelle spoke with her outside the restaurant, she was sitting on the bench contemplating suicide. As she wrestled with thoughts of ending her life, she told God that if He didn't want her to kill herself He had better send someone to talk her out of it. God answered her prayer. He sent Michelle.

Today, Michelle volunteers at a crisis center for teen girls. That night as Michelle left her job, she stepped into her purpose; and through her obedience God saved not one, but two lives.

During your time of training, God will allow your path to cross with many women who feel defeated and are ready to give up, and He will use you to speak hope into their lives if you make yourself available to Him. Never take it for granted when you find yourself in a weird place, at a weird time, and around... people who are different. Ah, you thought I was going to say weird people, didn't you? Truth is, we can all be weird at times. But, yes, God wants to use you mightily and will often position you outside of your comfort zone so you must rely upon Him completely.

ANN THOMAS

Metamorphosis – The Great Exchange

As I shared earlier, this book is based on and is inspired by the caterpillar metamorphosis process.

Metamorphosis is a Greek word that means to take on a striking change in appearance, character, or circumstances.

It's a total transformation.

As we Christians go through what I call a spiritual metamorphosis, our appearance, demeanor, and character changes. And how can I forget? Yes, our circumstances also undergo major changes. That circumstance that led or catapulted you into a time of refining is never the same when you exit the process. It's changed. It changes because you've changed.

This striking change in appearance and character is a radical one that begins on the inside. And what God is doing on the inside can't help but eventually showing up on the outside. Some of your changes will be strictly between you and God.

These changes will be shared in the secret and private place of deep prayers and tearful conversations that will stem from a heart that is transparent and repentant. The caterpillar is hidden away in her cocoon going through life-altering changes, and I am willing to bet that at times she probably looks quite hideous. She might look quite undesirable as she loses body parts, organs, etc.

Like the caterpillar, God hides and protects you as you deal with those unattractive character traits, sins, thoughts, and actions. As you lose and shed things that are no longer needed, you will initially feel incomplete and it *will* hurt. But God will draw even closer, squeeze you even tighter and will not release you from His loving arms until the work He began is complete.

When you emerge from your spiritual cocoon with God, you don't have to say a word to anyone. They will notice there is something different about you. Some might ask, "Girl, what's going on in your life? You are not the same." They will see it, and though you won't have to say a word, you must!

When God totally transforms our lives, we must not hold back. We must share the wonderful things God has done with others who are in need of hope. They need to know there is a God who loves them just as much as He loves you. And if He did it for you, He can certainly do it for them.

From her place of surrender and seclusion, the caterpillar emerges as a new creature – a butterfly. Her transformation is so extreme that if she tries to return to the old "caterpillar hang-outs," her former friends won't recognize her. She's different on the inside as well as the outside. She has more eyes, she no longer crawls, she flies using her big beautiful wings. She has a new purpose.

It's no different with you and me. When we emerge from our metamorphosis we will find it difficult to go back to those past places and hang with people who are unable to celebrate all God has done in and through us. That's good. There is nothing back there for you. Everything you need to move forward is in front of you, not behind. Trust me, as you go through the fire, you quickly learn who your true friends are.

Some will walk with you through the fire and others will be necessarily burned away.

The word metamorphosis means to change, but I prefer to view the process more as an *exchange*. In other words, it's more like giving up one thing to gain another. The caterpillar loses her legs to get wings. As we go through our time of refinement, we engage in a beautiful exchange with God. God doesn't just remove things from our lives; He replaces them with something greater. In our time of transformation God exchanges His joy for our sorrow. His strength for our weakness. His love for our rejection. His beauty for our ashes. His wisdom for our confusion. His peace for our turmoil. And His hope for our defeat.

Our God is a God of exchange.

The greatest exchange of all times was the death of His son Jesus on the cross.

Jesus died so we could live. Blameless and without any sin, He took all of our sins (past, present, and future) onto Himself so we could be forgiven and have a relationship with God and live in eternity, forever. Considering how Jesus was whipped, tortured, spat on, and crucified, I would say that we received the best part of that exchange. Wouldn't you?

When God looks at you and me, He sees us completed. He sees the end result. When I look at the caterpillar; I, too, envision and marvel at the end result, but I can't help but consider the caterpillar. For me, it's impossible to stand in awe of the butterfly's freedom without thinking about the caterpillar's surrender. When I see a butterfly soar, I think of the caterpillar's captivity. The caterpillar's sacrifice is the butterfly's success. The caterpillar dies so the butterfly could live.

The great news is...all of this does not happen overnight. And thank God! We don't want nor could we handle all of these changes occurring at one time. It's kind of like an onion. Things must be done in layers. In His great mercy, God often shows us an area needing healing, and when we allow Him to heal it, He does. But just like weeds in a garden, when you mess with one area, other things needing attention reveal themselves. Much of our hurts and disappointments are often attached to feelings that are deeper than meets the eye. Acknowledging one feeling often exposes another.

For example, a lot of women when they begin to deal with the issue of unforgiveness with their spouse or boyfriend often learn that the root of their unforgiveness started way before that man; often with a father or mother. This deep hurt might not reveal itself until she is forty-five years old, but in each stage of her life it existed.

Like us, the caterpillar goes through stages. And that's how I would like to end this chapter, discussing the four stages or cycles of a caterpillar's life. In later chapters, I will share with you the revelations God gave me to show the correlations of our life stages to the caterpillars. To get to the final stage, the caterpillar must endure and fulfill each stage. To become who God created us to be, we too must persevere through each stage. We can't bypass the stages or seasons we don't like – it's all necessary.

The Egg

The first stage of the metamorphosis process is called the Egg. This is the egg that was laid by the adult butterfly. Butterfly eggs are very small, round, and can be oval or cylinder shaped. The color, shape, and features of an egg are determined by the type of butterfly that laid the eggs.

Interestingly enough, when you look very closely at a butterfly egg, you don't see baby butterflies emerging. Instead you see baby caterpillars. The caterpillar does not initially resemble the butterfly, but was created in the image of the one who laid the egg.

Spiritually speaking, we are not born with the characteristics of Christ. Remember, we are born with the sin nature of Adam. But over time, the closer we are to God, and the more we pursue our destiny, we, too eventually resemble the one whose image we were created in – God. The caterpillar as she perseveres through each stage will ultimately resemble her butterfly parents.

We will call this first stage Creation.

The Larva / Caterpillar

The next stage is called the Larva or Caterpillar. In this stage, the caterpillar is basically eating all day so she can grow. She eats the leaves on which her egg was laid. When first born, caterpillars are teeny tiny beings that cannot get around. In other words, they can't leaf hop. So their mama has to make sure she lays her eggs on a leaf she knows her babies will like.

In this stage the caterpillars are eating a lot and are growing rapidly. Her skin doesn't stretch, so she sheds her skin several times. This process is called molting. As Christians, we should also experience spiritual molting. The more we chew on God's word and grow in Him, we must shed our old nature.

Once fully grown, the caterpillar seeks a new location to pupate. That's the process where she spins the cocoon around herself, and hangs upside down like the letter "J" in preparation for the change.

We will call this stage Preparation.

The Pupa

The third stage is called the Pupa. The caterpillar sheds her skin for the last time. Her soft covering becomes a jade color, which is called Chrysalis. In its final stages, the Chrysalis becomes stiffer, takes on a waxy greenish color, and is decorated with gold and black highlights. Many physical changes are already occurring to include shedding her eight pairs of legs and her head capsule that contained six eye lenses.

On the outside looking in, she appears to be resting, but drastic changes are indeed occurring on the inside. Tissues, limbs, and organs are changing to form the body parts of the butterfly. She is in her cocoon. The place where she is dying to the old ways and embracing the new.

The cocoon serves two purposes. First, it keeps her secluded so she can remain focused on the goal at hand. Secondly, it keeps predators out so they cannot hinder the necessary process.

It's a place of both isolation and protection.

While in the cocoon, her mouth and legs are becoming functionless. Did you get that? She can't speak and she can't run. Many of us when we are in our place of seclusion need to learn how to stay put and keep our lips sealed. More to come on that. She also develops more eyes and her antennae appear. This is all crucial to the change.

We will call this stage Consecration.

Adult Butterfly

The final stage of the life cycle is called the Adult Butterfly. In this stage, she emerges in the image of the one who birthed (created) her. It is said that the emergence typically occurs in the morning. As Christians, we too look forward to our morning because the Bible promises that joy comes in the morning (Psalm 30:5b). The morning represents the start of a new day. God's joy gives us a fresh start.

At first when she emerges, her wings are soft and wet due to a fluid called hemolymph. Hemolymph is pumped into her body to enlarge her wings. When she emerges, she must quickly find a place to stretch and allow her wings to dry. The stretching strengthens her wings. Once dried, she is ready to soar.

What's next for the butterfly you might ask? The cycle simply begins all over again. Male butterflies seek a mate so they can give birth to more butterflies. They raise another generation to keep the legacy alive. We will call this stage Transformation.

As we discuss the four stages: Creation, Preparation, Consecration, and Transformation, God will show you things about your own life that require change. You will be challenged to make difficult decisions, ask the tough questions, and be completely honest about where you are. No matter what God shows you, remember what I said earlier.

God reveals to heal.

He won't show you things and leave you to tackle it alone. He will walk closely with you and at times He will sweep you off your feet and carry you.

Like my hairstylist Nikki said, "Ann, you're the butterfly." That's what I say to you, dear sister. You're the butterfly.

You may feel like the caterpillar right now. But no matter how tough things look and how tight your space feels; know there is an end result from which you will emerge more beautiful and powerful than ever! Come on butterfly! It's time to soar toward your purpose and destiny in Christ Jesus! Woot-woot!

To get different results, we must do something different.

Reflection

It is said that only when we are sick and tired of being sick and tired do we allow God to make the necessary changes.

1. God wants to make radical, life-altering changes in your life. What changes are you excited about?
2. What changes are you apprehensive about?
3. The cocoon is a place of spiritual isolation. Are you willing to make the sacrifice to spend intimate time with God?
4. What things might you have to set aside or give up to make your time with God a priority?

"There is a time for everything, and a season for every activity under Heaven: a time to be born and a time to die, a time to plant and a time to uproot, a time to kill and a time to heal, a time to tear down and a time to build, a time to weep and a time to laugh, a time to mourn and a time to dance, a time to scatter stones and a time to gather them, a time to embrace and a time to refrain from embracing, a time to search and a time to give up, a time to keep and a time to throw away, a time to tear and a time to mend, a time to be silent and a time to speak, a time to love and a time to hate, a time for war and a time for peace." Ecclesiastes 3:1-8 *(New International Version).*

CREATION

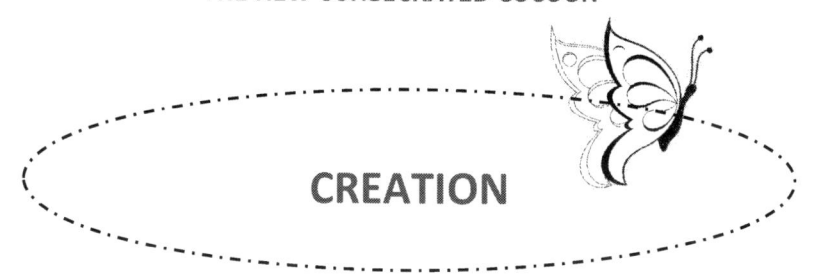

God is passionately and intimately involved in every aspect of His creation. He takes time to consider the shape, color, and size of a butterfly egg. So why wouldn't He invest even more thought and attention into His creation that is most like Him – humans.

God creates everything with the end result in mind.

The egg and even the caterpillar don't adequately reflect the beautiful butterfly that emerges from her cocoon. And the caterpillar's purpose (why she exists) is radically different from the butterfly's purpose. Yet, one must be embraced for the other to be fulfilled.

The parents, family, and circumstances you were born into greatly influences who you become. But they do not dictate your worth and identity.

These things help shape your personality, but only God commands your destiny.

Like the caterpillar and butterfly, where you begin isn't anywhere close to where you will end up. And only through an intimate and personal relationship with God can you come into the full understanding of why you were placed on this earth (your purpose). Until then, rest assured that everything about you, mental, physical, and emotional, are all part of God's unique plan for your life.

He plans on using it all, because everything God does is intentional.

ANN THOMAS

Born Identity

I can't begin to tell you the number of women I speak with who struggle with their self-worth and identity. Your identity is the unique, individual personality and character traits that make up who you are.

It's like a fingerprint – no two are alike.

Your identity is given by God and is the core place from which you draw your self-worth. Your self-worth is the confidence and satisfaction you have about yourself. If your perception about your identity is twisted, so is your understanding of your worth and value to God.

Feelings of unworthiness cause us to compare, settle, and compromise. Which leaves us miserably short of our potential in Christ. I can tell you from personal experience that my inability to become acquainted with my God-given identity set me up to encounter unhealthy relationships, painful experiences, and unrealistic expectations of myself and others.

Some of you may ask, "How do I know if I struggle with self-worth or identity issues?" Ask yourself the following questions: Do I feel undeserving to receive gifts or compliments? Do I allow what other people say about me to determine what I believe about myself? Am I in need of constant affirmation, attention, or reassurance? Do I compare myself to others to decide what I should have and who I should be? There are several other questions I could ask, but if you answered yes to one or more of the above questions – you more than likely struggle in these areas.

Everyone is born with a distinct identity. God created you uniquely different for a reason. You were formed in His image, which means you have His characteristics. Having an intimate relationship with God teaches you about His character. Knowing His character helps you understand who you are in Him.

THE NEW CONSECRATED COCOON

When you don't have an intimate relationship with God, the flip side is true. You lack understanding of who He is and who He created you to be. Sadly, you will seek your self-worth from elsewhere.

To truly understand and embrace your identity and purpose, you must go back to the originating source – God. The problem with many women is we don't consult The Source, we check with other sources, such as a boyfriend, husband, kids, parents, close friends, a career, ministry, or even the media.

We expect these sources to answer the deep yearning question, "How much am I worth?" Unless you ask God, the answer you receive will be subjective based on the source you consult.

For instance, your kids can tell you how much you're worth to them as a mom, but you were created to be more than just a mom. God saw the whole picture when He created you. God certainly will use you to impact the lives of family members, but He will also use you to influence the lives of many others.

Some of us are familiar with Bible verses that speak about our identity and worth and can even quote them quite well. As wonderful as they sound rolling off our lips, they don't mean a hill of beans if we don't' believe them.

Deuteronomy 28:13 says, "God will make you the head and not the tail. You shall be above and not beneath." What good is it to say, "I am the head and not the tail," if you are constantly looking for someone to initiate or take the lead when it comes to your life? Saying, "I am above and not beneath," sounds really powerful, but when someone asks how you are doing and you say, "Under the circumstances, I am…" you've just negated that Scripture. My sister, what in the world are you doing under the circumstance? Get out from under there! God created you to be an overcomer. You can't overcome anything if you see yourself as under it.

True change begins with our thoughts.

Our thoughts determine our words, and our words determine our actions. When we simply know Scriptures but don't believe or live by them, we become weak hypocrites whose walk doesn't match our talk.

God didn't give us Bible verses for our reading pleasure. We are to verbally declare them in times when strength and encouragement is needed. Say this out loud with me. "I can do all things through Christ who gives me the strength I need." You just stated Philippians 4:13. When you say it out loud, you are encouraging yourself. You are reminding yourself of a promise from God. God promises you can do anything when you choose to receive His strength. As a source of encouragement, you need to say that Scripture over and over again, as many times as needed until you own it.

I gave my life to the Lord when I was eleven years old. However, I did nothing to develop my relationship with Jesus. I did things to develop a religion. There is a difference.

Religion is about ritual, the things I *do*. Christianity is about relationship, who I *am* in Jesus.

I religiously memorized Scriptures for the purpose of self-accomplishment. "Look at what I know everybody." Don't get me wrong, we should desire to memorize Scriptures. We should become intimately acquainted with them so we can tuck them deep in our hearts until they become a part of who we are. As we own the Scriptures, our perspective, attitudes, and behaviors change. It's not the Scriptures or words themselves that have the power to change; it's our belief in the God who spoke the Scriptures that transforms us.

In my late thirties, I had a rude awakening. I encountered a very challenging time in my life and realized I had a lot of religion, which couldn't provide the strength, character, and faith needed to get me through. I desired for God to be my father, friend, and comforter, not a far off ritualistic antidote.

During this time, God sent a very special couple into our lives. This man and woman of God soon became spiritual mentors to my ex-husband and me, and later became

THE NEW CONSECRATED COCOON

Godparents to our sons. The husband, may God rest his soul (he passed away some years ago), was a man after God's heart. He was a six foot, seven inch, over three hundred pound Cuban. He was on fire for the Lord. On the outside he tended to be somewhat abrasive at times, but behind that seemingly iron clad demeanor was the biggest teddy bear you ever met.

When it came to his relationship with God he had one saying, "Everything is mind over matter. If God doesn't mind, then it doesn't matter." He was a servant pastor, with a huge heart and a smile to match. His wife, a wonderful, uncompromising woman of God was the perfect mate for him. They were in love with God and with each other.

When I first met them, I had a difficult time accepting his very direct nature. He didn't pull any punches, and being spiritually immature, I took his honesty personally. I interpreted what he said as an attack. Before I met him, I knew I had a bit of a sensitive nature, but somehow this brother found that one supersensitive nerve in my entire body, put a saddle on it, and rode it every time we got together.

I remember one incident in particular that really tested my spiritual and emotional maturity. I initially failed the test. Miserably so. However, God did use that situation to begin a process of needed healing in my life. He and his wife were having brunch with my sons and me. My ex-husband had been out of country for several months. Before he left, we all prayed together and agreed that our mentor would step in as a father figure. My sons absolutely adored him.

So there we were sitting around the table, laughing and having a good time until my older son, who if I recall correctly was around eleven or so, received his order of pancakes. As I had been used to doing, I took my son's plate, grabbed a knife and proceeded to cut his pancakes into smaller pieces. I did this all the time without even thinking. My mentor asked why my son wasn't cutting his own pancakes and I gave him a lame answer. I know it was lame because he came back at me again. He told me that at age eleven my son should be allowed to cut his own pancakes.

With a hint of attitude, I gave this deeply spiritual response, "He doesn't know how to use a knife and I don't want him to hurt himself."

"So teach him," my mentor replied.

Now, let me be transparent with you. This conversation had long ceased to be about my son and his pancakes and had become an issue of my needing to be right and having the final say.

Realizing this, my mentor pressed in a little more. He wasn't disrespectful, just insistent. The banter went back and forth for a few minutes. I'm sure at this point my son would have been willing to stack the pancakes like a sandwich so he could just eat.

After about five minutes had passed, I finally, being the humbled and mature Christian I was, agreed and told my son to cut the pancakes himself. NOT! I wish that were the case. Instead, it became pretty obvious to my mentor that I was emotionally vested in the outcome of the conversation and so he wisely and maturely moved on to another topic for the sake of peace. Of course, I thought I had won that battle. But I later learned that was not the case.

That evening, I tucked my sons in and returned to the living room where my mentors were sitting on the couch waiting for me. I was stubborn, but I wasn't stupid. I figured we would revisit the pancake situation – and we did. But not the way I thought.

We prayed before we began talking. Then he told me that as a man, he had been noticing some areas in which I was not allowing my sons to grow up and take on responsibility. He shared that in my ex-husband's absence, I was doing things that were treating my sons like babies. Oh no. Did he just call them mama's boys? I think he did. He shared with great concern that my low expectations had the potential to encourage laziness and not require them to step up to their potential.

THE NEW CONSECRATED COCOON

Of course I was highly offended. Who did this man think he was? He didn't *even* have kids. So how could he possibly tell me how to raise my sons? Needless to say, I did forget two things. He was the man God divinely placed in our lives to help raise our sons while my ex-husband was away. Also, he was just that, a man. I am not a man. I had never been and never will be a man. Therefore, I needed to respect and accept the fact that he actually had insight into what he shared.

Some of you single ladies need to hear my heart. If you are raising children by yourself; strive to be the best mom you can possibly be.

But don't try to be a father to your children.

God knew exactly what he was doing when he created the roles of mothers and fathers. They are distinctively different. It breaks my heart when I see mothers stepping outside of their God-given assignment as a nurturing mom, trying to fulfill the role of a dad. If a father figure isn't present in your children's lives at this time, do all you can to tell them about their Father in Heaven and how much He loves them.

Assure them that He will never leave them or abandon them. Also, pray for God to bring healthy and appropriate male figures into their lives that can prayerfully impart blessings and administer correction and guidance from a fatherly perspective.

My mentor continued to share some areas in which my sons should be more helpful such as, cutting the grass, washing dishes, doing laundry, cleaning, washing the cars, etc. Again, I wish I could share with you that I received this information with a thankful heart and a sense of deep relief. But that was not the case. I remained offended. Why? Because all I heard him say was, "You are a bad mother." At no time in our conversation did he say one thing about my mothering skills. But I perceived he was attacking my ability to be a good mom. And so I was not initially receptive to his suggestions or correction. Then this man of God simply asked me, "What's the real reason you are so upset with what I shared?" I didn't have an answer. But something didn't feel right and I knew it.

He let me off the hook for a few minutes and offered to help get my sons on the right path. We discussed their spending a weekend with him where he would teach my oldest to mow the lawn and find chores for my youngest. After my guard was down a little, he turned his attention back to me. Gulp!

Again he asked why I was so offended by what he said at the restaurant. I still didn't have an answer. He allowed that awkward silence to build and before I realized it, tears were rolling down my cheeks. I felt forced into a corner but deep down knew I needed to be there.

It was time to get real, so God could reveal, help me to deal and heal. Did you catch that? Real, reveal, deal, and heal.

Some of you reading this book have not faced your skeletons. You open and close your closet of hurts each day, pretending not to see them hanging there. You're in denial and are refusing to get real. You thought by pretending that pink elephant wasn't in the room it would all go away, but it hasn't.

I pray that that as you read this book, God's great love and mercy will bring to mind those people or events that caused you great pain. And as you remember, don't fight it. Instead, allow God to lovingly walk you through the process of finally moving beyond your disappointment, resentment, unforgiveness, and rejection. This process requires prayer, transparency, and the love and support of wise and Godly people around you.

With God everything is possible (Matthew 19:26).

With God, your healing is possible.

I didn't realize it, but my healing was on the way as we continued in prayer and conversation that evening. Led by the Holy Spirit, my mentor and his wife helped me understand what was happening at the core of my oversensitivity. At a crucial point in my life, rejection entered in and took up residence. Rejection moved in and evicted my identity in Christ.

My identity was now rooted in trying to be accepted and affirmed. Rather than my identity being rooted in Christ, it was steeped in what others thought of me.

I viewed correction or suggestions for improvement as a character assassination. In other words, when someone tried to correct an action of mine, I interpreted it as a personality failure or flaw.

I had a hard time separating who I was from what I did.

To avoid correction or constructive criticism, I became easily offended and even argumentative. This way I would not feel like such a failure.

I had learned how to reject before being rejected.

If someone had a view that opposed mine, I interpreted the opposition as a devaluing of my opinion. So I vehemently defended my need to be right. Being right brought about a sick sense of affirmation. Wow! This was an eye-opener for me. I grew up thinking that people just had it out for me and it was up to me to fend for myself. I don't know about you, but the constant battling and need to defend myself eventually became old and sucked the energy and joy out of me. Can I get an "Amen?"

He asked questions that delved into my past and we identified some key events that contributed to my unhealthy perception of my value and self-worth. However, looking into my past was not for the purpose of placing blame. It was to acknowledge those things that contributed to my way of thinking and my behaviors; so I could make a conscious decision to not repeat them.

Beloved, once you become old enough to make your own decisions, you lose the right to blame others.

Disappointment and rejection causes us to lose trust in people. Some women wear their mistrust on their sleeves for everyone to see. But others, like me, desperately wanted to trust people, and so the mistrust was not as obvious. My issues of mistrust hid themselves in my insecurity.

My insecurity caused me to develop a secret suspicion of others. When someone said they loved me, I truly wanted to take it at face value but was always expecting the destructive fine print to reveal itself.

Realizing this, my mentor assured me that everyone wasn't out to get me or to demean me. To make his point, he said one of the most profound things anyone had ever said to me. It may not be as deep for you, but I will share it with the hopes of blessing someone. He asked if I believed he loved me. I answered "Yes." He asked if I believed he would not intentionally harm me.

I truly believed he would not knowingly hurt me. So I answered yes. Then he said, "There may be times when I unintentionally and unknowingly hurt you by what I say or how I say it. However, before you think the worst, remember that I love you first and foremost and then seek to get clarification; rather than assume I am trying to hurt you." In other words, he asked me to filter his interactions with me through the knowledge of his love for me.

Wow. Think about it. It's our assuming the worst first that gives power to our offensive nature.

We give more power to assumption rather than clarification.

There is a quote that says, "We tend to judge others by their actions, but want to be judged by our intentions."

Personally, I would prefer others to extend grace toward my actions and seek to clarify my intentions before thinking the worst of me. Wouldn't you? Assumptions and quick judgments are rooted in feelings of fear and rejection or fear of rejection. We convince ourselves that we have already struck out of the game before the pitcher even steps onto the mound.

THE NEW CONSECRATED COCOON

What a revelation! His counsel was very practical and simple. I didn't say it was easy, but it certainly wasn't complicated and we tend to make things more difficult than they need to be. It's all about a choice and the choice was mine.

From there, the conversation shifted to what I believed about God's love for me. Whoa! It only got better, or gooder as I like to say. I learned that I truly didn't believe that God loved me. I didn't believe He loved all of me. The key word was "all." I brought God down to the level of man. Man puts conditions on our love for each other. We freely show our love to others when we're in agreement, are happy, and are having our needs met.

You may not realize it, but we place ultimatums on our relationships when we say things like, "I love you when or I love you if." That's not like God. God says I love you – period! In fact He says that nothing can separate us from His love (Romans 8:38-39).

There were parts of my character that I believed God totally loved about me, and then there were those other parts that I didn't believe He could ever love. There were things I did that had shame or guilt attached to them and I didn't believe that God could forgive me and fully accept me. There were areas in my life where I experienced rejection and I included God in the list of those who rejected me. I figured if the person(s) I trusted couldn't accept me fully and without conditions, why would God?

At the end of this conversation it became painfully obvious that I had some serious work to do. Or, actually, that God had work to do in and through me. My mentor made it crystal clear that God had placed him in my life to help me deal with the issue of my identity and value in Christ. Was I excited at that notion? No! Of all people, He gave me someone who refused to dance when I broke out my violin. Did I need it? Yes! And I thank God for my mentor's obedience. I did give him a hard time, but he gave it right back as he was determined to do what God required of him.

He didn't give in to my emotional and self-preservation tactics. Most of all, he didn't give up on me. He kept his gaze fixed on the "me" God created me to be. That evening, God released me from the burden of things I did or said in the past and gave me a new slate. I truly became a new creation in Him (2 Corinthians 5:17).

While at a cookout a year later, my mentor started messing with me. He was trying to get under my skin and I didn't become defensive or argumentative. He looked at me and said, "You aren't fun anymore. I can't upset you." We laughed; he hugged me, and told me how proud he was of me.

The truth is, I knew what he was trying to do and refused to give him the victory. Don't think I wasn't tempted to let his irritating remarks bother me; I am still a work in progress. Ha-ha. However, with my new awareness of my worth in God's eyes I was empowered to choose how I reacted.

As I write, I tear up thinking of how very special I am to God that He would send this giant servant into my life to help deepen my relationship with my Heavenly daddy, my wonderful creator. I will be forever grateful.

So how does your sense of unworthiness play out? What easily offends you? We often think it's a person that causes feelings of unworthiness, but people can't do to us what we don't allow.

Someone can't make you feel unworthy.

But depending on their motive, they can capitalize on what's already there. If your lack of self-confidence makes them feel great about themselves, they might just hang around you all the time. Believe it or not, an over critical personality can also be a sign of lack of self-worth. Criticism is a clever attempt to redirect or deflect the attention to another.

Feelings of unworthiness can be contagious. If you have kids, your overly sensitive or critical nature is easily caught. It doesn't matter what you say, your children watch what you do and how you react to others. If you constantly cut your kids off when they are trying to speak, they could feel devalued or believe their voice isn't important.

Feelings of unworthiness are like an odor, easily detected by one of two types of people: The first are people who seek to take advantage of ones who have poor self-esteem and lack a sense of identity. The other is those who want to join forces with you. You have low self-esteem, they have feelings of unworthiness, and together you make the perfect recipe for a codependent relationship.

For those of you who don't know what it means to be codependent, I will give you a very high-level definition. A codependent personality is one that displays overly passive or excessive caretaking qualities. Codependents tend to make excuses for other people's inappropriate behavior. They also become extremely pre-occupied with the needs of others while neglecting their own needs in an unhealthy manner. Ultimately, codependents believe they need someone or something else to make them complete. Codependency occurs in all types of relationships, not just in those between a man and a woman.

There are also parent and child relationships that are extremely codependent.

Codependents assume their identity from the person they are overly preoccupied or consumed with.

This preoccupation benefits the one who hooks up with a codependent for selfish gain. Ladies, if you are a highly codependent person, there is a controlling, selfish, manipulative, and extremely charismatic man out there who can spot you coming a mile away. You might already be married to this fella. Be careful of men with these types of characteristics. A man like this can also be deemed a codependent. He doesn't appear to be as weak or needy as you, but he really is.

If your identity is rooted in anything or anyone other than God, it's time to get it right. If not, you will live a life of striving to become someone you were not created to be.

The real you is not a figment of someone else's imagination.

The real you is who God says you are. Maybe while you were a young girl someone inappropriately communicated a message of unworthiness, and you've been operating in that lie for years. Maybe you've believed that your existence is a mishap, a misfortune, or a mistake. God wants you to know that there was nothing about you that is a "miss." He hit the mark when He created you. He hit the daughter lottery when you were born.

He doesn't just accept the parts of you that are serving in ministry, are a good worker on your job, or an excellent cook. He also accepts that part of you that yells at your kids. He accepts that part of you that feels discouraged at times. He accepts those areas in which you struggle because they all make up who you are – in Him.

After that time spent with my mentors, I adapted a saying that I wrote everywhere and constantly repeated to myself. "God loves me. He loves all of me." The key word is "all." I will not lie and tell you that it doesn't take work and lots of prayer to transform your thinking from being a victim to being a victor. It does take work. Hard work. But the benefits far outweigh the sacrifice.

At some point, you and only you must make a decision to believe what God says about you. You must read, believe, and accept the Scriptures that speak of how much you matter to God. You must not seek others or possessions to dictate your worth.

They become idols or little gods in your life. You will worship them and eventually accept their truth rather than God's truth.

What's the truth? God created you whole in every way. In Him, you lack nothing. God loves you just as you are. Even though you and your circumstances go through many changes, God doesn't change and neither does His love for you. There is nothing you can do that can cause Him to love you more or less. He is your greatest supporter. He is your biggest cheerleader. At times when you don't have enough confidence in yourself – God has faith in you. He knows your potential and sees the end results.

Start declaring who you are in God.

Stop declaring those negative words your mom or dad may have said about you. No longer accept those demeaning things spoken over you by our ex-husband. Refuse to believe the horrible things your unappreciative child said on the way out the door. What God says about you trumps everyone else's opinions and subjective remarks. And when God in His great love reveals areas where you fell short, ask for forgiveness. Ask for it and also accept it.

Then, ask person(s) you hurt to forgive you also. Put that old you in the past and leave her there. It's time to move forward in God's unwavering and unfailing love for you. He loves you more than you could ever imagine.

Today marks a new you! I've provided several Scriptures to give you a jump start on your new journey. These do not even begin to scratch the surface of God's many promises to you and me. But they are a great place to begin. Read them, write them down on sticky notes and paste them on your bathroom mirror. Speak them over yourself, meditate on them, and memorize them. Tuck them deep in the crevices of your heart and be prepared to whip them out when people or situations seek to redefine your identity.

By the way, it's important to get a good grasp on how much God truly loves you. Only then can you love others with a love that imitates God's love for you.

Scriptures

God gives you a fresh start, so don't hold on to the past.

"Therefore, if anyone is in Christ, he is a new creation; old things have passed away; behold, all things have become new." 2 Corinthians 5:17 (New King James Version)

God sacrificed everything for you so you could be saved and live with Him in Heaven forever.

"For God so loved the world that he gave his one and only Son, that whoever believes in Him shall not perish but have eternal life." John 3:16 (New International Version)

There is nothing you can do to stop God from loving you.

"Can anything ever separate us from Christ's love? Does it mean he no longer loves us if we have trouble or calamity, or are persecuted, or hungry, or destitute, or in danger, or threatened with death? No, despite all these things, overwhelming victory is ours through Christ, who loved us. And I am convinced that nothing can ever separate us from God's love. Neither death nor life, neither angels nor demons, neither our fears for today nor our worries about tomorrow - not even the powers of Hell can separate us from God's love. No power in the sky above or in the earth below - indeed, nothing in all creation will ever be able to separate us from the love of God that is revealed in Christ Jesus our Lord." Romans 8:35, 37-39 (New Living Translation)

God loves justice and He loves his people. He always has your back.

"For the Lord loves justice and he will never abandon the godly. He will keep them safe forever." Psalm 37:28 (New Living Translation)

God's love never fails and is a source of shelter and protection.

"Your unfailing love, O Lord, is as vast as the Heavens; your faithfulness reaches beyond the clouds. Your righteousness is like the mighty mountains, your justice like the ocean depths. You care for people and animals alike, O Lord. How precious is your unfailing love, O God! All humanity finds shelter in the shadow of your wings." Psalm 36:5-7 (New Living Translation)

God is with you, calming your fears and singing over you.

"For the Lord your God is living among you. He is a mighty savior. He will take delight in you with gladness. With his love, he will calm all your fears. He will rejoice over you with joyful songs." Zephaniah 3:17 (New Living Translation)

God's love is rich in mercy and full of grace.

"But because of his great love for us, God, who is rich in mercy, made us alive with Christ even when we were dead in transgressions - it is by grace you have been saved." Ephesians 2:4-5 (New International Version)

God has wonderful plans for your future.

"For I know the plans I have for you," declares the LORD, "plans to prosper you and not to harm you, plans to give you hope and a future." Jeremiah 29:11 (New International Version)

God's thoughts about you are rare, beautiful, and too many to count.

"Your thoughts - how rare, how beautiful! God, I'll never comprehend them! I couldn't even begin to count them - any more than I could count the sand of the sea." Psalm 139:17-18 (The Message)

God's love for you is larger than you can imagine, gives you strength, and makes you complete in Him.

"I pray that from his glorious, unlimited resources he will empower you with inner strength through his Spirit. Then Christ will make his home in your hearts as you trust in Him. Your roots will grow down into God's love and keep you strong. And may you have the power to understand, as all God's people should, how wide, how long, how high, and how deep his love is. May you experience the love of Christ, though it is too great to understand fully. Then you will be made complete with all the fullness of life and power that comes from God." Ephesians 3:16-19 (New Living Translation)

God promises He will never leave you or abandon you.

"Be strong. Take courage. Don't be intimidated. Don't give them (trials) a second thought because God, your God, is striding *ahead of you. He's right there with you. He won't let you down; he won't leave you." Deuteronomy 31:6 (The Message)*

When God forgives, it's a done deal. He doesn't bring it back up.

"He (God) has removed our sins as far from us as the east is from the west." Psalm 103:12 (New Living Translation)

Before you were born, God hand-picked and reserved special plans for you.

"Before I shaped you in the womb, I knew all about you. Before you saw the light of day, I had holy plans for you." Jeremiah 1:5 (The Message)

Your name is engraved in the palms of God's hands.

"Can a mother forget the baby at her breast and have no compassion on the child she has borne? Though she may forget, I will not forget you! See, I have engraved you on the palms of my hands." Isaiah 49:15-16 (New International Version)

God's love never quits!

"God remembered us when we were down, His love never quits. Rescued us from the trampling boot, His love never quits. Takes care of everyone in time of need. His love never quits. Thank God, who did it all! His love never quits!" Psalm 136:23-26 (The Message)

God's marvelous love is reserved for His children.

"What marvelous love the Father has extended to us! Just look at it - we're called children of God! That's who we really are." 1 John 3:1 (The Message)

God will cause the devil to flee when you remain humble before Him.

"Humble yourselves before God. Resist the devil and he will flee from you." James 4:7 (New Living Translation)

God comforts you in your time of trouble so you can comfort others who need it.

"He (God) comforts us in all our troubles so that we can comfort others. When they are troubled, we will be able to give them the same comfort God has given us." 2 Corinthians 1:4 (New Living Translation)

God doesn't allow you to be tempted beyond what you can handle.

"The temptations in your life are no different from what others experience. And God is faithful. He will not allow the temptation to be more than you can stand. When you are tempted, he will show you a way out so that you can endure." 1 Corinthians 10:13 (New Living Translation)

Reflection

1. Self-worth is the confidence and satisfaction you have about yourself. How would you describe your self-worth?
2. Do you regularly compare yourself to others?
3. What sources do you tend to take cues from about your self-worth or value?
4. Would you define your experience with God as one that is religious (what you do) or relational (who you are to Him)?
5. Do you struggle with oversensitivity? Are you easily offended?
6. Do you have a difficult time accepting constructive feedback?
7. Have you ever felt rejected? If so, how does that affect your relationships today?
8. Are you able to separate who you are from what you do?
9. Do you feel disrespected or devalued when someone disagrees with your point of view?

10. If you were to take a trip into your childhood, are there specific relationships or a particular event that caused you to feel inferior, inadequate or devalued?
11. Do you struggle with issues of trust? Do you question the authenticity of those who try to get close to you?
12. Do you assume the worst about people at first?
13. Do you believe that God loves ALL of you (even those areas you know are not pleasing to Him)?
14. Are you dealing with any issues of unforgiveness with yourself or others?

THE NEW CONSECRATED COCOON

Eve – Bad Apple or the Apple of God's Eye?

The more I learned about the characteristics of a Godly woman, the more I desired to understand God's purpose for my life as a mother, wife, daughter, sister, and friend. To truly appreciate why God created women in the first place, I went back to my roots. Not my West Indian roots, but my spiritual roots, back to the Garden of Eden. I wanted to know more about Eve – the first woman ever created. The name Eve is derived from the Hebrew word 'haya,' which means to breathe, live, or have life. Eve was the mother of all human life, so she was appropriately named.

Who was this Eve? Why was she created? What was God's plan for her? Did she fulfill that plan? Many people are familiar with the story of Adam and Eve in the Garden. Young and old, black and white, male and female; all could give some account as to what happened. The events can be summed up as, "God told Adam and Eve not to eat the fruit. They did. They blamed each other and were kicked out of the Garden."

Although it seems pretty cut and dry, a lot of what occurred in the Garden affects how we as women see ourselves today. And the events of the Garden also introduced unhealthy dynamics between male and female relationships, particularly in marriage.

There's no doubt in my mind that God did and still does have a very special purpose for women. Like Eve, His plans for you and me go beyond our sin.

Our sin doesn't cancel His plans, but it does delay them.

Just as Eve disappointed God, we too fall short of His standards. But He never stops loving us. The more I learned about Eve and her mess-ups, the more I understood and appreciated God's grace, mercy, and compassion toward us.

The bigger our sin, the greater His mercy.

Each of us is the apple of God's eye (Psalm 17:8). He delights in us. And when we make mistakes, He's our biggest cheerleader. He doesn't stop believing in us.

We often don't see ourselves as a whole creation. We tend to take cues about our identity from our individual roles.

If things aren't going well in our marriage or our children are in a rebellious stage, we view ourselves as failures. But being a wife or a mother isn't the sum total of your existence. For many, God's plan does include getting married and having kids, but I'm here to tell you - it doesn't stop there. And sadly, many women's self- worth is defined by these roles.

Yes, being a wife or a mother is crucial and you should desire to be all you can in these roles. But let's face it. No matter how wonderful you are, some husbands are going to cheat and leave. Some children are going to rebel and dishonor you. Some best friend is going to be disloyal or inappropriately butcher your character. When this happens, you must remember that your value isn't determined by the actions of others; it's determined by God's love for you. God loves you. He loves all of you.

Women were created to be game changers and difference makers.

Like Eve, we were created with power and purpose. When God doled out influence to both Adam and Eve, I believe He gave Eve an extra dose. I also believe that when He assigned the capacity for "number of words spoken in a day," He gave Eve a triple portion. Ha ha, we won't go there.

Truth be told, women are complex and unique creations. And what better way to express our uniqueness than the way in which Eve was created. Adam was created from dust, but Eve was formed from Adam's rib (Genesis 2:21).

I've heard different "man-made" theories as to why God used Adam's rib instead of another body part. It's been said that if God created Eve from Adam's brain, she might have been viewed as intellectually inferior. If God created her from

Adam's back, she might have been perceived as a burden. If created from his hand, she may have been mistreated by Adam. If created from his foot, he may have walked all over her. But she was created from his rib, so she could be close to his heart and by his side. She wasn't created to rule over him, nor was she created to be his doormat.

Though there are no scriptural verses to support these theories, I do believe that God was intentional about choosing Adam's rib, and I like the idea of her coming from the closest thing to his heart. I think that might explain why women are so emotional. At least it sounds like a great excuse. Can I get an "Amen?"

I also believe that the serpent targeted Eve because of her God-given influence, purpose, and potential. Another word for influence is to persuade. The enemy isn't going to waste time and effort on someone who isn't a threat. He knew the power God had given to Eve and knew she would be able to persuade Adam to eat the forbidden fruit.

Eve was created to be Adam's helpmate. Being his helper didn't make her subservient or inferior – it meant she would complement him. Where he may be weak, she would come alongside him and strengthen him, encourage him, support, him, love him, and respect him. And he would do the same for her. However, because of selfish desires hidden deep in her heart, Eve became Adam's HURTmate rather than a helper. As a result of their disobedience, sin was introduced into the human race and all are born with the propensity toward sin.

So what exactly happened in the Garden? First off, Adam and Eve had everything they could ever want in the Garden. They lived totally rent-free, didn't need to pay for utilities because they had running water and lights twenty four hours a day, seven days a week. They didn't have to budget for food because there were many trees with lots of fruit. And money for clothes wasn't an issue – they wore the same thing every day. Don't worry; you will get that one later.

God placed two trees in the middle of the Garden – the Tree of Life and the Tree of the Knowledge of Good and Evil. He told Adam that they could eat from any tree in the Garden, except from the Tree of the Knowledge of Good and Evil. There is something about human beings that desire to have or do something all the more once we're told not to. That greasy hamburger in the commercial never looked as good until the day you began your three-day fast. Can I get a witness? I am serious. That's how we are. Just when we are told we can't have it, we want it.

When I was pregnant with my first son, I remember craving a glass of wine or a wine cooler on more than one occasion. I wasn't even someone who regularly had alcohol. But I knew I was unable to have it during my pregnancy and that made it all the more desirable.

Satan is the voice of rebellion that waits for the right opportunity to whisper in our ear. Let's face it – we all have forbidden fruit. What's forbidden fruit? Anything God says you cannot have or should not partake in because of the pain and destruction it will cause. Here's a proven truth about sin. Sin always takes you further than you want to go, demands more than you want to pay, and keeps you longer than you want to stay. Sin looks appealing to the eyes, promises satisfaction to the flesh, and causes you to believe you will be better off for having done it.

Forbidden fruit is a great deception. It's trickery. Deception is all about twisting the truth. It's a trap. One of the most desirable forms of forbidden fruit today is inappropriate male/female relationships. Many are having sex without getting married, and ones who are married are having sex with people other than their spouse. Many are committing emotional adultery. That's when a married man or woman emotionally connects him or herself with someone other than their spouse. They share all of their feelings, desires, and even hopes and dreams with someone who has no honor or respect for the covenant of marriage. What are the repercussions for partaking in forbidden fruit? Fatal dis- eases, unplanned pregnancies, divorce, and devastated families to name a few.

Many women are walking around wounded, lonely, and desperate for attention. They are vulnerable and easy to take advantage of. Then there are men out there who have razor sharp antennas who detect this weakness and move in for the kill. Many of them are lurking around on the social websites, chat rooms, and online dating sites.

Are you spending a lot of time on the Internet chatting with guys? Old boyfriends? Your high school sweetheart? Or perhaps a married man? What are you truly searching for? Are you hoping to find Mr. Right? Whether you are married or single, your time is better spent in prayer asking God to help you become Mrs. Right. Whatever you are searching for that is outside of God's will, the devil will make sure you find it. Be careful that you are not setting yourself up to be bait for Satan, rather than a vessel for God's use.

Our desire to partake of forbidden fruit begins in our thoughts. So what are you meditating on? What's constantly on your mind when you lay down at night? Thoughts turn into feelings and then feelings can easily turn into actions. Isn't it interesting that Eve probably had thousands and thousands of trees to choose from, but she could not, or would not, resist the desire to eat from the *one* tree God said not to eat from.

It's so incredibly human to focus on the one thing we shouldn't have versus the many other blessings we do have. Eve's battle began in her mind. She secretly questioned and doubted God. She entertained two thoughts. First, she thought God was withholding something from her. And secondly, she wanted to be like God and know all things. Ladies, if you find yourself questioning God's motive or character because you can't have what you want – you are in a very dangerous place.

Eve was right! God was withholding something from her. He didn't want her to have the knowledge of good *and* evil. At this point all she knew was good. And God tried to keep it that way for her own protection. She and Adam didn't even realize they were naked. They had no shame. Sex was a pure and sacred act between husband and wife. There was nothing perverted about it. Evil was foreign to them, but not to Satan. He is very familiar with sin, rebellion, and the repercussions therein. He was banished from Heaven for becoming prideful and wanting to be like God. And since he couldn't get even with God, he turned his gaze on what God loves the most – the human race. Satan doesn't want to go down by himself, he wants to take a whole crew of people with him; particularly those who claim to love God.

Like Eve, Satan approaches you and me and plants seeds intended to question God's love and character. The serpent didn't cause Eve to sin. He simply capitalized on thoughts that were already there, as she desired to be like God. The Bible says that the enemy can only tempt or entice us with our own evil desires (James 1:14).

I need you to get a picture of that in your mind. He entices or lures us away using the thing that is already appealing to us. In other words, Eve was already eyeballing the fruit. And all Satan needed to do was walk up and say, "Looks good, huh?" Then Eve says, "Yes, it does."

"So what are you waiting for? Eat it. You know you want it."

"I can't." "Why not?"

"God said if I ate it, I would die."

"Surely he didn't mean you would *actually* die..."

When the enemy approaches you and me, he uses those things we have already been looking at in our mind's eye or in our thoughts. He targets those things we are already meditating on and desiring and builds a case for why we should have it. Do you get this? It's important you understand how the deceiver works. That's why the Bible says that we cannot say it's God who is tempting us because God would not stoop to such a level as to willingly destroy us. Satan will. His goal is not to just tempt you; it is to bring you down. It is to abort God's purpose and plan in and through you. He wants to diminish your usefulness to God.

Satan confronted Eve with a topic that was already appealing. His line of questioning was strategically designed to uncover her doubt regarding God's motives and commands. God told Adam that if they ate from the tree they would die. The serpent told Eve that they would not die, they would simply be like God, knowing good and evil. God is not a liar. If he said they would die, that's what He meant. And when they ate the fruit, there were two deaths: first a spiritual death and then a physical one.

Adam and Eve were not created to physically die. They were created to live forever. And after their disobedience, God lessened the average human life span from infinity to 900 years old. Imagine having kids when you are three hundred years old? And as man continued to rebel, the average life span became even less.

Not only did they eventually die physically, but they immediately died spiritually. When they ate the forbidden fruit, their relationship with God was injured. Before eating the fruit, they had a pure, deep, intimate, and transparent relationship with God and each other. Once they ate the fruit, they realized they were naked, felt ashamed, tried to cover themselves with fig leaves, and hid from God.

Isn't that what we tend to do when we mess up? We try to cover it up and then we hide from God. We hide from Him in the sense that our prayer life and church attendance becomes inconsistent and sporadic. We no longer feel worthy to tell others about Jesus because of our own guilt or shame.

Eve gave in to her desires and ate the forbidden fruit first. Then she gave it to Adam, who the Bible says was with her (Genesis 3:6). Time out! Where was Adam? The Bible didn't say she had to call out for him or tell the serpent she'd go get him and come right back. He was there. Right there! Earth to Adam. Assuming he was truly within earshot of the conversation, why in the world didn't he intervene?

There is a reason the Bible says the serpent was more crafty than all of the animals (Genesis 3:1). He was slick and is always looking for a two-for-one deal. He's never satisfied with bringing hurt and destruction to one life. He seeks to destroy entire families and more than one generation. Nine out of ten times when he attacks you, he is after your marriage and/or your children. But he knows in order to get to your husband and your kids; he must come through you first.

Remember I stated that Eve was the one with the most influence. I believe if the serpent tried to have Adam convince Eve to eat the fruit, things would have gone differently. Not because Eve didn't want to eat the fruit, but because she wouldn't want Adam telling her what to do. Don't forget – she was a woman. I could hear the conversation now. "Oh...Uh uh (shaking her finger at him and rolling her eyes), you're not going to drag me down in your mess, Adam. And you sure aren't going to tell me what to do. Sorry, honey, but you ain't the boss of me."

Adam, on the other hand, liked how calm things were in the Garden, so when Eve offered the fruit, he probably went along for the sake of keeping the peace - happy wife, happy life.

Obviously, I'm being humorous. I hope you smiled. But seriously, disobedience is nothing to laugh at. Obedience is God's love language. God knows we love Him when we do what He asks us to (1 John 5:3). Plain and simple. When we obey God, we invite blessings into our lives. When we disobey Him, we reap painful repercussions. And Adam and Eve's sin opened the door for destruction, allowing Satan to introduce several lies into the Garden.

When they sinned, lies about God's character, our value to God, relationships, and accountability were set in motion. Lies that we still contend with today. And like Eve, we also struggle with the desire to be like God. We want total control of our lives and desire to know everything.

The enemy is a deceiver and constantly dangles forbidden fruit before each of us with the promise of immediate

THE NEW CONSECRATED COCOON

gratification. This tactic makes me think of the great marketing realm of TV commercials. I especially think of those ads that sell medicine products. You know them; the ones in which the side effects are often more dangerous than the potential relief of the medicine itself.

Let's say it's a heartburn commercial. The spokesperson speaks of the immediate relief at a pace we can all follow and understand. But as the commercial progresses, the pace is intensified and hurried, almost like an auctioneer. "Side effects may include shortness of breath, an allergic reaction, swollen feet, dizziness, blood clots, and even death." Huh? Even death? Are they serious? At that rate I'll keep my heartburn, thank you very much. Satan uses that same marketing ploy. He promotes the instant pleasure, while leaving the devastating and painful effects to the fine print of the offer. Who actually reads the fine print? Not many and certainly not those who are seeking immediate relief. Satan's side effects to sinful behavior is written in fine print, not immediately noticeable and downplayed when compared to the so-called benefits.

He desires for God's children to be ignorant, weak, powerless, and selfish. Satan's ultimate goal is to have you turn your back on God, but he's not that obvious. He's clever. His first tactic is subtle. It begins with complacency. As you become complacent you get comfortable living a life of compromise and half-hearted commitments toward the things of God. You tell yourself that as long as you attend church each Sunday God accepts your behavior. But that's where you are sadly mistaken about the God we serve. He is an all or nothing God. He is not a "little dab will do you God." You are either fully surrendered or you are not. There is a saying "If Jesus isn't Lord of all, He's not Lord at all."

If you are attending a church that is truly seeking God's holiness, at some point you will not be able to sit Sunday after Sunday, hear God's word and not squirm in your seat due to the Holy Spirit's conviction. May I lovingly say, "If you are actively living in sin and you attend a church that inspires you and tickles your ears, allowing you to return home the same way you entered in, I have to wonder about your church."

Each time you enter into a church that preaches the uncompromised Word and truly allows the Holy Spirit to have His way; you should feel uncomfortable in your sin and desire to quickly get right with God. I'm just saying...

Any church were the pastor speaks messages that encourages man's comfort rather than Holy Spirit conviction is more than likely the *wrong* church for you. I pray you receive what I just shared with the utmost love.

So back to the enemy.

One of the enemy's most effective tactics is complacency. Being complacent causes you to have a false sense that everything is okay the way it is and there's no need to improve. You don't need to grow. So you slowly detach from God and no longer desire His daily input, correction, or guidance.

Your heart becomes hardened and less sensitive to the effects of your sin. As a result you begin to lose your effectiveness for the kingdom. Before you know it, there is a chasm between you and God and then you blame God for not being there for you. When in fact, you've made decisions that told God you no longer wanted His input.

Eve believed that God was keeping something from her and decided to take matters into her own hands. God was in fact keeping something from her, but it was for her protection. Sadly, Satan's strategies are just as effective today as they were in the Garden. Ladies, there are times when God does not reveal certain things to you. He's an all-knowing God. He sees the big picture and knows what's best for each of us. At some point, you must decide that you will trust Him. How do you know whether you like a certain type of food that you're not familiar with? You taste it. Well...if you're like my oldest son, you look at it and turn your nose in the air. But you truly can't say whether you like or dislike something until you've given it a try.

THE NEW CONSECRATED COCOON

That's what God wants you to do. He wants you to taste and see that He is good (Psalm 34:8). God wants you to take His promises for a test run. And trust me, once you've experienced His goodness, faithfulness, mercy, grace, and unconditional love, you will not want to return to your old self-sufficient and self-preserving ways.

Eve was the first woman who wanted to have total control over her life, but she wasn't the last. In our prayer time we ask God to open the doors He wants opened and close the ones He wants shut. Yet many of us get our faces smashed by doors God is closing because we're still trying to see what He's doing. We ask God to remove things that hinder our growth, yet tighten our grip when He tugs at those things. We tell God to have His way, yet we reason and negotiate with Him when He calls us out of our comfort zone. Our elegant prayers turn into acts of disobedience when God requires us to deny our flesh and harness our emotions.

Before their sin, Adam and Eve had it made in the Garden. They spent intimate time with God. Think about it. What son or daughter wouldn't enjoy spending one-on-one intimate time with their daddy? God loved Adam and Eve deeply. He withheld nothing. Yet, somewhere in Eve's heart she desired to be something God didn't create her to be. She lusted to have something God didn't intend for her to have.

Ladies, we still struggle with the same desire to please our flesh that led Eve to eat the fruit. We still desire to be like God – knowing everything and having control over it. To this day, we still believe the lies the serpent spewed at Eve in the Garden. As a result, we are still experiencing the curses or repercussions from Adam and Eve's disobedience. The cost they paid didn't stop with them. It continued to their children, their children's children, and so on. You and I are descendants of Adam and Eve and therefore, we too must pay the high price that comes with sin.

Most times, the gratification or pleasure that accompanies sin is immediate, but the repercussions aren't. Can I let you in on a secret? Satan has nothing to offer you but pain, strife, and loss; and ultimately a one-way trip to Hell. Your destiny and purpose comes from God. Every blessing and good gift comes from God – no one else (James 1:17).

Satan is an imitator of God. He wants to be like God.

So he pretends to give you something good. He pretends to give you something that God has told you that you cannot have or you cannot have it right now. If God has delayed a request you've made, He knows you are not ready. He knows if you get it now, it will bring destruction and pain; not glory.

If God says no to a request, then it's not for you to have. Satan comes in and he convinces you that you need it and you need it now. So he offers that forbidden fruit with the promise that you will not die. His offers always come with a price to pay and often requires compromise, ignoring your intuition, disobedience of wise counsel, a pushing of your own agenda, or our getting ahead of God by forcing a chain of events to happen a certain way or within a certain timeframe. There is never a true sense of peace with these tempting offers. When you are feeling pressured to make a decision or participate in something that you are uneasy about, remember that God leads and Satan pushes. Anxiousness is not of God. However, if you proceed, Satan will attempt to provide a false sense of peace to justify your desires.

There are times in my life when I know that my actions or words will net a desired outcome, and I am enticed by the immediate gratification. Before reaching for the fruit, I must consider the effects of my actions on my purpose and destiny. I must consider the effects of my actions on others. I must seriously contemplate what I am willing to flush down the toilet (integrity, ministry, trust, meaningful relationships). Not only can you lose the trust of man, but also God's trust. When God is able to trust you, He gives you special assignments and extra power to complete them. He gives you favor and His protection remains with you.

The more God is able to trust you, the more He will give to you.

THE NEW CONSECRATED COCOON

2 Chronicles 16:9 says God searches the earth for those whose hearts are fully committed to Him, so He can show Himself strong on their behalf.

God's grace and mercy are two of the most beautiful gifts He's given us. When we experience His grace, we get what we don't deserve. When we experience His mercy, we don't get what we do deserve. They are gifts that demonstrate God's unwavering love toward us. God loves us so much that at no point during our interaction with forbidden fruit will He not accept our sincere apology. So if you find yourself staring at and desiring the forbidden fruit and realize it's wrong, God is willing to forgive you. If you reach out and touch the fruit, forgiveness is readily available. If you grab the fruit and bring it close to your lips, God's grace and mercy still abounds. And even *after* you have tasted the fruit, God will not turn His back on you. God hears and is moved by prayers of repentance at any point that we cry out to Him.

Always remember that sin takes you further than you want to go – it's progressive. And the deeper you enter in, the higher the chances are of taking others with you. Like Eve, once you offer another person the fruit or accept someone else's offer to partake, lives are devastated and relationships are never the same.

As humans we struggle with forgiving others and ourselves, but God has no problem in this area. He is the great forgiver and His grace and mercy are available at every turn. I am so far from perfection. But I do perfectly strive to keep my heart tender to God's corrections and cautions on a daily basis. Yes, I know I will receive forgiveness after I've tasted the fruit, but I want to hear God's voice when I am staring at or thinking about that fruit for longer than I should. God's forgiveness comes with strength to help us overcome our sins, if we accept it. Rapid and immediate repentance is a great way to stop the progression of sin.

Before moving on, I want to speak briefly about what to do after you've partaken of the forbidden fruit.

Be encouraged, sister; there is life after sin.

Your ability to move forward is determined by decisions you make. Satan's goal is for you to hide yourself from God and isolate yourself from others once you've sinned. He wants you to walk under a cloud of shame and self-condemnation. He wants you to feel unworthy of God's forgiveness.

My precious sister, there is nothing you can do to forfeit God's forgiveness. The Bible says if we confess our sins and sincerely ask God to forgive us, He is faithful not only to forgive us, but also to cleanse us from all unrighteousness (1 John 1:9). What does that mean? It means that not only does He wipe our slate clean, but He also removes those things that keep us from being right with Him. God is faithful.

I hate to break the news to you, but God doesn't just magically remove your desire to sin simply because you ask Him to. You must ask with an honest heart and be willing to do the work needed to turn away from the sin – that's what it means to repent.

Repentance is a turning away from your sin and a turning toward God. Why turn toward God? So He can empower you to put your desire for that sin behind you. This is a job for two people: you and God. There is your part and then there is His. He will not do your part. Forcing you to do something you truly don't want to do is taking away your free will. And you cannot do His part. God's part is to fill you with power, cleanse you of unwanted desires, and give you a fresh start. God's part is in response to you doing your part.

Trust me, if there was ever a time for God to revoke free will it would have been in the Garden.

God knew that Eve would choose the fruit, but it doesn't mean His heart wasn't crushed when she did. If you're a mother, you understand this. It's like watching one of your children headed toward a painful situation because of decisions made, and knowing you can't control them. It hurts to watch. Imagine God looking at Eve and the serpent talking. How His heart must have broken as he observed the sly grin on the serpent's face. And then, Eve takes the fruit and bites it. When Eve did that, God saw each and every one of our faces. He saw your husband cheating on you, my sister. He saw the divorce you didn't want. He saw the molestation you didn't deserve. He saw the premature death of your child and the incredible pain it caused. He saw that accident that left you paralyzed. He saw that cancer that gripped your health. His heart was broken into many pieces by the choice Eve made. He didn't take away her free will and He is not going to take away yours.

God desires that when you ask for forgiveness, you mean it with your whole heart, and not because you were caught. Many are sorry they were caught in their sin, but are not sorry about the sin. Being sorry is not the same as having a heart of repentance. Your desire to be forgiven should be out of sadness because you've broken God's heart. It should be motivated by a desire to bridge the distance between you and God that was created by your sin. You should want to make things right between you and God again. Your request should be soaked in humility and genuineness.

God responds to a sincere heart. I know this to be true for as I type I am reminded of an inappropriate relationship many years ago. It didn't please God – bottom line. We were both professing Christians who prayed together in the midst of our sin. I now know that all that praying didn't matter a hill of beans, as they hit the ceiling and returned void. God was not pleased with our relationship and turned a deaf ear to our unified prayers.

On two occasions, I prayed by myself for God to remove all desire for this individual. The first time I asked God to help me end the relationship; I kind of sort of meant it. Have you been there? I knew it was the right thing to do. I didn't want others to be disappointed in me if they found out. But when it came to what was going on deep in my heart – I didn't mean it. I still desired that individual. I still wanted his affirmation. I enjoyed the way he made me feel. I craved the attention. I cherished the companionship. And so my praying to God was in vain. When I got up off my knees, my next action was to check my phone to see whether he called.

However, the second time, weeks later, I laid flat on my face, cried out to the Lord with tears of repentance, a desire to restore my intimacy with Him, and a desire to earn back His trust. I was shocked. God miraculously and immediately answered my prayer. I arose from lying on the floor, blouse soaked in tears, and feeling 100 pounds lighter.

I was lighter. I had lost the huge burden of knowing that I wasn't pleasing God. I lost the burden of the secretive nature of our relationship. I lost the burden of shame. And I picked up the forgiveness, unconditional love, and mercy of my Heavenly Father. Will it be that immediate for you? Maybe. Or maybe it will take a few days or weeks. But I tell you that when you ask God to do something, you must ask believing that He will do it and not doubt. The Bible says that those who ask and doubt at the same time should not expect God to answer their prayers (James 1:6-7).

When you cry out to God for help, cry out in faith and believe that He will reward you because you seek Him with your whole heart (Hebrews 11:6). Also, for goodness sake, give God something to work with. If I got up from all of that weeping, repenting, and believing and then called that man again, I would have taken matters out of God's hand and reclaimed it all. We must do what's within our power and then give it to God to do what only He can do. I was simply amazed at how God quickly answered my heart's cry because He knew I was finally sincere. That brother didn't know what hit him. The day before my prayer, I was a needy, clingy individual and he loved every moment of it. Then God got a hold of me and my desires turned from man to God. I desired the love and approval of my Heavenly daddy. Oh, the joy that filled my heart knowing my daddy was proud of me.

There is much to be said about experiencing a true intimacy with God. There is a freedom that cannot be explained. And when we give up that freedom, life just isn't the same. If you haven't experienced this intimacy, then you have no idea what I'm talking about. But for those who have, you understand. Losing intimacy with God means losing joy, peace, and feelings of self-worth. When you have true intimacy with God, the sin you initially enjoyed becomes short-lived. You lose your appetite for that unhealthy desire.

I've said a lot in this chapter, and now it's time to put the rubber to the road. I am led to ask. "Are you involved in a sin that you know is grieving God's heart?"

Are you struggling to have intimate prayer time with God because of your guilt and shame?

If so, my sister, in the precious name of Jesus, I lovingly ask you to stop it. Right now! But you say, "I can't stop." Yes you can. You don't want to stop. There is a difference. Your sin has become familiar. You depend on it for your value and self-worth. And yet there is no real value in what you are doing. You are using it to escape a deeper pain. Your healing can only come from one person – God.

Are you waiting to be found out? Will that make you stop? If so, the damage might be irreversible. Why wait for that to happen? Do you want everything God has for you? Then you must stop. And you must stop now!

God cannot entrust great things into your care because of the reckless way you are handling this situation. It's not too late. It doesn't matter what you've done – God will forgive you! If you don't desire to stop, pray and ask God to give you the desire to stop. Confide in someone you trust. Go to a pastor, leader, or spiritually mature friend. Be honest with them so you can be held accountable to stop what you are doing. There is practical help available for you. It may not feel like it, but there are people who love you and want the best for you.

And even more, God loves you, and He is ready to forgive you right now. If this pertains to you...stop and take a moment to sincerely ask God to remove your desire for this sin. Ask for His forgiveness. He's waiting. Right now, my sister, I agree with you in prayer that God will answer your heart's cry and this is your divine moment to step into the glorious, fruitful, and purposeful life God has for you! Remember, if you ask, God is faithful to forgive you.

Hallelujah!

Eve messed up. No doubt about it. And some might say she's the bad apple that spoiled the bunch. But I say hogwash. Please understand, disobedience isn't the end of the story. Even when we disobey, God doesn't revoke the gifts He gives us, cancel the purpose He has for us, nor withhold His love from us. But, living in disobedience eventually makes our gifts not as effective, and it does cause us to feel like God doesn't love us (unworthiness).

Sin separates us from God. But repentance reconciles us to Him. And when reconciled, we are empowered to step back into our purpose and destiny. The more we obey God and show ourselves trustworthy of the things He has for us, the more He blesses us and use us to radically impact the lives of others.

Although Eve disobeyed, God never stopped loving her and He never stops loving you and me. Psalm 17:8 says God will keep us as the apple of His eye, and hide us in the shadow of His wings. Isn't that beautiful? Not only does He love us unconditionally and is willing to forgive us, but He will also protect us from all that tries to harm us.

This is great news, and I pray that this chapter inspires you to seek after a deep intimacy with God. Desire to be and remain the apple of His eye. Desire to live a life that pleases Him. Remain transparent before Him. When our hearts are truly surrendered to God, He answers the requests of our hearts and not the demands of our flesh. And when you mess up, repent, accept His forgiveness, and move on. Move forward in confidence knowing you are the daughter of the King, equipped and empowered with God's mercy and grace.

Reflection

1. Are you actively involved in a sin you know does not please God?
2. If so, have you prayed and sincerely asked God to remove the desire for that sin?
3. Like Eve, have you wrongly influenced someone else to partake in your sin?
4. Have you blamed someone else for a 'sin' decision you made?
5. Do you incorporate repentance into your daily prayers?
6. If married, do you take responsibility for your personal disobedience to God without first focusing on your husband's shortfalls?
7. Do you believe that God still loves you even when you disappoint Him?
8. Are you currently gazing on something or someone that can be used by the enemy to tempt you into sin?
9. Eve did not have enough faith in God to believe He knew what was best for her. Is there an area in your life where you lack faith and are trusting in your own feelings?

"It's impossible to please God apart from faith. And why? Because anyone who wants to approach God must believe both that he exists and that he cares enough to respond to those who seek Him." Hebrews 11:6 (The Message).

ANN THOMAS

Created to Be Blessed - Not Cursed

I am a firm believer that we must understand where we came from in order to strategically determine where we need to go. Making different choices and moving in a new direction doesn't just happen, it must be intentional. When we mess up, we must acknowledge what we did, seek to understand why we did it, and put a plan in place to not repeat the same behaviors. Adam and Eve messed up. We know what they did, and why, but we haven't discussed the impact of their sin in detail. It's important to understand the effects of their behavior on our lives today.

Adam and Eve's disobedience introduced sin into humanity, and as a result we, their descendants, still struggle with the propensity toward fulfilling the desires of our flesh.

We struggle with wanting to be our own gods. We want to control everything. We struggle with desiring the things that are not good for us. We struggle with the temptation to blame others and not take personal accountability for our behavior. We can't trust our flesh. It's greedy. It's self-serving and manipulative. For many years of my adult life, my flesh embraced certain emotional behaviors that eventually contributed to a breaking point in my marriage.

Prior to that painful event, I thought that being loud, controlling, and even confrontational was a part of marriage. Did I like it? No. Did I get good results? No. But had I seen or experienced this type of behavior before? Yes. Like I said, I thought 'This is what married couples do, and then they make up and move forward." I finally learned that this type of behavior eventually causes a marriage to implode, and sooner or later an outward explosion follows.

In 1999, just days before Christmas, my ex-husband and I separated. Our sons were two and seven at the time. I was hurt, disappointed, and filled with anger. But most of all, I was in a serious state of denial. Though my ex also contributed to our painful separation, I was in denial about my own contribution. I prayed constantly for God to change him. My prayers sounded something like this. "Please God change his heart. Give him a revelation so he can be the husband I need him to be. Help him to see how wrong he was." I prayed these prayers every single day.

Looking back, I obviously thought I was doing the "Christian" thing by praying for him. Amazingly enough, I didn't think to pray for me. Nor did I think to ask God to search my heart. I saw myself as the victim. I constantly looked outward to cast blame. Did I realize I was doing this? Not really. I actually thought that the few feeble attempts I made toward being the wife God created me to be exempted me from God's scrutiny.

Victims are good at shining the light elsewhere to avoid taking personal ownership.

The thought process of a victim is to deflect the problems unto others in an effort to not have to look at them self. I went to church. I served in ministries. I taught Sunday school. What could possibly be wrong with me? Looking back, I was definitely a piece of work.

During that awful time of separation, I struggled with a serious bout of depression. I lost my appetite and almost thirty pounds in a little more than a month. Getting out of bed was difficult. Each morning, I would open my eyes and immediately think of my husband's whereabouts. Every night before going to sleep, my thoughts were consumed with him. For the sake of my sons, I managed to drag myself out of bed and somehow make it to work each day. At work I made several trips to the bathroom to cry in the stalls. I'd sit in my car for my lunch hour and sob my eyes out. God's grace allowed me to somehow maintain my job and a little bit of sanity for our sons. But I was in bad shape.

Every day I mustered up smiles for my sons, took care of their needs as best as I could, and tucked them in each night choking back a massive flow of tears as they asked for their dad. Then I would hurry to my room and cry myself to sleep. Unfortunately, life had very little meaning to me. I didn't feel like I had a purpose. I had lost all hope to live. I entertained thoughts of suicide but could never follow through because of the boys. Thank God.

The first two weeks of our separation, I awoke with swollen eyes just about every day. However, without fail, I would pray and ask God to change my husband. One particular morning I tried to sit up in bed and was physically wiped out. I had no energy. I was drained. So I rolled to the edge of the bed and kind of flopped onto the ground. I pulled myself up onto my knees and prepared to offer my ritualistic prayers over my husband. But while on my knees, something different happened that morning.

God interrupted my routine.

His presence filled my bedroom. God came in and knelt down beside me. I felt Him there. Tears streamed down my face as I closed my eyes. Suddenly, I saw a vision. I saw a big screen – like one at a movie theater. And then, the next thing that happened blew my mind. I made the big screen.

I saw my husband coming home from work. He was dejected and tired. He had been emotionally and spiritually beaten down by the world. He came through the front doors of our home and stepped into a place that should've been a safe haven. Then I entered the scene, yelling, pushing, and calling him names. The names dishonored him. They chipped away at his manhood. They belittled his role as a provider and as a husband. I watched it all play out.

We were both on the screen, but God brought extra attention to me. I began to see myself for who I really was and it stunk. I started weeping at the side of my bed. My sobs were coming from somewhere deep. I was broken like never before. Honestly, I was overwhelmed with a deep conviction. And I instantly began to ask God to forgive me out loud. "God, I am so sorry. I didn't realize I was being so hurtful." I was sad over what I saw.

THE NEW CONSECRATED COCOON

All of a sudden, an incredible warmth came over me. I didn't fully understand it at the time, but I do believe that God wrapped His arms around me. And as He held me, I felt His grief. And then I felt His forgiveness. This went on for almost thirty minutes. When I got up from kneeling at the side of my bed, the bed sheet was soaking wet. But I felt so much lighter. I took a deep breath and was about to go wake my sons when another feeling overwhelmed me. Shame.

The images began to replay in my own mind. But this time it wasn't God replaying them, it was the devil. He wanted me to feel ashamed rather than set free. He began to whisper in my ear... "So what kind of wife are you? You'll never change. You've always been that way." Was the devil being truthful? I was forced to ask myself the tough question – why? Why did I behave that way? Why was I so angry? I had questions and needed answers. And I needed these answers whether my husband and I would reconcile or not. I needed them for me.

That week, I sought counseling through my company's Employee Assistance Program. But let me be brutally honest. My first session was with a non-Christian counselor and served as a band aid for my problem. This woman must have been burnt by a man in her own past. She fueled my anger. Egged on my independence, and basically advised me to drop that zero and find a new hero. Well...not in those exact words, but close enough. Then she gave me all of these "self-help" tools. Self-help? Lady, are you serious? I am the daughter of Adam and Eve. They tried to help themselves and you see where that got them. I tried to help myself and you see where it got me. This "Take matters into my own hands" stuff wasn't going to work this time.

After my session with her, I prayed that evening and asked God to direct me to the right counselor. Going through a secular program would not exactly position me for Christian counseling, but I prayed and called the Assistance Program the following Monday. I asked whether the counselors listed their ethnicity or their religious affiliation. The representative said they rarely listed race and definitely didn't list their beliefs. She located a female counselor closer to my home and said it appeared she was African American. How about that? Her race was in fact listed. I asked for her name and number. I figured nothing could be worse than the woman I had already seen.

I called the office that day and was told that the counselor was booked solid and her next available appointment was within four weeks. What? I explained to her assistant just how special my situation was. Surely, what I was going through had to be more important than any other calls they were receiving. Obviously I am being facetious, but don't we think like that sometimes when going through a struggle; our problem is a priority over all others? She assured me that she had done her best – four weeks. I cried. Then she said she could put me on the waiting list and if they had any cancellations they would notify me.

Let me tell you a little something about the God of Heaven that I serve and love with all of my heart. He showed tremendous favor to his daughter whom He loves so much. I received a phone call on Wednesday about a cancellation and by Thursday I was sitting in the counselor's office. She was a beautiful, strong, educated sister from Jamaica. Being from the West Indies, I felt at home with her accent and demeanor. But I tell you...I never felt more at home as when I realized this woman was sent by God. She was a Christian. And I don't mean a "mamby pamby" Christian. I mean a Holy Ghost filled believer who helped me understand myself through God's eyes. No "self-help" here. It was all "God help."

Some Christians don't believe in counseling. My thought on counseling is this... When our hearts are truly broken and repentant, God will heal our hurts and help us make the necessary changes as we yield ourselves completely to the process. Trust me, God doesn't need any help. He can do it all. However, there are times when practical steps must be taken, accountability is needed, or mediation is necessary. For these scenarios, God provides a host of resources and counseling is one of them. Counseling is never the answer; it's a resource the Holy Spirit uses to help facilitate healing, forgiveness, and restoration.

Counseling serves two purposes: information and implementation. The information God spoke through my counselor was eye-opening and gave me hope. Remember I said the devil was really doing a number on me? I arrived in her office believing I was the worst wife and mother on the face of the Earth. Through answering tough questions about my parents, siblings, grandparents, events, relationships, etc., we were able to identify key relationships and events that molded my perceptions and influenced my behaviors.

Why was this important? Because I realized that some spaceship didn't land on planet Earth, drop off a "jacked up" woman named Ann Thomas and go back into outer space. I didn't just wake up one day a disgruntled, hurt, disappointed, codependent, needy individual. But this is what the devil wanted me to believe.

I learned that things happened and things were said that etched these unhealthy perceptions on the heart of my identity. My healing truly began when I acknowledged these truths. I acknowledged what was said to me. I acknowledged what was done to me. Not for the sake of placing blame, but for the sake of no longer carrying a burden that wasn't mine to carry. In other words, there were things that I heard, saw, and that happened to me that I should not have experienced. But I did experience them and they influenced many of my life decisions. And it's the same for you.

The information helped me identify those areas where I needed God to heal hurts and disappointments and to fill voids where I was empty, lonely, and afraid. I needed God to restore me to who He created me to be and to give me the courage to forgive those who knowingly or unknowingly harmed me. Information – the "what" I needed to know to make better decisions.

Then came implementation – putting actions to all I had learned and taking ownership for my own behaviors. That was the most difficult part of the counseling sessions. Taking action is not for the faint at heart. It's not for the ones who want to remain in the same place. It's for ones who are sick and tired of being sick and tired and are ready to live a life of freedom and purpose. It's for those who are willing to get into a process and not quit when the going gets tough.

It's about making new decisions daily, and even hourly. It's a needed time of restoration and reclaiming all the enemy stole from you. No more blame game; it's about choices. When God asked Adam and Eve whether they had eaten from the tree, they had two choices. Respond in humility, come clean about their actions, and ask God to forgive them. Or, in pride, choose to self-preserve and take no personal ownership for their decisions.

Guilt and shame causes people to become defensive, offended, and self-protective. Back in my bedroom in 2000, when I made my big screen debut, I experienced two sharply contrasting emotions that morning. First, I felt the loving conviction of the Lord as he showed me the areas He needed to heal. But soon after that came another feeling – condemnation.

Condemnation is not from God. It's from the devil.

When feeling condemned, we struggle with feelings of unhealthy shame, guilt, and lack of worth. Think about how clever Satan is. Right after I felt God's loving touch and was drawn toward God, he stepped into my thoughts with feelings designed to create distance between me and God. He wanted me to run away and hide myself. Sounds familiar? Conviction breaks (humbles) us and draws us closer to God because when God reveals, he wants to heal. Condemnation is Satan's counterfeit for conviction. It's intended to spiritually and emotionally break (crush) us and pull us away from God. That's the same thing that happened in the Garden of Eden. Adam and Eve felt condemnation and therefore felt unworthy to face God. So they hid from him.

Imagine how that must have broken God's heart. If you are a mom, you can easily identify with this. You've given your

THE NEW CONSECRATED COCOON

kids everything they could possibly want or need. In the Garden that translated to food, shelter, dominion over the earth, and a personal and intimate relationship with God. In our world today, that translates to clothes, shoes, cell phones, computer games, hobbies, extracurricular activities, etc. We drive them to and from school, events, and even chauffer their friends around. And they seem to appreciate it until we have to put our foot down on that one thing. All of a sudden they forget all of the other things we've done for them. We say they can't have something and like Adam and Eve, they reach out and grab the fruit anyway.

Doesn't that hurt? It hurt God to know that Adam and Eve were willing to forfeit all He had given them, including His trust and their intimacy with Him to satisfy their flesh. Our kids are sometimes also willing to sacrifice our trust for what they want. Don't get on your high horse just yet. You and I do the same to God. We make decisions that choose our fleshly desires over what we know pleases Him. Just as we grieve over our kid's choices, God grieves over many of our choices.

Did you hear these words when you were growing up? "This hurts me more than it does you." I believe God said that somewhere in the Bible and they forgot to document it. It hurt God to have to instill correction for Adam and Eve's disobedience. Come on, moms. You can relate. Doesn't it hurt when you have to take something away from your children? Our heart is to give them the world. But, the Bible says God disciplines those He loves (Hebrews 12:6). And we also must discipline our children out of a heart of love, not anger.

The key word is love and love is at the core of discipline, but not at the core of punishment. There is a difference. As moms our goal is to discipline, not punish. Discipline is about correcting a behavior. It communicates they did something wrong. Punishment is designed to inflict pain, communicate disappointment, and often introduces shame into the situation. Correction communicates, "You did something wrong." Punishment says, "You are something wrong. Something is wrong with you, the person." One speaks to an idiotic choice; the other speaks to their identity.

Never tell your son or daughter you are a liar. Instead you say, "You told a lie." One speaks to the action or behavior, whereas the other declares or attaches an identity to them. Feelings of anger, bitterness, and resentment often accompany punishments. Many times, the person imposing the punishment is upset and concerned about what others might think of them. Do you see the difference? When your children disobey, prayerfully seek to correct the action, not damage their character. Let them know you don't approve of what they did, but nothing they do will ever change your love for them.

Unfortunately, Adam and Eve's disobedience resulted in a lot more than disciplinary action – or even punishment for that matter. Adam and Eve were cursed because of their sin. What is a curse? It is a pronouncement of misfortune. It's the harsh results of our violating and opposing God's commands. The opposite of a curse is a blessing, which is basically a pronouncement of good fortune.

God's children are blessed when we obey His commands and walk in His ways. Both blessings and curses begin with one generation and are often passed to many generations that follow. These are called generational or family curses.

Do generational or family curses exist today? Absolutely. The secular world calls it generational patterns, but I am keeping it scriptural. It's a curse.

A family's finances can be cursed. Generational curses such as, alcoholism, abuse, divorce, and sexual perversion (rape, molestation) can run rampant in more than one generation until someone recognizes and breaks it. The unhealthy behaviors associated with curses are caught, not taught. Someone who grows up in an alcoholic household simply believes that their way of life is normal. That doesn't mean they like it, but they assume that heavy drinking, passing out, and the other disruptive behaviors are just a part of life. The dysfunction distorts their perception of who they are and how they view relationships.

Generational curses can be broken. Breaking curses that have gripped your family for generations will not be easy. When Satan has had a hold on a particular family or generation for a long time, he is not willing to just throw in the towel. Therefore, you will have a fight on your hands, but you are equipped to win. As a Christian, you have the power to do be victorious.

1 John 4:4 says, "Greater is he who lives in you (Jesus) than he who is in the world (Satan)." You have Jesus' power living inside of you. By His power you can reverse, cancel, and void curses. As a mother, you have the spiritual authority to cancel curses over your children. As you do, be sure to replace the curse with a blessing. Speak and declare blessings over yourself and your entire household.

Some curses are more deep rooted, control- ling, and destructive, and so you might need to seek spiritual counseling to help sort through the wounds and relationships affected by this. Identifying and breaking generational curses is necessary for Christians to walk in complete freedom.

So let's revisit the Garden.

Adam and Eve ate the fruit and immediately realized that something changed. Their eyes were opened. They saw things differently from how they saw things seconds earlier. They looked at themselves and each other and realized they were naked. So they immediately covered themselves.

Genesis 3:8 says after eating the fruit, Adam and Eve heard God walking in the Garden and hid among the trees.

Come on, people, this is God. As if He couldn't see them. When we sin, we do such foolish things, don't we? Verse 9 says God called out to them (even though He knew exactly where they were). And God still does that today. When you and I sin and try to hide ourselves or avoid Him, He comes looking for us and He knows exactly where we are (emotionally, mentally, spiritually). When He calls out to us, He's giving us an opportunity to respond. He's giving us an opportunity to come clean.

God called out to them and Adam replied, "I heard you walking in the Garden, so I hid. I was afraid because I was naked." So God asked how they knew they were naked and whether they had eaten from the tree. Well...this would have been the perfect place and time for Adam to simply fess up and come clean. But what does he do? What many of us do at times when we are busted – look around to see who we can possibly blame for our actions.

He told God that the woman God gave to him offered the fruit and he ate it. Then God looked at Eve and asked her, "What's up with that?" She looked around and realized there wasn't anyone left to blame but the serpent, so that's what she did.

We, the descendants of Adam and Eve still play the blame game today. We tell God, "It's the father or husband you gave me." We run from assuming personal responsibility for our own actions and say things like, "When I was growing up, my dad was never there for me. So I looked for love in all the wrong places, and that's why I have three children by three different dads."

Once we become adults, the blame game becomes obsolete. Revisiting your past to understand the relationships and events that contributed to who you are is one thing. But revisiting your past to identify people to blame for your indecision to move forward today is a cop-out. If we aren't careful, we can use our past as a crutch to not stand on our two feet today. As a new creation in Christ (2 Corinthians 5:17), your past indicates who you were. God doesn't consult your past to determine your future and neither should you.

I will say as a side note that I have met women who enjoy hanging out in the past because of the attention it brings. People feel sorry for them and feed their needy victim mentality. This behavior is often caused by rejection. A victim mentality totally goes against what Christ died for. He didn't die for you to be a victim. His painful, excruciating death was to give you the freedom to be a victor. Each time you choose to remain a victim, you are basically saying that Christ's death wasn't enough.

Adam and Eve played the blame game.

I am sure the serpent wanted to blame someone too, but he was out of luck. The buck stopped there. God pronounced a curse on Adam, Eve, and on the serpent.

The serpent or snake was cursed in two ways. Many religious scholars believe the serpent was walking when he approached Eve, so the first part of the curse was that he would now crawl on his belly. And secondly, the serpent would be at constant war or enmity with the woman and her offspring. In other words we, Eve's offspring, would constantly struggle with the enemy and his offspring (ones who serve him). Even more, Eve's most powerful offspring to walk the earth was Jesus and Satan is constantly at odds with Him.

However, if you've read the end of the book, Jesus wins, and that means you and I win too.

As for Adam, God told him since he listened to his wife, he would now have to struggle to make a living. He would sweat and work hard. No more "Easy Street." He had to step his game up and provide for his family.

The curses God spoke over Eve are the main reasons for my writing this chapter. Some of our struggles are Eve's fault. Let me just put that out there. Thanks to Eve, women now experience painful child birth. Yep. In Genesis 3:16a, God says, "I will sharpen the pain of your pregnancy, and in pain you will give birth." Gee, thanks a lot, Eve! And if that wasn't enough, God also cursed Eve by giving her a desire to control her husband, BUT, her husband will rule over her. Oh, my. I know I've got someone's attention.

One Bible translation says that Eve's "desire" will be for her husband. And yet another translation says she will "long for" her husband. We can potentially glean from the various translations that Eve would either yearn to be number one in her husband's life or yearn to take over his life. Either way, she wants to be in control. And so, the truth be told, Eve was officially the first controlling, codependent woman, which brings a tremendous amount of strife into any relationship, especially marriage. These behaviors don't allow husbands to freely lead their homes because they are too busy contending with a needy or dominating wife.

Eve's sin introduced an imbalance in the marriage relationship that is still very prevalent today. Don't believe me? Watch any sitcom or reality show that's on TV today. It's hard to find a woman whose self-worth isn't wrapped up in hostility or sexuality. She's either a b-word because she's mean or a babe because she's hot.

Where can we find a healthy depiction of women who are comfortable in their own skin and don't need to loudly express or expose themselves to get attention? I'm not looking for a religious image of a woman either who thumps the Bible, is judgmental, and is wearing a potato sack to ensure she's not showing too much. God is about balance. The devil is about extremes and you need to ask yourself, "Where are the extremes in my life?" What behaviors are you displaying to advance a personal agenda?

Eve had a personal agenda. She wanted to be like God. She wanted to know it all. Hmmm. I think some of us still struggle with that one. Busybodies, wanting to be in-the-know about everyone. Wrapping gossip in prayer requests and cloaking judgment in pretentious concern. Okay, I will move on.

Ladies, most of you are probably not surprised to learn that you have power. But some are probably surprised to learn that the power (influence) you have is given by God. This means there are things He wants you to use that power to do. And it's not to control your husband, kids, or anyone for that matter. If you are misusing your God-given power, it's time to stop.

Here are a few ways we tend to misuse our power:

- **Words.** Words carry the power of both life and death. Choose to speak life. Encourage others rather than tear them down. Pray for them.
- **Beauty.** God gave you that gorgeous face or body to attract people to Him, not to your bedroom. You are not merchandise, so stop trying to sell yourself.
- **Victim Mentality.** It's not always about you, and the world doesn't revolve around you. Use your ability to draw people closer to tell them about God, not your woes.
- **Tears.** The ability to have emotions is a gift. Do not use them to control, manipulate, or win people to your side. Instead cry tears of compassion over the things that break God's heart.
- **Strength.** Don't become proud and constantly talk about your accomplishments. Instead highlight your successes to give God the glory, acknowledging that without Him you can do nothing.
- **Money.** It's not about having the next new thing. It's about ensuring your needs are met and then seeking to meet the needs of others who are not as fortunate.

You are blessed to be a blessing to others.

You have been given a power. That power is to be used to influence others for God's kingdom. To draw them closer to God. The more you walk in obedience and choose to live for God, the greater his ability to work in and through you.

Deuteronomy 30:19 says, God has given us the choice between life and death and between blessings and curses and He tells us to make a choice. And He earnestly hopes we will choose life.

My precious sister, the choice is yours. God never makes up our minds for us.

Choose life! Choose blessings.

Remember, you were created to be blessed by God so you can in turn be a blessing to others.

Reflection

1. When you pray, do you give God permission to search your heart and point out anything that doesn't please Him?
2. Is there an area God wants to heal but you won't allow due to pride, shame, or denial?
3. A lot of who you are is due to pivotal relationships and experiences in your life. Have you acknowledged those things that were done or said to you that formed unhealthy behaviors?
4. Are you dealing with an inappropriate or unhealthy situation in which you are self-preserving or self-protecting?
5. Do you understand the difference between condemnation (from the devil) and conviction (from the Holy Spirit)?
6. When in trouble as a child, were you exposed to discipline or punishment? Do you understand the difference?
7. Based on your answer to the previous question, how has that affected your relationship with God?
8. Do you believe who you are is separate from what you do?
9. Are there unhealthy or unholy behaviors in your life that were also prevalent in your parents' and/or grandparents' lives?
10. Have you done anything that's causing you to hide from God?

"If you listen obediently to the Voice of God, your God, and heartily obey all his commandments that I command you today, God, your God, will place you on high, high above all the nations of the world. All these blessings will come down on you and

spread out beyond you because you have responded to the Voice of God, your God: God's blessing inside the city, God's blessing in the country; God's blessing on your children, the crops of your land, the young of your livestock, the calves of your herds, the lambs of your flocks.

God's blessing on your basket and bread bowl; God's blessing in your coming in, God's blessing in your going out. God will defeat your enemies who attack you. They'll come at you on one road and run away on seven roads. God will order a blessing on your barns and workplaces; he'll bless you in the land that God, your God, is giving you." Deuteronomy 28:1-8 (The Message)

PREPARATION

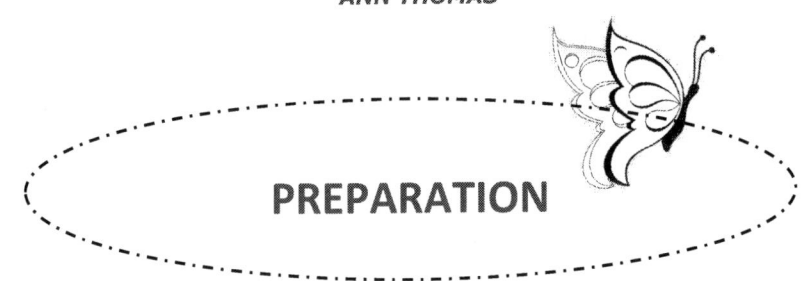

Devouring the leaf on which her egg was laid, the caterpillar eats, grows, and sheds her skin. She eventually seeks a secluded, protected place to settle in and prepare for the next stage of her life.

The mama butterfly strategically chooses the right leaf for her eggs, setting her precious babies up for success. Abandoning her eggs on the wrong leaf could have undesirable lasting repercussions.

Like the mama butterfly, parents must also create a healthy and thriving environment that encourages their children to grow physically, emotionally, and spiritually. This growth process is one that involves being stretched and strengthened. It's a time when God reveals areas of immaturity and lack for the purpose of making us more complete in Him.

This period prepares us for the refining process we must all go through to become the women of God we were created to be. Just like butterflies are in no way ordinary, neither are we. We were extraordinarily created to do extraordinary things for God's kingdom.

THE NEW CONSECRATED COCOON

Parents – Set Up or Set Back

I must be honest and share that I had the most difficult time writing this chapter. Not only were the words challenging to come by, but in the midst of writing I experienced spiritual warfare of a different kind.

Guess which area of my life was attacked? You guessed it – my parenting.

I had not been down this path before and so I was unsure how to respond. And one day while lying flat on my face crying out to God, He showed me that He was refining me even more in a specific area that would not only bring healing in my home, but take me to a deeper level in Him. And guess what? You get to come along.

Going deeper with God is never easy, but always worth it. I accepted His precious invitation and so here I am with a heart that is bursting to share.

I am a work in progress as God regularly molds my character and transforms my thinking so I can hear His heart in each situation I encounter. That's the ticket to parenting – hearing and communicating God's heart to our children. I finally settled it some years ago that my sons do not belong to me. They are on loan. And the day that I stand before God He will ask me to give an account for the type of mom I was. My desire is to see God smile and nod with pride as I describe the days when I desperately sought to love them like He does.

Parenting is one of the most difficult and yet rewarding assignments. I would venture to say it's the highest calling and most powerful ministry on earth.

Parents are the primary influence in the life of a child and have the ability to support or sabotage God's plans and purposes for them. I do not speak about this topic with the delusion that I have arrived; because I am far from the mom God created me to be. However, I do believe that God has graciously granted supernatural insight to this topic and will use this information to facilitate healing, renewal, and restoration of relationships, dreams, and hopes. I am simply a willing vessel and have prayerfully emptied myself of all personal preconceptions and notions so God will have His way.

When God showed me the word "sabotage" I thought, wow, that's a strong word. But it literally means to destroy, hinder, hurt, or hamper. And that, my friend, is the power parents hold. Parents hold the ability to knowingly or unknowingly place their child on a path of good or bad decisions and healthy or unhealthy relationships.

Parenting is serious! It's not for the faint at heart.

It's not for wimps.

We can't do it alone; we need God every step of the way. As parents we either set our kids up for failure or for success.

Parenting is not about how much stuff we can buy our kids, being their best friends, or giving them unlimited freedom. In fact, it's the opposite. It's about giving them the stuff money can't buy, being willing to be the unpopular adult, and setting healthy boundaries around all aspects of their lives. There are things children need that can only be received from their parents.

When God created Adam and Eve (the first parents), he intended for their roles to be very different and yet complement each other. Single parenting is so incredibly difficult because it loses the sense of balance God intended. There is something all kids need to receive from their father and there is equally something all kids need to receive from their mother.

I am not in any way knocking single parenting because as I write, I am a single mother. It's not impossible for a child from a single parent home to receive all God has for them. But I am saying that a single parent situation complicates things and makes the already challenging process of parenting even more difficult.

THE NEW CONSECRATED COCOON

Moms and dads impart different things into their children's lives, and what's needed is different for a male child versus a female child. What a son needs from his mother is very different from what he needs from his dad. And it's the same with a daughter. I've heard it said that the most powerful role model in the life of a child is the parent of the same sex. In other words the mom is more powerful in her daughter's life and the dad is more powerful in his son's life.

I'm no psychologist by any stretch of the imagination. And thought I do not disagree completely, I do believe that each parent, same and opposite sex of their children offers valuable and vital characteristics needed to raise a well-balanced child.

Yes, I totally agree that a mom can't teach her son how to be a man. Got that! And certainly it's the same for a dad and his daughter. However, while the father helps his son become the man God created him to be; his mother helps create his expectations for his future wife. And the same goes for a daughter.

When done right, a daughter will seek a husband like her father because her dad loved, protected, and respected her in preparation for her husband-to-be. And the same with a son; his mother sets the stage for the type of woman he should seek, one who honors her husband, is modest, nurturing, etc. So I don't disagree with the importance of the parent of the same sex in a child's life, but God created the ultimate parenting scenario with both a mother and a father.

Now, with all of that being said, a child can in fact live in a home with both a mom and a dad and still not receive what he or she needs to become a healthy and well-rounded adult. The stark reality about parenting is...parents can't give what they don't have. And even more, we often don't know what we don't have until we are face-to-face with an incredible void. If we don't know something is lacking or broken, then how in the world can we fix it?

Parenting requires a tremendous amount of grace. First, we must be willing to give grace to our own parents, and secondly, we ourselves need grace to raise our own kids. Make no mistake about it...there are things our parents did right and things they absolutely did incorrectly. And if we aren't careful, we can repeat the same mistakes – but for God's incredible grace.

You might wonder why in the world I'm spending so much time on the topic of parenting in a book that speaks to our refining process. Because our time of refining is also a time of defining. Or should I say re-defining.

Our initial response to our consecration process or a time of squeezing will be to exude learned, comfortable, and familiar behaviors. And for each of us, there are certain responses, emotional and otherwise that we caught from key relationships that helped define who we've become.

We all have experiences that defined our perceived self-worth and value. From the time of birth until now, these defining relationships and events wrote on the heart of our purpose and whispered in the ear of our potential. They either encouraged our hopes or pushed us closer to hopelessness. They were our biggest cheerleader or a major stumbling block. And in our time of refinement, God desires to do away with the old, unhealthy behaviors and replace them with ones designed to launch us closer to being the woman of God we were created to be.

The most defining relationships for every human being are parents. And how you and I respond to correction, authority, and challenges is heavily determined by what we experienced or didn't experience as kids. Our ability to humble ourselves, trust, and be transparent with others is based on what was modeled for us over the years. Our response to a certain scenario was influenced by how we saw others react to them growing up. Think about it. When conflict arises, are you eager to put on your boxing gloves and jump into the ring, or does the very thought of emotions flying everywhere make you want to retreat into an invisible corner?

THE NEW CONSECRATED COCOON

I can't begin to tell you the number of women I speak with who are adults in the physical, but are still little girls emotionally.

They consciously and subconsciously seek affirmation, security, attention, and nurturing that should have been provided when they were little girls. Interesting how God created us in His image and therefore we desire the same things He does.

God desires intimacy with us and so He created us to desire intimacy with Him and others. God wants us to love Him unconditionally and put Him first, and isn't that what we long for in our relationships as well? We are created with desires that our parents are to fulfill when we are young.

Parents are a baby's introduction to and first impression of God.

Wow! That's heavy, isn't it? But it's true! As the most influential people in the life of a child, parents are to be "God with skin on" to their children. A child's emotional and spiritual needs from birth to early teenage years are to be met by her parents. Then, as she grows and enters into the teenage years, the role of her parents is to model and encourage the development of a personal relationship with God so she will seek God to meet her needs and desires directly.

What needs and desires am I referring to? The desire to feel secure, protected, nurtured, loved unconditionally, and affirmed. So the million dollar question is...what happens when a child doesn't receive these things from her parents? You got it – she seeks them from elsewhere. When unfulfilled, these desires don't dissipate. They simply grow stronger.

Do you know any grown men or women who absolutely must be the center of attention? Or someone who requires constant pats on the back? Or a woman who has a difficult time nurturing her children? Unfortunately we can tend to look at these behaviors and mumble, "Grow up." That's the problem – they haven't. The little girl or boy inside still yearns for what they should have received. Coming to the realization that we are lacking in certain areas of our lives is a hard truth to accept, but it's the truth nonetheless.

There is great power in acknowledging and accepting truth. John 8:32 says, that knowing the truth sets us free. Free to do what? Free to make different or better decisions than we did in the past. But some people have a hard time coming to grips with the truth and would rather make excuses or cast blame. At some point we all must take full responsibility and ownership for what's ours. We must acknowledge those things that were outside of our control and then set our gaze upon what we can control.

When we are willing to take control of our own actions we then are free to forgive past hurts and unmet expectations and release our parents from the guilt of not being able to change the past. This ability to let go of all expectations of a better past is at the core of forgiveness, which we will discuss in more detail later.

The mother butterfly lays her eggs on a leaf that she knows her baby caterpillars will be able to eat from, gain nourishment, grow, and ultimately become butterflies. She doesn't just drop them off in the middle of a mud pile and expect them to fend for themselves. She sets them up for success. Unfortunately, some parents knowingly and unknowingly drop their kids off in a spiritual, emotional, and mental mud pile, setting them up for failure. Their children are forced to learn about the sacred things of life from someone else or through a painful experience. Rather than having the blessing of a parent's protection, they quickly learn to protect themselves. But this need to self-protect often leads to self-preservation, self-sufficiency, and the inability to trust that other people genuinely have their best interest at hand.

Rejection is one of the most, if not the most hurtful experience.

Especially when the person doing the rejecting is someone we love or trust. Jesus definitely knows what it feels like to be rejected and cast aside. It's not God's desire for any of us to experience such pain, especially at the hands of our parents. But many children do.

Rejection can begin at the time of conception from a mom who desperately wants to abort her baby. And if she chooses to keep her baby, the rejection might continue as she pawns him or her off on other family members to care for or she allows TV and video games to become a substitute for her attention. This is sad and it breaks God's heart. That is not what God intended for the privilege of parenting. Parenting is a gift.

I believe that the characteristics of a parent are 25% taught, and 75% caught. In other words, our kids immolate more of what they see us do rather than what we say. A parent can tell a child how much they love them until they are blue in the face, but if their actions don't align with their words, the child will believe and draw conclusions from the behavior. There is a phrase that says, "Your actions speak so loudly, I can't hear what you are saying."

Sadly enough, without realizing it, children adopt and repeat unhealthy behaviors. Oh, but there are some who realize these unhealthy patterns exist and make a vow to not be like their parents when they grow up. Unfortunately this drive to be the total opposite leads to an all-consuming mission to be nothing like their parents and swings the pendulum way to the other side – which is equally as unhealthy and extremely draining.

To some degree, we have all struggled with issues surrounding our moms and dads. For some, the issues are not life altering, and for others it's been an issue of life or death.

If you are reading this chapter and your relationship with your parents is totally awesome, I celebrate with you and give God all the praise.

For those who still struggle with feelings of rejection, abandonment, unforgiveness, or resentment, I do believe that God wants to finally heal you and set you free from the bondage of unhealthy relationships. Many fail to realize that our inability to respect and love our parents has a profound impact on other relationships.

Ephesians 6:2-3 says to honor your mother and father so things will be well with you and you will enjoy a long life on earth. This Scripture also says that this is the first commandment that has a promise attached to it. In other words, God promises that if you obey this commandment, He will bless you. The blessing is a long life on earth.

That word "long" isn't just quantitative, it's also qualitative. It promises a life of peace, joy, love, unity, etc. Do you want things to be well with you? Do you want to prosper in school, your job, or ministry? Do you want a blessed marriage? Do you want your children to honor you? Do you want to leave behind a legacy of love, grace, and security for your own children?

That's what the Scripture means when it says, "It will go well with you." I don't know about you, but this is the kind of life that I desire. And I don't desire it just for me. I desire it for my children, their children, and so on. I also desire it for other family members. I want to leave this type of legacy. And it starts with honoring my mom and dad.

Unfortunately, many are not willing to extend honor toward their mom, dad, or both until they show signs of deserving the respect. That's where the grace of God comes into play.

Grace is undeserved favor. Key word – underserved.

Grace is what you and I received when God sent His son Jesus to die for and save us, while we were still sinners. Did you get that? God sent Jesus before we deserved that kind of sacrifice - before we deserved that kind of love. So while in your eyes your parents don't deserve to be honored, Jesus' sacrifice says they do.

Honor is another word for respect, and you can respect your parents even from a distance. We respect them by what we say to them and about them. We respect them by the thoughts we have toward them. We respect them by praying for them and speaking blessings over them; even or especially when we feel they don't deserve it. Honoring your parents requires your view to change from how you see them to what God says about them. God says they are worthy and deserving of great grace.

When you truly understand what it means to honor your mom and dad, you can respect them whether they are living or deceased. Yes, you can still honor parents who are no longer with you. If your mom or dad passed away and you didn't have a chance to make amends before they died, you can set some things straight today and begin to honor their memory. After all, they did at least one thing right – they had you.

It is my prayer that in reading this chapter you will be enlightened, gain new perspective, make new decisions, take responsibility for your own actions, release your parents and determine to become the best woman, mother, wife, sister, and friend you could ever be. It's time!

Father and Daughter Relationship

Ever wonder why fairy tales like Sleeping Beauty and Cinderella are so popular? Could it be that they pull on the heart strings of our desire to be swept off our feet and carried away by our prince charming? Do they cater to that yearning for a "happily ever after life?" I believe God placed the desire in each woman's heart to be pursued, captured, and whisked away by her prince charming. And yes, there is the desire for our earthly prince charming to do this; but do you realize you also have a spiritual prince charming?

You sure do. His name is Jesus. He is our ultimate prince charming.

He is the ultimate groom. He will outlive and outlast any prince we can find on earth and he will out love them all as well. His love for you and me is matchless and will last for all eternity. And one day, our prince charming Jesus will return for his bride (the church), scoop us up, look into our eyes, and declare his everlasting love for us. And just like a bride prepares for her wedding day in the natural, our consecration process is preparing us for our spiritual wedding day when Jesus comes to join Himself to us. I get excited just thinking about it.

As I reflect on several married women we might consider powerful or prominent in both the Christian and non-Christian circles, many of them have awesome, supportive, strong, and loving men by their side. And many of these women will tell you that without their husbands, the fame and notoriety has little to no meaning. Even with all of our God-given talents and ambitions, most women desire to have our prince charming by our side, believing in us, encouraging us, and loving us through our ups and downs. We want to know that when we grow old, our prince will be there to care for us, hold our hand, and still tell us we are beautiful.

So when and where does a prince charming enter into the life of a woman? At birth. Yes, I said at birth. That prince charming would be her earthly father (biological or otherwise). There is a powerful bond between a girl and her father that has the ability to set her up or set her back in preparation for both her earthly and spiritual prince charming.

Your dad should be the first man to ever touch you. He should be the first man to hold you, hug you, stroke your face, run his fingers through your hair, and have you sit on his lap. Your dad should be the first male to plant a loving kiss on your lips, cheek, or forehead. For those of you who had or have a very close relationship with your dad, you understand what I'm saying. For those who didn't experience these things, what I'm sharing may sound a bit weird or strange. But stay with me.

When you were a little girl and couldn't fend for yourself, your dad's strong arms, presence, and assuring words were designed to usher in a sense of safety, security, and protection.

THE NEW CONSECRATED COCOON

Growing up, my dad was an entertainer. He had a melodic voice that many compared to Nat King Cole. He sang at various locations that often required an overnight or weekend stay. My sister and I were daddy's girls, and so we missed him when he was gone. He was funny and full of energy. But what I remember most about his coming home after a few days away was the sense of protection over our home. If someone were to try and break into our house, I believed my dad would protect us at all costs. In my heart I knew my dad would give his life for his family. Back then we didn't have a security alarm, but we didn't need one as long as dad was home.

When my dad picked me up, I felt swept off my feet. When holding his hand and walking down the street, I felt special, like his princess. There was a pride that radiated from him as people complimented me. When I curled up in his lap, I felt like nothing or no one could get to me. I didn't feel abandoned nor did I ever worry about him leaving me. Deep down I knew he would always be there for me, no matter what.

I didn't realize it then, but this was my first impression and introduction to both my husband-to-be in the natural and Jesus, my spiritual husband. My dad's display of unconditional love, pride, protection, and comfort created an expectation. From birth until around eleven years old, what I just shared described the epitome of my relationship with my dad. If I were to get married at ten years old, guess what my expectations of my husband would be? You got it. I would expect that he would protect me, show me off, tell me how pretty I was, hold me, love me until his eyes fell out of their sockets, not allow anyone or anything to get closer to me than him, and that he would never leave or abandon me. My earthly father created these expectations. He didn't tell me these things; he showed me.

If I were introduced to Christianity during these formative years, guess what I would expect from my relationship with God? The same thing I received from my dad - security, protection, unconditional love, intimacy, and so on. These are all characteristics of God that would have been easier to embrace in a far off God because he had the same characteristics of my up close daddy.

Then...came the teenage years. In the earlier (formative) years, parents attempt to build a foundation of love and stability; brick by brick, mortar by mortar. Each brick soaked in blood, sweat, sacrifice, and tears. Only to have the foundation tested for authenticity and fortitude by that child who has now become a teenager.

Unfortunately, my relationship with my dad changed during my teenage years as I experimented, sought popularity and affirmation, tested boundaries, etc. Moms, I hate to break the news to you, but if your teenager is doing these things, it's all a part of their growing up. So chill out, they are not weird, ungrateful, or rebellious. It's not the things that they do or say that will mold their future. It's your response.

Based on his own upbringing and experiences, my dad was not emotionally equipped to walk me through this new territory in a way that helped me find a good healthy balance. His response was to pull away due to his feelings of inadequacy in these areas. I know I'm talking about dads in this section, but, moms, when your children are struggling through stuff and their attitude is anything but desirable; that's the time to draw closer to them and not detach or withdraw your love.

As a teenager, the way you and dad show your affections for each other will be different than the earlier years. You might not sit on his lap anymore, but you can walk hand-in-hand with him at the mall, or you can rest your head in his chest as he holds you while you cry. He can open doors for you and tell you how beautiful you are even though five horrid pimples have taken up residence on your face, with the biggest one on the tip of your nose. Ouch.

He can show you the proper way for a guy to hold you when you have your first slow dance. He can encourage you to wear clothes that are modest and don't display all of your private body parts because you are more than an object to be lusted after. He can affirm that you are worth the wait and any guy who is rushing you to lose your virginity doesn't value you as a person. And most important, he can show you how your future husband should love and respect you by the way he treats your mom.

He can tell you all about Jesus and his unyielding love for you. And although your dad loves you more than words could ever express, Jesus loves you more. He can assure you that in the times when he can't be there for you in the physical, Jesus will always be there with you and for you. He can tell you that there isn't anyone in this world who is able to communicate your true value and self-worth better than Jesus. He can tell you all about the great sacrifice Jesus made for you by dying for your sins so that you can live forever in Heaven with Him.

He can tell you that God has a plan and purpose for your life and that there will be people and things that will come into your path to steal that from you, but you must fight for what's yours. He can promise that as long as he has breath in his body, he will fight with you and for you.

The picture I am trying to paint is one that communicates the tremendous power a father has in the life of his princess daughter. That's why the father gives away the bride at a wedding. His giving her away is symbolic of a transfer of authority. Before the marriage, dad comforted, protected, respected, and provided for his princess daughter. Now, her husband agrees to step in and pick up where her dad leaves off.

Does this sound unrealistic for a dad? Well, it shouldn't. That's what God expects of all fathers. Can a dad do these things in and of himself? No! A dad of this caliber must walk closely with God. He must be a man of integrity and humility, be teachable, correctable, willing to quickly ask for forgiveness when he messes up, and willing to easily forgive when others hurt him.

Where does a father learn all these things to impart to his daughter? Possibly by watching his own father love, protect, and honor his mother. Maybe from being mentored by a spiritually mature man who is willing to pour wisdom into him and help him become the man he was created to be. And last but certainly not least; he can learn these things from God Himself. The Holy Spirit is the greatest teacher that ever lived, and if we are willing to learn from God, he is more than willing and happy to teach us what to do.

The sad reality is that most fathers didn't have this type of relationship modeled for them and some had very little or no relationship with their own fathers. If your grandfather didn't have these qualities within, then he couldn't pass it on to your dad, who in turn could not pass it on to you. And if you didn't receive this type of love, protection, etc., from your dad, you more than likely sought it elsewhere.

Or...maybe you received the opposite. Rather than unconditional love, you had to perform for your dad's approval. The five A's on the report card was never enough because he constantly focused on the one B. Maybe your dad had a critical spirit, so rather than praise and affirm your good characteristics, he constantly looked for something negative to talk about.

Maybe your dad didn't know how to enforce correction in a healthy manner, so he punished you physically and then emotionally by not speaking to you for days after. Maybe your dad never held you, so the first guy that wrapped his arms around you sparked a desire for that type of intimacy with men and so you became promiscuous.

The Bible says that before you were born all of the days of your life were written in God's book. This means that your potential, your purpose, and your destiny were also written down. When the devil took a sneak peek at your written future, he panicked and was filled with intimidation. So he dispatched a plan to sidetrack and dismantle God's plans for your life. His first strategy was to hinder your mom and dad from giving you all God had for you. And second, he introduced counterfeits or lousy substitutes for the real thing.

THE NEW CONSECRATED COCOON

Where unconditional love was lacking, he deposited love with conditions. Conditional love produces a striving spirit - one that learns to perform for affirmation. This is where we get our perfectionist tendencies. Where security and protection were lacking, he deposited the inability to trust and the desire to self-protect. Where intimacy and affection were lacking, he introduced the desire to exchange sex for love in return. And sadly, these counterfeits cannot compete with the real thing God has for you, so you become a black hole. Meaning, it doesn't matter how much of the counterfeits you receive, you still have a gaping void in your heart.

How does all of this relate to your consecration process? As God is allowing you to go through a difficult time, you may draw from these counterfeit experiences and emotions. Therefore, you might believe that God is punishing you and doesn't love you anymore. When in fact it's His great love for you that's allowing the trial. Why? Because trials test your faith, faith produces perseverance, and perseverance strengthens you to press in and obtain all God has for you, so you will lack nothing in Him (James 1:3-4).

As you go through a challenging time you might feel like God has abandoned you because your father did, but God says He will never leave you (Deuteronomy 31:8). You might be inclined to perform for God's approval and say or do all the right things in the hopes He would be pleased with you. After all, that's how it was when you were growing up. But God's love is unconditional with no strings attached. There is nothing you can do to make Him love you more or less and nothing can separate you from His love (Romans 8:38-39).

So what happens when your life is filled with counterfeits? Well...you then begin to settle for counterfeit blessings, counterfeit relationships, and a counterfeit prince charming. The Godly man you say you want can walk up and kick you in the rear and you still wouldn't recognize him. Or if you are fortunate enough to get the real deal, you can't appreciate him because he doesn't cater to your unhealthy emotions and demands.

Women are attracted to one of two types of men – those who are just like their father or those who are the complete opposite. If your dad deposited the right things, not perfect, but modeled a respectable and loving relationship, then it's a no brainer why you would be attracted to a man just like him. His character and personality are familiar.

But negative characteristics are also familiar. Dads who are abusive, controlling, neglectful, and emotionally unavailable leave their mark as well. And believe it or not, we can be attracted to that kind of man, not because we like it, but because it's familiar. We know how to respond to that type of dysfunction, and so we go with the flow because change is a more foreign and seemingly tougher process to embrace.

If I were a therapist counseling a man who is about to marry a woman with major daddy issues, I would not only raise a red flag. But I might slap his face to make sure I had his attention and then explain the following things.

First, the voids in her life will cause her to knowingly and unknowingly want him to meet unrealistic expectations. And second, if he does something that remotely reminds her of her father, he is going to get the response she gave or wishes she gave to her dad. He will be punished for the mistakes of her father. It's a no-win situation for that brother. Actually for either of them.

These are issues that should be resolved *before* they walk down the aisle and say for better or for worse. And I do mean before. This leans heavily to the side of "for worse." The challenge with having a counterfeit view of ourselves is the inability to have an authentic, healthy, and transparent relationship with God and others. Why? Because most males we encounter in life are consciously or sub-consciously measured up to or are compared to our fathers. We are human and it's very easy to do. Our perspective of men and God are through the eyes of our father. This perspective is shaped by the good, the bad, and the ugly.

A dear African American friend of mine struggled with feelings of inferiority toward white women for many years. For a long time, she didn't understand why. She just knew she felt very insecure around them. She didn't trust them. She hated seeing a black man with a white woman. And then, her own husband had an affair with a woman of another nationality, and it devastated her. It added insult to injury. During their time of separation, God revealed how she came to this unhealthy dislike and complex. Her father was s serial adulterer. Each time he had an affair, he chose a white woman. And when they divorced, he remarried a white woman.

Unfortunately, it took many years before she realized that her dad's sin, selfishness and insensitivity injected the poison of racism into her blood stream. When God revealed, He also wanted to heal her and she allowed Him to. God set her free not only from the bondage of racism, but also from inferiority, jealousy, and lack of self-worth. Today, her circle of friends resembles the rainbow and consists of every color and race imaginable.

God is so good!

Mother and Daughter Relationship

Your earthly dad ultimately should be a good example or model for the type of man you might choose to date, marry, etc., and he's also your first impression of God, your Heavenly father. Your mom, on the other hand sets the stage for the type of woman (mother, daughter, friend, sister) you will ultimately become.

Funny how stories like Cinderella don't exactly paint a warm and fuzzy picture of mother to daughter, or female to female relationships. Yes, Cinderella's prince rescues her, but he rescues her from a cruel, hateful, and suppressing family environment. Cinderella is treated like a second class citizen and has little to no value in her stepmom's eyes.

Sadly enough, some women can relate to that type of icy cold, non-nurturing, and self-absorbed motherly demeanor; which is the total opposite of what God desires for mother and daughter relationships. As the parent of the same sex, moms are to impart the following to their daughters: a nurturing spirit, a healthy emotional, physical, and spiritual self-image, a hunger to pursue goals and dreams, and a loving respect for her earthly father and husband-to-be. Let's look at each of these.

Nurturing

I believe God created women to be natural nurturers. In other words, He created us to lovingly encourage growth, provide a safe, warm, soft, and always welcoming place of comfort. For many, this comes easy. I'm not saying that dads can't be nurturers; some are really great at it. However, moms kiss the boo-boos, cheer for you even when you strike out, don't believe in an ugly class picture, and will give you her last, even when you don't deserve it or don't appreciate it. The nurturing love of a mom gives you the shirt off her back before you even ask.

When I meet women who are not the nurturing type, I usually learn after some probing that their moms were not very nurturing. Or something happened when they were young that stole their ability to be vulnerable, caring, and giving. When I also speak with ladies who have "women" issues, it's typically because of a strained relationship with their mom.

Sadly enough, if a mom constantly criticizes her daughter and doesn't instill a nurturing spirit; the daughter often grows up feeling closer to men. She grows up believing she can only trust men and not women. She views women as catty and full of drama and gravitates toward male relationships. These women also develop a hardened exterior and find it difficult to let people draw too close, keeping most people at arm's length. Is it possible for a mom to contribute to such a warped sense of female relationships? The answer is yes.

Women who have been hurt, rejected, and or betrayed by their moms are tough candidates for meaningful female relationships, but it's not impossible. Ultimately, a woman who is hurt in this way can eventually open up to another woman after time and proof. They need time to observe a woman's sincerity and consistency. And they seek proof or evidence that she will not be like others who were untrustworthy, petty, judgmental, and condescending.

These women will test your love. They will even push you away just to see if you will keep coming back or if you will be like everyone else and give up. And if, by God's grace you are persistent over time...they will slowly allow you to get close. You must earn that intimate place of sisterhood.

If you are the type of woman I've just described, male relationships are okay. But trust me when I say that the commonalities of a female-to-female relationship are matchless. Woman to woman, there are things you will instinctively understand, embrace, celebrate, and encourage each other through. There are intimate things of the heart you can share with a trusted girlfriend and know beyond a shadow of a doubt that she totally understands.

Self-Image

Moms are probably the most influential figures when it comes to a daughter's spiritual, emotional, and physical self-image. I am led to address the physical self-image first. I'm sorry but it amazes me when a mom is surprised by or criticizes her daughter's wardrobe – too tight, too revealing, or too short. Yet, the mom's wardrobe is one that communicates an unhealthy desire for attention.

It's hard enough to combat the demeaning images portrayed as femininity on TV and in music videos; but when mom's closet is filled with blouses that regularly show cleavage and skirts that constantly show thighs; how can she possibly expect her daughter to understand or embrace modesty? How can she expect to correct her? Seriously.

I'm sorry, but I must go here. This type of revealing clothing is not only popular in our secular circles, but is also prevalent in the church today. And it's not just the single women who are wearing provocative clothing. There are way too many married women dressing inappropriately because their "husbands like it." I'm sorry, but I have a problem with any "man of God" who doesn't mind other men drooling and gawking at his stuff. 1 Corinthians 7:4 says the wife's body belongs to the husband and the husband's body belongs to the wife. And ultimately whether married or single, our bodies belong to God (1 Corinthian 6:19).

Ladies, whether your husband gives you the thumbs up or not, it's unacceptable to dress this way for two reasons. One, it communicates to other ladies (especially the younger generation) that this is acceptable and their worth and value is determined by their physicality. And second, it's a stumbling block or temptation for others. Why would you want to cause another man to lust after you? If married he should desire his wife. If not married, he should be cultivating a desire for his wife-to-be.

2 Corinthians 6:3 says we must not live in such a way that causes others to stumble or find fault with our ministry. What's our ministry? To win others to Jesus. How we go about it (method or talents) might differ, but ultimately we lead them to Christ by our example. So, how can you expect to win a man, woman, boy, or girl, to Christ if your clothing, actions, words, or attitude causes them to think sinful, lustful, or sexual thoughts? You can't!

As we discussed earlier, a dad helps his daughter understand how a man should treat her. Whereas a mom helps develop her self-image (what she thinks of herself); which ultimately communicates how she expects others to treat her. It's all connected.

THE NEW CONSECRATED COCOON

Remember I said earlier; we need both parents.

As I reflect on my days as a pre-teen and teenager, I do not remember my mom wearing provocative clothing. My mom was definitely beautiful on the outside, but she was loved and respected for her inner beauty. Until we were teenagers, my mom selected and purchased my sister's and my outfits. She would actually bring them home, which means we were not there to say we didn't like this and that. We were grateful when she bought something and gladly wore it. Then, when we became teenagers, I chose my clothing knowing my mom and dad had the final say as to whether I could keep and wear it.

I did go through a period in my early twenties where I wore a few outfits that were out of character. As I think back, I wore them but never felt one hundred percent comfortable getting the attention the outfit beckoned for. Even though I was not attending church at that time, I was still very much aware of when my clothing revealed too much.

The more I reflect on my childhood, I don't recall my mom flaunting a lot of sexy lingerie or sleepwear in front of my sister and me. Having girls, I guess she could have exercised a little freedom in what she wore around the house. But she didn't as to not awaken unhealthy curiosity before the right time.

I do remember when doing laundry, I would occasionally run across some of my mom's undies. They were very different from my thrift store brand. They were frilly, full of vibrant colors, and very feminine. I thought she had the coolest underwear and considered that type of underwear for married women. In today's culture that type of thinking would seem strange as middle school girls wear their pants without belts to display their thongs. God help us.

Moms, it's time to wake up. Our daughters are watching us and are taking their cues from what they see us do. They observe the clothes we wear, how we hug men, and how we carry ourselves.

They watch our emotional outbreaks, our drama-queen moments, our attention-seeking schemes, and who we talk about and how (gossip). They pay attention to whether we are a "Sunday-only" Christian. Do they see us hoot and holler on Sunday and swear and lie Monday through Saturday? Do they see us wear a certain type of clothing to church and another type during the rest of the week? Do they see us crack our Bible open daily and close ourselves off for private time with God? Do we incorporate praise and worship music into the music we listen to regularly; or is that type of music reserved for church and spiritual events? They are observing everything we do to determine what's right and what is acceptable. And they are paying more attention to what we do rather than what we say. Remember that.

Pursuit of Goals and Dreams

There is nothing more wasteful than a woman who has allowed all of her passions and gifts to lay dormant or even worse - die. If you are a wife, did you know that God created you to be more than a wife? If you are a mother, did you know that God created you to be more than a mother? He has gifted you with talents, a personality, and favor to impact the lives of specific people with whom you will come in contact. We were created to impact lives outside of our immediate family circle. If our daughter only sees us catering to her needs or the needs of our husband and not do something we enjoy; it sends the wrong message.

Don't get me wrong – our marriage and families are our primary ministry.

But they are not our *only* ministry.

Don't lose sight of that. If all we show our daughter is the life of a wife and mother, then they will grow up believing that's all there is – marriage, kids, kids go to college, parents retire, and then they die.

With Godly balance, you can be there for your kids and husband and still pursue your calling.

Let your daughter see you doing something for you. Let her see you doing something that brings you great joy. This will give her permission to develop and pursue a passion without feeling selfish or neglectful. Again, this is all done with a Godly balance and it's okay for your daughter to see you mess up, get off track, and then get back on track by the grace of God.

Whether it's your daughter or yourself, it's never too late to discover what you enjoy. For your daughter, point out her strengths, unique talents, and personality traits. For yourself, ask others what they see as your specific talents and skills. Then, ask God to show you where and how they can be put to use. I've heard it said that every assignment God gives each of us is a solution to someone else's problem. Be encouraged. Develop a heart of a servant by being a problem solver for God's kingdom.

Displaying Honor

Last but certainly not least, a mother can instill the wonderful gift of honor and Godly submission into her daughter. It's important for each of us to honor all God-given authority figures in our life. Who are our authority figures? First and foremost God. Then we have parents, husbands, spiritual leaders, teachers, bosses, police officers, and so on.

The Bible addresses the importance of honoring our authority in Romans 13:1-2. In the nutshell it says we should surrender to or respect our authority because they are appointed by God. And those who resist the authority also resist the order God has put in place and our resistance brings judgment. So yes, when we dishonor or are disobedient to the authorities appointed or allowed by God we are ultimately dishonoring God.

The best time to learn about honor is when we're young. If you have children, now is the time to instill this important value that will help them become adults who have a healthy respect for authority. A person who disrespects authority is typically one who has a rebellious spirit. And if you are a woman with rebellion issues; I have a bit of bad news for you.

As long as you are alive, you will always have people of authority in your life.

One day I was driving my son and two teammates to their basketball game. I relied upon the GPS to get us there quicker than the route I was most familiar with. The new route veered from the highway and placed us on several back roads. We were moving along pretty well until we came upon an extremely slow moving SUV on a two lane strip. I tried to be patient but this guy was frustrating me. I didn't know the speed limit, but surely he was going slower than what was allowed. I thought I saw a turtle moving faster than we were.

Eventually, I inched toward the middle of the road so I could see around the SUV and there was no oncoming traffic. I checked the yellow lane divider and it was dotted, so I could in fact go around him. Awesome! I floored the gas pedal to gain momentum, jumped into the left lane and began passing this slow SUV. But the SUV wasn't the only thing moving slowly. The chain of events I'm about to share also seemed to shift into slow motion.

As I passed the vehicle, I noticed (again in slow motion) what looked like a police mirror on the side of the SUV. For a brief moment I thought, "Could this be...?" But I continued on my mission to pass him before oncoming traffic appeared. Just as I pulled in front of the SUV I saw a speed limit sign that seemed to be strategically placed at the point where I had overtaken the SUV. The sign said 30 miles per hour and as I glanced at my speedometer, I was doing 39 miles per hour. A bad feeling quickly developed in the pit of my stomach as the speed limit sign, plus the weird looking side mirror seemed to make a really bad combination.

Just as the chain of events transitioned from slow motion back to the pace of reality, flashing lights beckoned me

THE NEW CONSECRATED COCOON

to pull over. Yes, you guessed it. I had passed an undercover police officer who while patiently driving the speed limit watched me zoom pass him doing almost ten miles per hour more than he was. That stunk.

I quickly pulled over and reached for my license and registration as the officer approached my car. My son and his friends didn't even realize what was happening until they saw my window go down and the police officer staring into the vehicle. As I attempted to look at him with an innocent demeanor, he said one word, "Whoopsies." I am dead serious. I chuckle now as I think about it. I knew exactly what he meant. It was painfully obvious that I had made a colossal boo-boo. I chose the wrong vehicle to overtake. What could I say? I simply agreed with him.

He asked where I was headed in such a hurry. I explained. I also told him that I was not from that area of town and had been unfamiliar with the speed limits. However, I agreed that I did in fact violate the speed limit. I handed him my license and registration as he inquired about my driving record. Praise God I had a wonderful record. I believe the last time I received a ticket for speeding was in 2001.

As I sat waiting for his return I told my son and his friends that if I got a ticket I clearly deserved it because I violated the speeding limit. I also quietly prayed and asked God for favor, this one time...even though I need his favor all the time. The officer approached the window again, gave me my information back, and said, "Ms. Thomas, I don't believe you have $254 to throw out the window, do you?"

"No, sir, I don't," I quickly and might I add, "humbly" responded. He let me go with a verbal warning due to my impeccable (as he called it) driving record. I thanked him, shook his hand, and blessed him.

According to the GPS, we had about eight minutes left to arrive at our destination. That was the longest and slowest eight minutes of my life as I refused to go over the speed limit, as I led a slew of cars at the speed of a funeral procession. One of the cars being the officer who was probably making sure I was headed where I said.

I could have said a lot of things to my son and his friends to belittle the officer and his authority. I could have accused him of driving slowly and trying to entrap me. I could have said he was being condescending with his first word – whoopsies. I could have tried to justify that I didn't know the speed limit, and so on. But instead I shared that I fully deserved a ticket and I thank God for his mercy by not giving me what I deserved. Trying to justify myself would only plant seeds of dishonor and disregard for the law. And even worse, the desire to sidestep the repercussions of breaking the law.

How we respond to and talk about authority molds how our kids perceive and respond to authority as well. That boss that you dislike, that pastor that corrected you, or that teacher that tried to discipline your child; all authority figures are appointed by God and are deserving of our respect and honor. Even when an authority figure might be unfair or rude, we must trust God to give us the right response. A response that pleases Him.

How did your mom treat your dad? Did she cook for him? Did she make his plate and serve him? Did she support his decisions and dreams, and honor him as the head of the household? Or did your mom openly and defiantly disagree with your dad in front of you, call him names, or talk about him when he wasn't around? Was she emotionally or physically abusive to him? However your mom treated your dad planted seeds in your mind about husband and wife relationships, whether you realize it or not. And the relational messages you caught, you more than likely have repeated – good and bad.

A mom who honors her husband gives a great gift to her watching son and daughter. To her son she displays the type of honor he *should* expect from his future wife. And to her daughter she sets an example of how she is to honor her future husband.

THE NEW CONSECRATED COCOON

The biggest challenge we women have with displaying honor or respect to our husbands is the vulnerability and humility submission requires. Yes, I said the "S" word – submit.

Trust me ladies, submission is not a cuss word.

Otherwise God would not have placed it in the Bible. Submission is not something you do; it's an attitude. True submission is a voluntary position of the heart, despite what the secular world says. Those who don't understand submission see it as a weakness or bondage. But when you choose to submit yourself you find strength and freedom rather than captivity.

The word "submit" means to permit oneself to surrender to the authority of another. A wife who truly submits to her husband in love has already submitted herself to the Lord.

True submission begins with God.

Submission to God may begin as an obligation as you try to obey His commands. However, your submission should eventually change from obligation to relational. The more you get to know God, the more you love Him. And the more you love Him, the more you want to show your love to Him by submitting to His will and His ways.

1 John 5:3 says we can know we've come to the place of loving God when we obey His commandments. In other words, God's love language is obedience. What greater act of obedience is there than to completely surrender or submit your will to His? What greater way to display your love for your husband or your parents than to obey their leadership, surrender your need to be right, and honor their role in your life?

Ephesians 5:22 says wives must submit themselves to their own husbands in the same way they submit to the Lord. In other words, your submission to your hubby should be the same as your submission to the Lord – out of love, honor, and respect. "But what if my husband doesn't deserve it?" Submit and honor him. This is similar to our discussion about honoring our parents. The commands are not contingent upon whether they deserve it or not, it's about honoring their God-appointed position in your life.

Before ending this section, the word submit does not in any way mean to subject yourself to repeated physical, emotional, or mental abuse.

These situations should not be condoned and must be addressed. A husband who is a repeated adulterer is equivalent to an emotional abuser. Do not accept this as normal or acceptable behavior. This is a stench in God's nostrils and must be addressed in the proper way. Submission is never meant to be used as a way to enslave a woman, strip her of her dignity, or treat her any less than the precious daughter of God that she is.

Mothers, as your children see you submit yourself first to God, to your husband (if married), and to other authority figures, they will learn to extend that same level of respect to those above them, including you. If you are a woman who struggles with authority, this is an area that God needs to heal.

A woman who struggles with submitting to earthly authority is a woman who will not surrender to spiritual authority. One affects the other.

As we wrap this chapter up, it's imperative that you see the correlation between your perception of your relationship with God based on your relationship with your parents; and also your relationship with your own children based on your relationship with your parents. It's all one big cycle. Just as your parents were to be your first impression of God; so were you to your own.

If we don't see ourselves the way God sees us, we will struggle, resist, and even curse God in the midst of our time of refinement because we will question His motives for allowing it. Sometimes refining comes as a result of a wrong decision we made. Sometimes it comes from a decision someone else made, but there is still something for us to learn from it. And sometimes, refinement happens when God is ready to move us to a new spiritual level and there are some things that must be removed before we can move forward with God.

Regardless to how or why you find yourself amidst a trial, it's imperative that you view God as a loving, guiding, and even corrective father who will never abandon you in the process. In your trial, God is also like a mother. He holds you, nurtures, and comforts you when you are hurting.

Parents are God's conduits. A conduit is a channel through which something is conveyed or passed through. Sometimes parents make themselves available and are able to deliver what God intended. And other times, the delivery is hindered by parents who are unwilling or unable to deliver His message.

God's goal is to make sure whatever you may not have received before, you will certainly receive by the time He releases you from that precious place of refinement. Ultimately, that's what the process is all about; making us complete in God.

I am not making light of what your parents did or did not provide. But I am saying that what God intended for you is still yours and in that quiet and secret place of the cocoon, get ready to receive all you need from the original source – your Heavenly daddy.

I pray this chapter has inspired you to chase after God to get what's yours. Get what God has for you so you can in turn be the conduit God intended for you to be.

Reflection

1. Do you consider yourself to be a nurturing person? For example, do you like to give/receive hugs, kisses, and are touchy-feely?
2. How would you describe your relationship with your mom?

3. If you could change one thing about your relationship with your mom, what would that be?
4. Do you feel more comfortable with male friends?
5. Do you have at least one close female relationship?
6. If you answered yes to the above question, what do you value most about the relationship?
7. Growing up, did your mom influence or control your clothing choices?
8. How would you describe your wardrobe? (Trendy, modest, form-fitting, or attention-getting)
9. Do you realize you were created to be more than a mom and a wife?
10. What have you learned from your parents about honoring or submitting to earthly authority?
11. Did your mom honor your dad as the head of the household?
12. Does the word 'submit' make you feel uncomfortable? Does it arouse feelings of being controlled? Does it cause you to want to rebel?
13. Are there things you did not receive from your mom or dad that you need from God today?

"So you also are complete through your union with Christ, who is the head over every ruler and authority." Colossians 2:10 (New Living Translation)

THE NEW CONSECRATED COCOON

Leaving and Cleaving

Based on all we discussed in the previous chapter, the values our parents instill - or don't instill - heavily influence the following: Who we become as adults, how we embrace relationships, and how we endure hardships.

The behaviors they modeled before us provided a successful roadmap for maneuvering through life, or a tedious treasure hunt to find out things as we go. Sadly, there are "treasure hunt" adults all around us who are still trying to figure out life and relationships.

When born, we are completely dependent upon our parents, and the goal of parenting is to prepare us to one day "do life on our own."

I once hear a pastor say, "I don't mind feeding baby Christians. But I do have a problem moving their beard out of the way to feed them."

Did you get that visual? Not very attractive is it? Bottom line – we all have to grow up. And treating adults like kids does them a great injustice.

In the womb, babies are attached to their moms by the umbilical cord. The cord is the baby's lifeline. It keeps the baby close to her momma, but even more importantly is essential to her growth and development. Babies receive food through the umbilical cord because they're unable to eat for themselves.

However, once she's born and can eat and receive nourishment through breast or bottle-feeding; the cord is cut. Makes sense, right? We don't see babies being pushed around in a carriage or sitting in a car seat with the umbilical cord still attached to their mom.

The cord is cut in the physical, but we're still connected to our parents by a spiritual and emotional umbilical cord and there is a time to be attached and a time to detach. In other words, the older we grow, we should be developing emotionally and spiritually so that we're no longer feeding off of our parent's emotions and their spirituality – we are developing our own.

Not only do we have adults who have a hard time detaching from their parents or have detached in an unhealthy manner, we also have parents who for one reason or another don't want to let them go.

One of the primary reasons we see parents holding tightly to their child is the fear of not wanting to deal with a marriage that has been rooted in the children. In other words, once the kids leave, the marriage doesn't have a leg to stand on. The parents believe the longer they keep the adult children around, the longer the survival chances for their marriage. So they emotionally breast-feed a son or daughter and end up crippling their growth and ability to detach.

When we become adults who can fully provide for ourselves, it's time to cut the physical and emotional cord from our parents. And that age will vary. Some cut the cord when they get married, some when they join the military or leave for college. And others just simply get a job and move out.

Sadly, some leave or detach from their parents in an unhealthy or destructive manner. They leave with anger, resentment, or unresolved hurts. Others do leave physically, but remain emotionally attached.

When we leave from under our parent's authority, it should be done in a way that positions us to be blessed. The detachment should be one that releases the son or daughter to go after who and what God created them to be and do it with confidence – not emotionally broken or crippled. But some adults detach or remain attached in a way that hinders all other relationships.

The challenge with an unhealthy detachment or unhealthy attachment is how it affects our ability to then attach ourselves to others – primarily a spouse. This ability to attach ourselves to others is what the Bible refers to as "leaving and cleaving."

In Matthew 19:4-6, Jesus basically says that from the beginning of time, God created man and woman to be united or joined in marriage. And for their marriage to be what God intended, the man should leave his mother and father to be joined (cleaved) to his wife and become one. Once they become one, instead of two (individuals), no one should split or divide what God put together. The word "cleave" means to hold fast to or stick to with an unwavering loyalty.

Based on this Scripture, how we leave determines how we cleave. And the opposite is also true. How we don't leave hinders how or whether we are able to cleave.

Unhealthy Detachment

A son or daughter who departs or detaches from their parents with unresolved issues cannot experience God's blessings in their life. Why? Unresolved issues breed resentment, unforgiveness, and anger. Your anger will cause you to dishonor your parents, and dishonor forfeits your ability to receive all God has for you (Ephesians 6:2-3). The blessings the Bible speaks of aren't just for you. They are also for those relationships closest to you.

I moved out of my parent's home when I was somewhere around 20-21 years old. I left with disappointments and unresolved issues in my heart. My parents didn't know this, as I masked my departure under the guise of needing to be on my own. I really didn't need to leave, but struggled with some of the family dynamics. I was running from things that I didn't want to deal with anymore.

The problem with running "from" something is we ultimately end up running "to" something. Human beings are created with the desire for spiritual, emotional, and physical attachment. God made us that way. First we attach to our parents, then we attach to God, and if we get married and have kids, we attach to our husband and children. So, when we detach from one thing, we seek to attach to another. We were not created to be lone rangers.

Ideally, we were created to detach from our parents and attach to God. In other words, transfer our dependencies on them to our total dependency on Him. And then if we get married, we attach to our husband. Detaching from our parents in an unhealthy manner, not attaching to God, and then attaching to a spouse sets us up for failure. The ideal way to enter into a marriage is having a healthy one-on-one relationship with God, with whom all of your expectations are placed and met. Then, when you get married, the expectations you have of your spouse are realistic.

You are not approaching your marriage expecting your husband to rescue you and fix all of your problems.

It's easy to detach from our parents in an unhealthy manner, keep rolling and think, "Thanks for nothing. I don't need you anyway. I don't need anybody." But that's not true. There's no place on earth you can run to and hide from the trials of life that will ultimately expose those areas of pain and disappointment. We all have to deal with them eventually.

Remember I stated that when I became a teenager, my relationship with my dad changed. As a result, I sought male relationships for all of the wrong reasons. There was a male void in my heart that I desperately wanted to fill. My dad was there physically; he just became emotionally unavailable. He was still a provider and took great care of our physical needs. We didn't want for much. Sadly, that's the mistake many men make today. They believe that if they are keeping a roof over their kids' heads and food on the table, they are fulfilling their fatherly duties.

As a teenager, the emotional attachment is what we need most. It's what helps establish security, builds confidence, and assures us of our inner and outer beauty. If dad doesn't affirm our worth as daughters, we will seek another man to do this. So my detachment was, in fact, very unhealthy because I left home searching, desiring, and yearning for something that only my dad and God could provide. I didn't turn to God, which means I turned to other human beings. Other humans tried to meet some of my needs, but could never meet my unrealistic expectations. I did not leave or detach with my father's blessing.

A dear friend of mine learned as a teenager that her dad was cheating on her mom. Who told her? Her mom. Wanting to protect the dad's image, her mom didn't want to share this with her family members or close friends. Believing her daughter was old enough to handle this type of information, she confided in her daughter. Unfortunately, this decision caused two things to happen.

First, the relationship between the father and daughter changed drastically. She now knew for sure, through her mother's tears that her dad was being unfaithful and causing great pain for her mom. Rather than see her dad through the eyes of a daughter, she now began to see him through the eyes of her mom. She lost all respect for him and developed dishonor in her heart. Of course, this mom didn't realize the daughter would respond this way to the news. And the daughter didn't let on to her mom just how much respect she had lost for her dad.

I believe in my heart that her mom was broken, discouraged, and simply needed an outlet. She probably thought that her daughter's unconditional love for her father could weather that type of information. She probably thought the daughter's love for her father would not be diminished by this news. But what the mom didn't realize was, the daughter didn't stop loving her dad, she stopped liking him.

The second thing that happened is the daughter developed major resentment toward her mom. She didn't realize it at the time. But when she got older, got married and began having her own marital issues, she realized that she silently resented her mom for not taking a stand with her dad and demanding that he stop having the affairs.

My friend later learned that marriage and relationships are not that cut and dry, especially when kids are involved. She learned that her mom thought it was best to try and keep the family together for the "kids' sake" and so she put up with the affairs. Unfortunately, this mom set her daughter on a vicious relationship cycle. Not only did she inadvertently communicate unhealthy messages regarding how a husband should treat and value his wife; but also how a wife should value herself.

My friend totally loved her mom. So she had no idea this resentment had built up until she was a wife facing hardship in her own marriage and was unable to share her full heart with her mom and receive advice from her. She did realize years later, through conversations with her mom, that her mom was reenacting the same thing she experienced growing up.

As life would have it, her mom's father was very much an adulterer and her grandmother didn't like it and was hurt by it, but condoned it to keep the family together; which, by the way, didn't work because he eventually left her for another woman. But the unhealthy behavior and cycle had already been passed down to her mom and siblings, and so it continued to my friend and her siblings.

Today, she and her mom have a really good relationship as she prayerfully gave all of her disappointment and resentment over to the Lord. Sure, she could have gone to her mom and shared that her mom's behavior set her on a bad path. She could have shared that her mom put her in a really bad spot by divulging things about her dad that she didn't need to know and quite frankly, wasn't sure how to process. Sure, she could have told her mom that by enabling her dad's sinful behavior she had set her up for a cycle of repeating the same. But my friend came to this realization. Her mom was powerless to change the past. And sometimes people live a life of regret over their inability to make a better yesterday. She didn't want to place that burden on her mom. She wanted her to live the years she had left to the fullest.

This is where a relationship with Jesus is so incredibly necessary and crucial. As you read this chapter, you will

THE NEW CONSECRATED COCOON

ultimately see two things: areas where your parents have handled things inappropriately and some mistakes that you yourself have made.

When God reveals these things to you, you will have one of three choices.

First, you can play the blame game and justify your actions. However, this really is *not* an option. So really you have two choices.

Second, if your parents are still alive, you can prayerfully share your disappointments with them. You can ask them to forgive you for harboring these feelings and then forgive them for the things they did or said that caused you pain. Sometimes, it's important to get these things off of our conscience, into the open where the enemy can no longer control or torment our thoughts. Satan has the most power in our thought life, and if he can debilitate you by getting you to nurse and rehearse disappointments, he will. He (the enemy) realizes that revisiting old pain keeps it fresh as if it happened yesterday. He'll make sure your ill-feelings don't expire. If kept in your mind, you give Satan power. But when exposed and put into the light, you take that power away from him. In asking for forgiveness and providing forgiveness to others, you acknowledge the wrong done to you, and also take responsibility for your own actions and decisions.

If you do decide to speak with your mom, dad, or both, be sure to pre-bathe that conversation in lots of prayer. Be sure that you've spent a lot of time with God so your motive in sharing is not one that is seeking revenge, but instead one that is seeking restoration and reconciliation. Your intentions should be motivated by God's love. And only God's love.

Finally, your third option is to give your disappointments to God, release your parents, and work it out between you and God. If the parent you need to make peace with is deceased, this will be your only option, as you can't speak with them face-to-face. Don't worry; God can give you peace even in this situation.

However, for some of you, your parents are still alive and they are not who they were when you were growing up. They've made their mistakes, but they are truly seeking to live a better life. You realize they did the best they could with what they had. You realize that in their way, they still loved you and their intention was not to harm you. You realize that bringing up these things will cause more harm than good. For you, your option, like my friend is to let God heal you. Let God give you what you need. Let God meet your unmet expectations.

In releasing your parents you will find that you can finally detach from them in a healthy manner and therefore, will be able to attach to others in a healthy manner. Attaching in a healthy manner means you can trust, rely upon, be honest with, and have healthy expectations of others. And if you have children, there is no greater gift to give them than the gift of seeing you live a life that is free from unresolved bitterness, anger, resentment and regrets. Put to death the unhealthy detachment and attach yourself to God. Gain your nourishment and encouragement from God. Let Him grow and mature you. Let Him heal you. Let Him meet your unmet expectations. Amen? Amen!

Unhealthy Attachment

This one is a little trickier. Unhealthy detachments are often self-telling. A person's inability to function in other relationships due to damaged or broken parental relationships is fairly easy to identify. But what about the ones whose relationships with their parents look like they are wonderful on the surface, but the core of the relationship is an unhealthy codependency?

How you leave is how you cleave.

Or on the flip side of the coin – if you don't leave, then you can't cleave. Remember, we said cleave means to hold fast to or stick to with an unwavering loyalty. A man or woman in a marriage cannot cleave or stick to each other with an unwavering loyalty if they are more loyal or committed to their mom or dad.

In other words, the marriage relationship that is supposed to consist of three persons – wife, husband, and God – actually consists of four people: wife, husband, God, and an overly involved mother-in-law.

Ladies, I strongly caution you to limit what you share with your parents about your marriage. Actually, with any of your immediate family members. It is one of the biggest mistakes a lot of married couples make. When the emotional umbilical cord is still attached to mom or dad and something goes wrong; the attached spouse has no problem picking up the phone and soliciting advice from a parent. Or worse, they pack an overnight bag and head to their parent's house.

Do you remember those wedding vows? You promised to love him in sickness and health, through the good times and the bad. You probably didn't say I promise to not run back home to mom and dad when he is sick or we have a falling out – but that was implied when you said "I do." Running back to mom and dad doesn't only apply in the physical sense, it also applies emotionally. When things go wrong in your marriage, your mom and dad are not to come to your rescue.

You are a big girl now!

When advice is needed, this is where a mentor, pastors, or someone who is more mature spiritually comes into play. This is not, I repeat this is not, the time to go running to your parents or any other close family members. We human beings have what is called a memory. And though we think we choose what we remember and what we don't, it's all stored away waiting for the opportune time to be recalled. Just when you don't want your family members to remember how much of a jerk you told them your husband was, they will.

A dear friend of mine is very close to her mom. Her mom is pretty much her best friend – like a lot of us. And if that's you, it's great. The challenge with sharing marital problems with your mom is her tendency to take your side most times.

Yes, yours. And truth be told, that's why you are sharing with her. If you knew your mom would take your husband's side, you wouldn't go running to her each chance you get. My friend's marriage was going through a rough patch as she learned her husband was engaged in online pornography.

While surfing the Internet, she discovered he had been visiting a lot of inappropriate websites. She was crushed. Their relationship seemed to be okay, but their sex life was not very active or vibrant. After having their second child, she struggled with her weight gain and didn't feel confident with her husband seeing her body. So their sex life had diminished. Her husband, not wanting to cheat on her with another woman, turned to online pornography.

Please note that pornography is still a form of adultery.

She was disgusted, embarrassed, and disappointed. She felt demeaned and dishonored over the images. She called her mom and shared everything with her. This wasn't the first time. She regularly shared their personal marital ups and downs with her mom. And so this was no different. She laid it on the line and her mom was devastated for her and upset with her husband. She shared the types of sites, how often he visited them, and that he had a secret email account he used to set up user name and passwords for some of the sites.

Unfortunately, what she did not share with her mom was the fact that she had withheld physical intimacy from her husband for over eight months. She didn't share that her husband regularly initiated love-making with her only to be turned down over and over again. She didn't share that on numerous occasions he tried to have conversations with her so they could acknowledge what was wrong and try to fix it; but she refused. She didn't mention that he asked her to consider seeking counseling through their church, but she refused. But she did share her husband's response, which made him out to be the total bad guy in her mom's eyes.

I am not in any way trying to excuse or justify this husband's response to his wife's unhealthy behavior. But I am saying that it takes two to tango and, ladies, we are not being fair when we report only our half of the story.

Wives, we are not to starve our husbands of sexual intimacy. All studies show that men express their love and feel loved through physical intimacy and women express and feel loved through emotional intimacy. And so we enter into an exchange; fulfilling their needs to have our needs fulfilled.

A man washing the dishes and bringing home flowers for his wife is positioning himself for a night of hot and steamy romance. A woman who genuinely meets her husband's bedroom needs will find her husband doing the laundry, rubbing her feet, and unexpectedly picking up the kids from school. It's the great, yet beautiful exchange. It's the two becoming one like it speaks of in Matthew 19:6. You are no longer looking out for your own needs. You are seeking to meet your husband's. And he is no longer looking out for his own needs; he's seeking to meet your needs. And with this, you can become one and cleave to each other with an unwavering loyalty.

However, if your loyalty is still to your parents or other family members, you will not cleave to your husband and ultimately invite them into our marriage; thus allowing the opportunity for division to enter in.

My friend told her mom all of the sordid details of her husband's porn addiction. Things blew up and her mom took the liberty of confronting her son-in-law. He was embarrassed and ashamed that his wife had shared this with others. He also felt completely betrayed.

Fortunately for them, once it all came into the open they were willing to seek counseling from their pastor. Over a period of time their relationship healed. But one thing did not heal. The secret feelings her mom still harbored toward her son-in-law. Though their marriage was able to be saved and restored, her mom continued to be suspicious of her son-in-law and treated him differently.

In her mind, she was looking out for her daughter. She wanted her daughter to be respected and treated as she deserved. In essence, the mom wasn't wrong for wanting the best for her daughter. But the unhealthy attachment between she and her daughter hindered the daughter's ability to truly cleave to her husband.

Sometimes the unhealthy attachment is between a mother and son.

Maybe you're dealing with a meddling, controlling, and over-opinionated mother-in-law. Here are questions to help identify an unhealthy mother-son attachment: Does your husband allow her to dictate things in your home? Does he invite her into the intimate details of your marriage? When she visits, does she behave like the woman of the house?'

All of these are signs of a son who has not detached from his mom in a healthy manner. He is still emotionally attached and allows her to treat him like a baby, when in fact he is a man. This goes for unhealthy detachments or attachments to fathers as well.

If God has revealed to you through this chapter that you or someone you are close to is struggling with unhealthy detachments or attachments, it's time to seek healing and a healthy release from these unhealthy ties.

Remember, the idea is to detach from your parents in a healthy way so you can attach to God and others in a healthy manner. I'm not saying you shouldn't have a close relationship with your parents. You absolutely should.

However, be sure that your relationship is one that has healthy "adult" boundaries around it. Your relationship should not be one of unhealthy codependency that hinders your ability to become an independent adult.

We all must get to the place of total dependence on God.

When your total dependency is on God, you are free to enter into a healthy marriage; one that consists of two interdependent beings, rather than two codependent persons or one independent rebel.

Detaching from our parents in a healthy manner releases a blessing that frees you to live the life for which you were created. A life that is completely dependent upon God for all of your needs. He knows all of your needs and will meet them even before you ask.

Reflection

1. Are you harboring any bitterness, resentment, or unforgiveness toward your mom, dad, or both?
2. Unmet expectations due to unhealthy parental relationships can contribute to unrealistic expectations of others. Are you expecting people to do what only God can do in your life?
3. If married, who do you share intimate details about your marriage challenges with? Has it proven to be a wise decision?
4. How involved is your mom or dad in your personal/marital affairs?
5. After reading this chapter, have you identified an unhealthy attachment (codependent, emotional neediness) to one or both of your parents?
6. Have you identified an unhealthy detachment (bitterness, resentment, etc.) from a parent or both?
7. If you are a parent, have you identified an unhealthy attachment to or unhealthy detachment from an adult child?

"This is your father you are dealing with, and He knows better than you what you need." Matthew 6:8 (The Message)

CONSECRATION

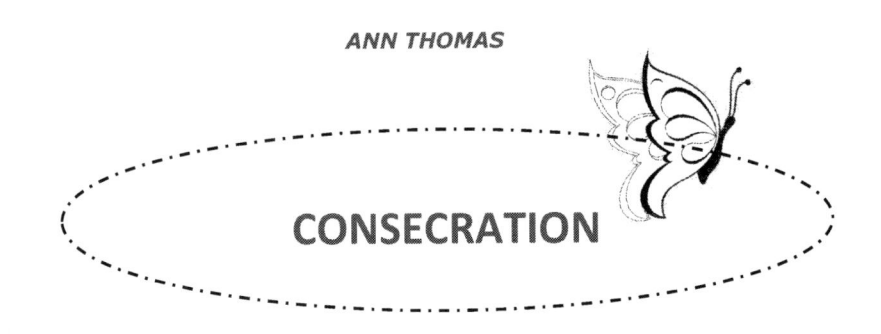

This is the stage where the change occurs.

In the caterpillar's metamorphosis cycle the third stage is called the Pupa. She sheds her skin for the last time. She spins a cocoon that soon becomes a place of isolation, maturation, and protection.

To the onlooker it appears she is resting, but she is anything but resting. She is engaging and embracing changes that are life-altering. It feels lonely in the cocoon, but she's not alone. God, her creator, is right there ensuring everything goes as planned. He won't allow anyone or anything to hinder the process. He's removing the old to make room for the new.

Like the caterpillar, we too must embrace our process of change. For change to occur, God must have our undivided attention and our full cooperation. In our cocoon we learn to wait on God. We learn to surrender. We receive His unconditional love. We experience His faithfulness. We draw closer to Him and He draws closer to us.

He strips away everything that hinders what He's doing in you and replaces it with only those things that will launch you into your new season with Him.

Once refined, He prepares and positions you to be released with greater power and an even greater purpose.

THE NEW CONSECRATED COCOON

Set Up to Be Set Apart

I have been eagerly anticipating this section of the book.

This is where things become both exciting and challenging, but mostly exciting! This is where the rubber meets the road. Or even better, this is where you truly meet God.

All previous chapters were designed to get you to this place.

In everything God led me to share, I wanted you to understand that before you were even born, God had a plan for your life (Jeremiah 1:5). And based on the following: Adam and Eve's behavior and repercussions, significant relationships and events in our lives, and our own decisions – those plans were side-tracked. However, God promised to complete the good work he began in each of us (Philippians 1:6); the work needed to carry out the plans He has for us.

So let's get back on track!

Many of us are taught to create a Plan A and being wise, have a plan B as a backup. Well, in seeking God, He showed me that our Plan B should be simply another way to return us to Plan A. In other words, it's not a deviation from it. If you are hearing from God and act accordingly, Plan B is simply the delayed version of Plan A. It returns or restores us to the original plan.

God's delay is not His denial.

As you work through your Plan B, your faith in God should increase, your trust should be renewed, and your resolve should be strengthened.

And if by chance God does deny you – His denial is for your protection. He knows what's best for you and me and He also knows what we can handle. When we are truly seeking after God's will for our lives, He will not allow things or people to come into our life for the purpose of destroying us. He loves us that much.

People who restore old, run down, dilapidated houses and make them look like new have nothing on God. He is the original and ultimate restorer! He is all about restoring His children back to His original plan for our lives. And often times, that's what this concentrated time with God is all about – refocusing, rejuvenating, restoring, and releasing us into God's original plans.

God does not have nor have need for a Plan B.

Jeremiah 1:5 says before you were born and before you were formed in your mother's womb, God consecrated you to do good works for Him. Other words for consecrated are sanctified, set apart, chosen, hand-picked, and separated from the rest. Wow! God really thinks the world of you and me!

Consecration is not a one-time deal. It's an ongoing and necessary process designed to purify us, clean us up, and make us holy, pleasing, and ready for God's use. And since we live in a sinful world, there are things that enter into our lives knowingly and unknowingly that hinder us from being used by God for the work He hand-picked us to do. And so a time of consecration is needed to remove these things and set us back on the path God has for us.

Many times, the sins that enter into our lives are distractions for our destruction.

Did you get that? Distractions are often subtle. They creep into our daily activities and are designed to quietly woo us away from the direction God needs us to go.

Remember, the enemy doesn't play nice, and the distractions, though they may seem harmless, are placed in our path to ultimately destroy our God-assigned purpose and destiny. And so God, in His great love and mercy calls us back to Himself to clean us up, love on us, and put us back on track.

THE NEW CONSECRATED COCOON

It's important to understand that we must be completely available to God based on the work He has for us to do. This means there can't be any sin, idols, or strongholds (things that keeps us bound) in our lives that prevent us from surrendering our full selves to God. We must give ourselves completely over to God.

2 Timothy 2:20-21 says in a wealthy or rich home, there are utensils made of gold and silver, and some of wood and clay. The expensive utensils are used for special occasions and the cheap ones for everyday use. If you and I keep ourselves pure or clean, we can be used for special occasions. As we keep our lives clean, God will use us for good works.

I need you to fully understand why your time of consecration is so incredibly important. When you say, "Lord use me," He takes you seriously and He responds to your request. Let's examine these Scriptures a little deeper so God can bring it closer to home. To do so, I'm going to quote the Message Translation. If you don't have a Message Translation Bible in your possession, I highly recommend you get one. You don't have to use it as your primary Bible, but use it as a supplement to your study time as the language is "real talk." It's in your face and makes it pretty plain.

"In a well-furnished kitchen there are not only crystal goblets and silver platters, but waste cans and compost buckets – some containers used to serve fine meals, others to take out the garbage. Become the kind of container God can use to present any and every kind of gift to his guests for their blessing." (The Message).

Wow, this is a sermon that will preach! Let's start from the top. In a well-furnished kitchen speaks of a mansion or a place that is filled with wealth. This is a word picture to describe Heaven – God's kingdom. And in this well-furnished kitchen, if you can envision this in your mind – there are crystal goblets, silver platters, waste cans, and compost buckets.

For those of you who are forty-something and older, remember those china cabinets our parents or grandparents had? The cabinets where the finest "don't touch" dinnerware were carefully stored? The chinaware sat in the cabinet waiting for that special guest or special event where their presence signified a time of honor and blessing. Those who ate from the china knew they were special and this was no ordinary event.

The china was not for everyday use. There were another set of dishes and glasses available for that. They were hidden away in the kitchen pantry. Were they used? Absolutely, but not for the same purpose as the china. The Scripture goes on to talk about other things in this well-furnished kitchen. There were also waste cans and compost buckets. These were more than likely sitting in a lower place, such as on the kitchen floor. They were used to discard things. Were they used? Absolutely, but the reason they were used didn't even come close to the noble use of the crystal goblets and silver platters.

The Scripture goes on to encourage us to become the kind of container God can use to present a gift to His guests for what? For their blessing. There it is in a nutshell.

Why does God consecrate us? Why does He set us apart? So that we can look good and be seen as something special in our own eyes or in the eyes of man? No! He sets us apart so that we can be a blessing to others. And not just any kind of blessing, but the blessing that they need and the blessing that God requires.

Woo! Can we just stop here and take a deep breath?

I don't know about you, but this passage really speaks to me. You and I were created to be crystal goblets and silver platters. But life has a way of dragging us down. Life's events can demean and discourage us. And some of you reading these words see yourself as a garbage or waste can – only good for receiving what others dump on you.

Come on, now! I'm talking to somebody. And not only do you view yourself as that, but you've allowed others to see and treat you that way.

This grieves the heart of your Heavenly father. He sees you living way below the potential and purpose for which He created you. And like any good daddy, He won't just sit by and watch this happen. He's gotta do something about it. And He does. He calls you back to Himself for some "daddy/daughter time." This...my sister, is what your time of consecration is all about. It's time for you to curl up in your daddy's lap so He can love on you.

To help encourage you about this precious time, I purposely labored in the earlier chapters to paint the picture of what God intended, what happened, and now we are back to what God intended. You've been dumped on and dumped in. At this point, it doesn't matter by whom. We are no longer putting a face to the perpetrator. All who tried to steal from your purpose (knowingly or unknowingly) wear the same face. The face of our enemy, Satan. It's all a part of his plan to steal, kill, and destroy God's purposes in and for you.

Your time of consecration is one of isolation and protection. During this time, God must have your undivided attention and He will go to whatever lengths it takes to make this happen.

Isolation – Lonely but Not Alone

I may have shared this in an earlier chapter, but my time of consecration was the most beautiful, yet loneliest time of my entire life. Was I surrounded by people? Yes, all day and every day. Was I surrounded by praying people? Yes, all day and twice on Sundays. Did they pray for me? Yes, regularly. Were their prayers powerful? Yes, absolutely. Did they empathize with my pain and trial? Yes, they felt for me, cried with me, and held me tight. Could they stand in proxy for me? No. Could they come join me? No. This was a time that was strictly between me and God and it got lonely. Boy, did it ever get lonely on some days.

There were days when I was in my cocoon and it felt dark. It felt cold. It felt like I was completely closed off from the world. And some days, just when I thought it couldn't feel any colder, darker, or lonelier - things kicked up a notch. Some of you may be there right now.

I was very aware of God's presence. He never left me. But, I initially yearned for human company. However, this time was designed for me and God alone. Don't think I didn't try to invite others into my cocoon at first. You know how we do. I picked up the phone and spoke with very dear and trusted sisters. I shared my heart. I cried. I wept from the depths of my toes. They listened. They cried with me. They sympathized with me. But guess what? They couldn't join me. They couldn't take up my cross. It was mine to bear.

The whole time I kept trying to reach out for someone to comfort me, God simply watched my endeavors, and waited for me to get a clue. He was so patient. He wanted to be the one to comfort me. He wanted to wrap His arms around me. He wanted to tell me it was going to be okay. And when I finally fell into His arms, His reassurance was greater than any human being could offer.

Don't get me wrong. There is a time for us to tap on those around for encouragement and to help lift our arms when we are too weak to lift them ourselves.

In Exodus 17, the Amalekites and Israelites were engaged in a war. And Moses went to the top of the hill and took Aaron and Hur with him. As long as Moses held his arms up, the Israelites were winning. But when Moses dropped his arms, the Amalekites started defeating the Israelites. Aaron and Hur saw he was getting too weak and the battle was not over, yet his arms were drooping. So they each took an arm, each on one side and held up Moses' arms until sunset, when the Amalekites were soundly defeated.

We all need Aarons and Hurs in our lives.

We need ones who will see our weak arms and be willing to come alongside us and hold them up. Real prayer warriors don't need to know the intimate details of your struggle; they simply see the need and they answer the call. They see you battling and lock shields with you.

I had some mighty women of God who on many days came alongside me and held my arms up. Sometimes I was able to convey my weakness, but most times, like Moses, I just stood there speechless with drooping arms. And whether I had the strength or good sense to ask for help, my Aarons and Hurs came around me and stood with me.

There's a time to keep our arms raised and fight, and there are times to lower them and allow God to fight the battle for us. When God steps in, the party is over. The lights go out. The music fades. The people go home and it's just you and Him. And He lovingly woos you into a place of seclusion and protection; while He handles His business.

Though our consecrated cocoon can feel terribly lonely, when you finally surrender it will be the most loving experience you'll encounter. It's the place where God wraps His arms around you and draws you close to Him. So close you can hear and feel His heart beat. Hear His heart beating with great joy to hold His daughter close.

The situation that draws us to this place is almost never pleasant. But once here, we recognize our desire to be here is just as strong as God's desire to have us here. We realize our desire to see God's face just as much as He desires to behold ours. We desire to know that our daddy loves us beyond our actions and accomplishments. He loves us for who we are. We are His daughters, beautifully and wonderfully made in His image.

Some of us end up in this intimate place kicking and screaming, while others arrive totally exhausted and depleted. And all we can do is flop into His arms. We've tried to do so much but it wasn't enough. We've tried to please people, but still fell short of their expectations. Our accomplishments were underappreciated, while our mess-ups seem to be over exaggerated. Have you been there? In this private place we desire to hear that our daddy is proud of us. We desire to know that there is more to do, more to receive, and more to become.

When we finally embrace this beautiful place, we realize it's a place of refining and re-firing; restoring, and refueling. We receive strength and strategies; after all, this will not be the last battle we'll face. Trust me...there is more to come.

However, how we enter in and how we exit this time with God determines how we will respond to the next trial.

In this beautiful place, we begin to see ourselves as God has always seen us.

Protection not Punishment

Once we surrender to the consecration process, we realize the hidden value of this time alone with God. However, before we settle in and embrace the process, we often view a time of isolation as torturous and punitive. We believe we did something drastically wrong and this is God's way of correcting us.

Here's the reality – we typically end up in a place of needed consecration for one of two reasons. First, we made some sort of unwise decision that got us terribly off track and God wants to help us get back on track. Or secondly, God is ready to takes us to a new level in Him and He needs our undivided attention. Many of us say we want more of God and want to do more for Him. Newsflash! New levels means more responsibility and God needs to know we can handle it. So He tests us or allows a test to come our way to see how we respond. After all we need to show ourselves trustworthy to handle more treasures of the Kingdom.

You aren't the first person to be called into a place of isolation – into a dry and barren wilderness. Both Moses and Jesus were led, by God, not Satan, to a place of isolation so He could prepare them for the great things He was about to do in and through them.

THE NEW CONSECRATED COCOON

I know this truth may be hard for some of you to receive. However, regardless to how or why you end up in this place, God loves you and will take advantage of having you tall to Himself. If you remain with Him, He promises that you will emerge from your experience a new woman – a woman of renewed faith, authority, and power.

When we are in our spiritual cocoon or our time of consecration, the war is still being waged all around us. The battle is still being fought. However, we can't be touched. God strategically hides us while fighting on our behalf. He keeps us safe!

One of the reasons the caterpillar is hidden away during her transformation process is to keep predators at bay. Her cocoon is designed to prevent them from hindering the process or attacking her during a time of complete vulnerability.

Like the caterpillar, we too are vulnerable during our time of consecration and God knows that – so He hides and protects us. Psalm 91:4 says, God protects us under His wings. His wings are our place of refuge, protection and escape. Escape from what? The war that God is winning on our behalf.

This time of isolation is not about punishment; it's about purification.

Remember you were set apart, which means you can't act like everyone else. You can't think and talk like everyone else. You can't respond to trials like everyone else. So He pulls you out of the world and sits you on His lap so He can talk to you. So He can speak with you one-on-one and face-to-face.

This is a special time designed for reflection and repentance. A time to listen to your daddy's heart as He shares the things that grieve Him. This is a time where He lovingly asks you to take a long, deep, hard look at your life, relationships, priorities, passions, and pursuits and figure out where He is in all of it. This is a time where He reveals your man-made idols that took Jesus off the throne and became self-appointed saviors. He wants you to dethrone them and put His son Jesus back where he rightfully belongs.

This is also a time for you to share your heart with Him. Share your disappointments. Share your desires. Give Him your hurts and pain. Ask for forgiveness and forgive those who have injured you. Give Him your rejection.

Often times man's rejection is God's protection.

Interestingly enough the caterpillar metamorphosis process points out that the cocoon is a place of protection from predators. Inside the cocoon, the caterpillar is defenseless, vulnerable, and submitting to the process. This is true for us as well. In our time of consecration we are letting our guard down. We are dropping our defenses, allowing God to be our defender. We are no longer self-protecting. We are trusting God to hide us from our enemies.

While the caterpillar submits to the process, other larger insects or animals can easily take advantage of her. It's the perfect opportunity to catch her off guard.

Guess what? It's the same for you and me. Don't think everyone around you wants to see you become the butterfly you were created to be. Some would like to hinder your metamorphosis process and see you remain a caterpillar – just like them.

While you're in a place of vulnerability some may seek to take advantage of you. Saying or doing things in an effort to persuade you to be a lifetime member of the caterpillar club. They don't want you soaring high above with other butterflies.

Beware of those who are trying to rescue you from a time God has set aside specifically for you and Him. They will try to give you a way of escape. They will tell you that you simply need to move on. They encourage you to go around your process of healing instead of *through* it. They will say things like, "That husband didn't realize how good he had it, but there's a man out there for you who will love you the way you deserve." They might even try to quickly set you up with someone. They'll tell you this isn't a time to be weak, but instead this is a time to be strong. These ones will encourage self-focus rather than God-focus. Beware!

A word of wisdom: During this time, seek to surround yourself with other spiritual butterflies. Surround yourself with those who have submitted themselves to God's consecration process. Those whose lives are totally surrendered to the Lord and can coach you through the process using the wisdom of God. Stick with those whose lives bear fruit of their surrender and transformation.

Matthew 7:16 says you will know them by their fruit. Who is them? Those who are serving God with their whole heart and are fully embracing His will, not their own. And what's their fruit? Their lifestyle. Their walk matches their talk.

This is important because anyone who is truly growing and is being used by God is like a tree that bears fruit. The health and usefulness of a tree is determined by the quality of its fruit. A fruit-bearing tree that bears no fruit is useless to a farmer. In the Kingdom of God a non-surrendered, non-yielding Christian is useless to God.

Watch out for non-fruit-bearing men and women who want to snatch you out of your place of growth, refuge, and protection and thrust you into the line of fire for the enemy to defeat you.

Those who truly love the Lord will encourage you to remain in that secret, intimate place with Him until He releases you.

We often don't view isolation as something positive. Yet God regularly calls us into focused times of quietness and complete intimacy with Him. He is a jealous God and He will not allow His daughters to place anything or anyone as a priority over your relationship with Him.

Reflection

1. Have you ever felt like God delayed an answer to your prayer or denied your prayer request?
2. Is there an activity, task, or relationship you now realize is a distraction?

3. Reflect upon your lifestyle over the last year. If God were to place you in his House, would you be fine china, everyday eat ware, a waste can or something else?
4. Have you fought against times of isolation with God? If so, what methods did you use (example: TV, working late, etc.)
5. When you need encouragement or prayers do you let others know or do you hide or keep it to yourself?
6. Have you been an Aaron or Hur to anyone lately?
7. When was the last time you had some one-on-one time with your Heavenly Daddy?
8. In your intimate time with God do you give Him permission to search your heart and reveal anything that doesn't please Him?
9. Do you share your deepest disappointments, pain, and struggles with God? Why or why not?
10. Examine your inner circle. Are you currently surrounded by mostly caterpillars (those who are at the same spiritual and emotional level as you) or butterflies (those who are more mature or experienced and can help support/guide you where God is taking you)?
11. Deuteronomy 6:15 says God is a jealous God. What does that mean to you?
12. Has God been beckoning you to abandon some things or relationships in order to spend more focused time with Him?

"As the deer pants for the water brooks, so my soul for you, Oh God. My soul thirsts for God, for the living God. Deep calls unto deep at the noise of Your waterfalls; all Your waves and billows have gone over me. The Lord will command His lovingkindness in the day- time, and in the night, His song shall be with me – a prayer to the God of my life" Psalm 42:1-2, 7-8 (New King James)

THE NEW CONSECRATED COCOON

I Surrender All

So what's really going on inside the caterpillar's cocoon? I'll tell you what's happening. Surrender, submission, acceptance, and transformation. There is a death taking place in preparation for a birth.

The caterpillar is dying so the butterfly can live.

She is hanging upside down in a way that resembles the letter 'J' and she's allowing the necessary process to take place. Her caterpillar limbs, tissues, and organs are changing to form body parts needed for a butterfly. She's losing her eight pairs of legs to make room for two beautiful wings. She's anticipating a whole new mindset. No longer will she see things from a "worm's-eye view" but instead she will soar high above seeing things from an aerial perspective. There's a whole lot of changing going on.

So what's going on inside of our spiritual cocoon? Pretty much the same thing. Old patterns, habits, attitudes, and mind- sets are being removed to make room for new ones. The old fleshly woman is dying to make room for the new and improved woman of God that will emerge. Our flesh is being crucified and that hurts!

Often, in my times of worship with God, I stretch my arms wide and think about Jesus on the cross. No, I don't have the excruciating nails in my hands and feet like He did; but there is something about that posture that begs surrender. With my arms stretched wide and eyes closed, I feel fully exposed and ready for God to do whatever He wants to do in me.

Remember I said earlier that the refining process is one that requires the metal to be held over the fire until the silversmith sees his reflection in it? Well, it's the same with our consecration process – God will not release us until He sees more of Himself in us. And seeing more of Himself means seeing less of us. We can't become a new creation in Christ while hanging on to the old stuff (2 Corinthians 5:17). It just doesn't work that way.

Consecration requires major humility. Humility is not a sign of weakness; it's actually strength of character. It takes courage to be humble. Anyone can be prideful. Pride is a mask. It's a cover up. Humility, on the other hand, requires vulnerability and transparency. We are never more like Christ than when we humble ourselves. Pride protects and holds tightly to achievements, accolades, position, and manipulative power. Humility releases and exposes; giving God the glory for all He does in and through us. It allows and desires for God to point out anything within us that doesn't please Him.

This precious time with God is designed for us to let go of things that He needs us to release, so we can grab a hold of the things He needs us to embrace. For each of us, those areas will differ. But for the sake of this book, there are seven areas I want to address. The number seven symbolizes perfection or completion. And God's goal is to perfect and complete us in Christ Jesus. Amen? Amen!

The areas are: sexual immorality, unforgiveness, control, our words, our thought life, pride, and our intimacy with God. If we can allow God to be the master of these areas in our lives, we will emerge from our spiritual cocoon armed with greater kingdom authority and power. Eager to stand firm when the enemy attacks. Are you ready? Let's go deeper.

Sexual Immorality

For many women, this is an area that is difficult to conquer. Not because we are sexual beings per se. But because men are. And we realize that the way to tap into a man's emotional intimacy is through sexual intimacy. Many women are willing to take the gamble and risk giving themselves over to a man with the hopes that this will finally provide the security and affirmation we all crave.

THE NEW CONSECRATED COCOON

Look around you – everything is sexually influenced from the music, movies, videos, reality shows, to sitcoms. And oh my, now we have to deal with commercials that are filled with half-naked women. Notice how many of these commercials strategically air during shows that a lot of men watch? Hmmm. Raising two sons, TV often opposes the Godly values I strive so hard to instill.

For God's sake, the commercials are just as sexually inundated as the TV shows. We can't go one night without having to endure a commercial that talks about tampons, lingerie, male enhancement, or woman pleasing products. Give me a break!

With the increase trends of sexting, chat rooms, and online pornography, people can live out their sexual fantasies without leaving the privacy of their homes. It's easy to hide behind words. These venues give those who might otherwise be shy in person a false sense of boldness that opens the door to unhealthy and ungodly communications. There was a time when we associated "soul ties" with the physical act of sex. Today men and women are creating emotional and sexual bonds through other modes of communication such as text messages.

For many women, our sexuality is a big deal. We struggle with weight, low-self-esteem, and lots and lots of unrealistic competition. And it's very easy to associate our worth with what a man thinks or doesn't think about our physique.

Let's be clear about what the Bible says about sex. Sex outside of marriage is a sin. Ladies, we are to honor God with our bodies. Our bodies do not belong to us, they belong to God (1 Corinthians 6:18-19). Sex with a married man who is not your husband is considered adultery and that's a sin (Deuteronomy 5:18). Sex was made for the marriage union. God is pleased and receives glory when a husband and wife give themselves to each other.

I will be the first to admit that remaining sexually pure isn't easy. Especially in today's sexually saturated society that glorifies adulterous affairs and one-night stands. Looking back at my own past, I have certainly messed up and disappointed God more than once. And now that I am single again, I have to diligently guard against opening doors of temptation for this sin to enter into my life.

Sexual immorality is a major place of deception for many Christians. We somehow feel that this is the one sin that God turns a blind eye to. We say God created us for intimacy so He understands. He created us for intimacy with Him first and foremost. And through our intimacy with Him, we are prepared for intimacy with a husband.

Ladies, the best way to guard against sexual immorality is to stay clear of situations that open the door to temptation. Beware of those things that set your thoughts in the direction of physical intimacy. Many movies encourage feelings of lustful desires. Certain types of music can incite erotic feelings and thoughts. I call those types of songs "mood music." This type of music might be okay for a husband and wife to listen to together, but it may not be a good idea for lonely singles.

Texting a man on a regular basis who has expressed interest – especially at night – opens the door to temptation. There's something about nighttime that heightens one's sense of being alone. The enemy is crafty. The conversation could begin as simply as this. "What are you doing? Lying in bed. Oh really, what are you wearing? Wouldn't you like to know? Yes I would. Seriously? Absolutely." That's why moms, you should know who and when your teenagers are texting.

Reading romance novels can open the door to sexual fantasies. They paint pictures of this hunk of a guy, who by the way is the most romantic guy in the world, and he knows how to really treat a woman. Before you know it, you are checking out the men around you, even in your church to see who possibly fits that mold. Then, if you spot a guy you believe fits this image of perfection, it's possible to begin fantasizing about

THE NEW CONSECRATED COCOON

him. Whatever we rehearse in our thoughts over and over again, ultimately seeks to play itself out in real life.

The one thing I have learned about the devil is – he loves to oblige. Ladies, whatever you are seeking, he will make sure you find the counterfeit version of it. He looks like the real thing and says all the right things, but he's a counterfeit. Counterfeits consume a lot of our time, energy, and emotions and are designed to be major distractions.

When I re-entered the single scene, I shared with my mentor that I am a "marriage-minded woman." I don't like being single. I love the idea of growing old with my soul mate. I desire to serve my husband. I want to pray and worship with a man who loves the Lord with all of his heart. And I will never forget what my mentor told me.

She said, "Before God sends your Isaac, the devil always sends an Ishmael first." Woo!

If you're familiar with the story of Abraham in the Bible, God promised Abraham and his wife Sarah that he would give them a son (Genesis 15:4). The problem was...Sarah was well beyond child-bearing years. And rather than believe and wait on God's promise, they decided to speed things up.

Sarah suggested that Abraham have sex with her servant, Hagar (Genesis 16). And like any good, obedient husband he did.

Yeah, right.

Hagar became pregnant with Ishmael and started showing Sarah attitude. Sarah got upset with Abraham and told him to put Hagar in check. Abraham didn't handle the situation, so Sarah took matters into her own hands. She was cruel to Hagar, which caused Hagar to run away. And Abraham became the first "baby daddy" in the Bible. It's classic Jerry Springer stuff.

Abraham and Sarah eventually had Isaac as God promised. But this was after the damage was done and several lives were affected in a way God did not intend. Ishmael was not God's promise – Isaac was. Be careful in growing weary while waiting on your Isaac that you don't create and/or accept an Ishmael. Stand on God's promises and wait on Him.

I hear you, Ann, but what do I do while I wait for my Isaac? Two things. First, allow God to meet your deep craving for intimacy. How does He do it? I can't explain it – it's supernatural. I just know He can and will if you trust Him and spend lots of time in the secret place with Him. Secondly, while you are waiting, become the woman of God who is worthy of the man of God you desire.

Until God sends your earthly husband, let Him be your husband. After all, He is our bridegroom and we are His bride. Let's do all we can to remain without spot or blemish, blameless, and pure before Him (Ephesians 5:27). And if you mess up, quickly repent and turn away from that relationship. Ask the person you sinned with to forgive you for including them in your sinful behavior. Ask God to forgive you. And most importantly, forgive yourself. The enemy would love nothing better than to torment you with self-condemnation.

If you need to enter into a relationship of accountability to live a Godly single life, I suggest you do so. The enemy's power is diminished when we expose him and keep things in the open.

Pursuing intimacy outside of Christ and marriage will leave us lonelier than ever. We are designed to have sexual intimacy with a husband, not with boyfriends and friends with benefits.

1 Corinthians 6:16-20 says, *"There's more to sex than mere skin on skin. Sex is as much spiritual mystery as physical fact. As written in Scripture, "The two become one." Since we want to become spiritually one with the Master, we must not pursue the kind of sex that avoids commitment and intimacy, leaving us lonelier than ever - the kind of sex that can never "become one." There is a sense in which sexual sins are different from all others. In sexual sin we violate the sacredness of our*

own bodies, these bodies that were made for God-given and God-modeled love, for "becoming one" with another. Or didn't you realize that your body is a sacred place, the place of the Holy Spirit? Don't you see that you can't live however you please, squandering what God paid such a high price for? The physical part of you is not some piece of property belonging to the spiritual part of you. God owns the whole works. So let people see God in and through your body. (The Message).

Unforgiveness

Some of my relatives and friends are totally amazed that I do not harbor any animosity or ill-will toward my ex-husband. All I can say is God's grace is truly sufficient. His grace empowers me to do what I can't do on my own. And when we delight ourselves in God, He does give us the desires of our heart (Psalm 37:4). My heart's desire is not only to be free of harboring unforgiveness, but to take one step further and speak blessings over my ex. And I do.

I wish more people would understand that unforgiveness is bondage. Unforgiveness is driven by a spirit of control, only to realize that you are the one being controlled. Unforgiveness is a self-erected prison. We think that by holding a grudge we are somehow avenged, but in fact we are the ones imprisoned by our inability to move forward. Unforgiveness keeps us from fully stepping into our purpose and destiny, whereas forgiveness releases and launches us one step closer to what God has for us.

Unforgiveness is like a cancer. Not only is it deadly to the one who is unwilling to forgive, but if not quickly treated, it spreads to others around us.

We are never more like Christ than when we forgive.

My ability and desire to forgive others has very little or nothing to do with whether I feel like it or whether they deserve it. It has everything to do with my desire to be obedient to the Lord and I also want His forgiveness. Matthew 6:15 says God will not forgive us of our sins if we don't forgive others. I pray you get this into your spirit today. You can't expect God to forgive you for the things you do on a regular basis that breaks His commands and breaks His heart; and not be willing to extend forgiveness to others.

Put plainly, unforgiveness is disobedience, and disobedience is sin. If God says not to steal and you steal, you are sinning. The same goes with if He says or commands us to forgive and we do not forgive, we are sinning against Him.

The greatest example of forgiveness is Jesus on the cross. Right before He died, He asked God to forgive those who crucified Him (Luke 23:34). He asked God to forgive them while they were mistreating Him. Wow! For some of us, it's been years since that person hurt you and yet you are still unwilling to forgive. How many precious years of joy and peace have you forfeited with your unwillingness to forgive?

Some of you might say regarding Jesus, "I wasn't physically there. I didn't personally crucify Christ. So that doesn't pertain to me." It does pertain to you and me. In fact, it pertains to all sinners. It wasn't a physical person who crucified Jesus. It was our collective sin that nailed Him to the cross. Jesus, who was absolutely sinless, took on our sins, died for us, and forgave us for crucifying Him. Wow! If Jesus can forgive us, how much more should we forgive others who hurt us? Do you want God to forgive you? Then, forgive others.

Now, don't get me wrong. Forgiveness isn't easy.

I have in no way mastered this wonderful and Christ-like trait. During my divorce, I had moments when my thoughts definitely were not Christ-like. I'm just keeping it real. Forgiveness is not a natural act. It goes against the very fiber of who we are. It contradicts our pride - a pride that wants to protect our hearts from being hurt again. Forgiveness is a supernatural act. It's one that cannot be achieved by our flesh. We need to exercise faith in order to forgive.

THE NEW CONSECRATED COCOON

I often say that forgiveness is an instantaneous process. Meaning, the decision to forgive is instant, but the healing happens during a process.

By "faith" you choose to forgive today. Faith believes the things you are asking for has already happened before you see any evidence (Hebrews 11:1).

For many, forgiveness requires you to "faith it" until you make it.

Faith operates in the spirit realm, not the natural. Forgiveness is not a natural act of the flesh. It is the supernatural will (decision) of the spirit.

Many of us have a hard time forgiving because we believe forgiveness gives others permission to hurt us again or it communicates we are okay with what they did. This is not true. Forgiveness acknowledges the wrong, but it also acknowledges the need to move forward.

You cannot move forward with unforgiveness in your heart. Matthew 5:23-24 says if you are at the altar presenting your gift to God and you remember that a brother or sister has something against you (or you against them), leave your gift, go be reconciled and then return to offer your gift. Unforgiveness prevents you from stepping into your purpose and destiny with Jesus. That's what that gift represents. That gift is your talents, treasures, sacrifices, work, love, and obedience to the Lord. God will not receive these things if you are presenting it with a heart that's not reconciled to His. There may be times when the person may not accept your apology. That's okay. As long as you did what God requires of you, give that person over to God and pray for God to heal their heart.

The biggest thing I want you to understand about unforgiveness is that it does not change the past. Holding on to the pain, holding on to a grudge, and repeatedly punishing the perpetrator will never ever undo what happened. The most powerful phrase regarding forgiveness I ever heard is, "Forgiveness is letting go of all hope of a better past."

Let's also be clear about the results of forgiving someone. Forgiveness might result in reconciliation, but will not always result in restoration.

Restore means to reinstate or reestablish.

There are times when the person who caused the pain is not someone God wants us to reestablish the relationship with. If re-establishing the relationship means subjecting yourself to constant abuse of any kind or participating in the other person's sin, restoration should not be pursued. Put this matter before God in prayer.

In the case where unforgiveness lies between parents and children, forgiveness is vital so that honor and blessing can go forth. As parents we are to bless our children. We are to pray for them. As children we are to honor our parents. We are to pray for them. Unforgiveness hinders these things from going forth. Forgiveness releases us to embrace a repaired relationship with those who have hurt us and also with God.

It's difficult to have a healthy and transparent relationship with God when we harbor unforgiveness. When it comes to our relationship with God, unforgiveness is like the pink elephant in the room. Everyone knows it's there but tries to pretend it isn't. Everyone sees it, but no one wants to acknowledge it. But at some point it has to be dealt with. You can't go to God daily and request for Him to bless you, move on your behalf, give you favor, forgive you, and all of these other things knowing you have unforgiveness in your heart toward someone. It just doesn't work that way.

In the nutshell, forgiveness is for you. When God transforms you into a butterfly you must be able to fly. You must be free. Unforgiveness is like a ten pound weight on your wings. You can't possibly soar until the weights are removed.

There are three more things I would like to share regarding forgiveness. First, it's important that you ask others whom you've harmed to forgive you. We knowingly and unknowingly hurt others. It's not a one-sided thing. The need for forgiveness goes both ways.

First, it's important to take ownership and acknowledge the pain you have caused someone. If you have kids, it is vital that you model forgiveness before them on a regular basis. Do you want your kids to come to you and ask for forgiveness when they've done something wrong? Of course. Then you must be willing to go to them and ask for their forgiveness when you do something wrong as well. You can't expect them to do something they don't see you do.

I ask my sons to forgive me regularly for things I knowingly do or say that offend or hurt them. However, I also sometimes ask for forgiveness for things that might have hurt them and I didn't realize it. In other words, I didn't think I hurt them nor did I intend to. But their demeanor says they are wounded and reconciliation is needed. Asking forgiveness is an act of humility and is even more humbling when you don't think you did something wrong, but value the relationship more than you value being right.

The goal of reconciliation is to clear the air and prayerfully prevent future misunderstandings. Use those opportunities to change your delivery method or the way you approach a similar situation the next time. I try to model this before my sons so that they will become grown men who are not too prideful to ask for forgiveness.

Secondly, forgiving is not forgetting. I can't tell you how often I hear people say "Forgive and forget." Human beings are not capable of forgetting. Everything is stored in our minds, whether or not we are able to recall them at a particular time. However, God does have the ability to forget (Hebrews 8:12). He chooses to forget. He doesn't bring it up anymore.

As for us, I say remember. Don't remember to hold a grudge, but remember to learn from it. In every mess-up, there is an opportunity for a teaching moment from God. God's always teaching us about ourselves, others, and Himself. If you were hurt as a result of a foolish or unwise decision, remember the pain it caused. Remember the lives affected and let that be motivation enough to not repeat the same mistake again.

Finally, we must also learn to forgive ourselves. There are times when we ask others to forgive us and they say yes. Then we ask God to forgive us and He does just that. But somehow we struggle in forgiving ourselves.

Don't you know that when God forgives you it's a done deal? Psalm 103:12 states that God removes our sin from us as far as the east is from the west. God doesn't have to think about it when we ask. He doesn't give us conditions or a list of things to do before He forgives us. We ask with sincere hearts and He immediately answers and grants our request. God throws our sins into the sea of forgetfulness. It's not that God actually forgets. After all He is God. But God chooses to forget; not allowing our past sins to dictate our future victories. Not only do we not forget, but we also take note of which sea God tossed our past sins into so we can go fishing, pull the past stuff out, and then have a pity party with the devil.

When God takes it away, let Him. If you need to, put up a sign, "No fishing allowed."

Please understand that the goal of pity parties hosted by or attended by the enemy is about your un-wrapping the gift of hopelessness. If the enemy can convince a person that things will never get better, he has them eating out of his hand.

Romans 5:5 says that hope in God will not lead to disappointment because God loves us so much that He gave us the Holy Spirit. In times of disappointment and pain, the Holy Spirit comforts us and reassures us of the plans God has for our future (Jeremiah 29:11).

I believe that a Christian who commits suicide is one who has lost all hope. People who don't have a relationship with Jesus have no hope because they cannot be sure of their future. But as a Christian, we can be one hundred percent positive that we have a future, not just here on earth, but also in eternity. And therefore we know that sadness or feelings of hopelessness may endure for a night, but we have a hope that joy will come in the morning (Psalm 30:5). The morning referred to in this Scripture is not the literal morning – it's figurative.

The morning symbolizes the moment our trial is behind us and joy is before us. On this morning, it's not about when the sun rises, but when the Son of God arises on our behalf. Hallelujah! This should cause you to rejoice because it's a promise of the joy that is coming to you if you don't give up.

Forgive yourself. It's the greatest gift you can give back to Jesus. Jesus died on the cross to take on your sin, shame, sickness, and hopelessness. Isaiah 53:5 says that Jesus was pierced for our rebellion, crushed for our sins, beaten so we could be whole, and whipped so we could be healed. The ability to forgive and be forgiven is that "wholeness and healing" the Scripture refers to. Each time you refuse to forgive yourself, you tell God that the sacrifice His son made wasn't enough. You tell Jesus that He needs to do it again, because His sacrifice didn't cover your situation.

Of course we know this isn't true. Jesus died once and for all – for all sins past, present and future. Believe and receive that your sins are covered. Walk in the freedom that Jesus hung, died, and resurrected for.

You're well-known as good and forgiving, bighearted to all who ask for help. Pay attention, God, to my prayer; bend down and listen to my cry for help. Every time I'm in trouble I call on you, confident that you'll answer. Psalm 86:5-7 (The Message).

Jesus is NOT your Co-Pilot

The area of control is one that I've struggled with in the past, and I must diligently guard against it today. Control is a learned behavior and is primarily birthed out of the need to self-protect. It's rooted in fear, disappointment, lack of trust, and lack of confidence. It's the desire to dictate the outcome of things. It's okay to pray that people's hearts will change in order for a situation to be resolved. But when we try to manipulate the situation to get the outcome we want; that's control.

If you are anything like me, God keeps me on a need-to-know basis in situations where I am a little over zealous. Sometimes I am not very patient when God takes His time to answer my prayers. Quite frankly, when He doesn't move fast enough, I am inclined to help Him out. And He knows this, so He doesn't divulge the work He's doing behind the scenes. God knows me inside and out and realizes that once I know what's going on, I will be tempted to reach over and take the wheel out of His hands.

I cringe whenever I hear people say that Jesus is their co-pilot. Seriously? You must really think very highly of yourself if you believe Jesus sitting next to you giving pointers is the best use of his infinite power. Jesus doesn't need a captain's license. He made the airplanes, He made the sky, and He certainly doesn't need your permission to take over. In fact, I want Jesus to be the pilot, the Holy Spirit as co-pilot, and then when they believe I'm ready – they can invite me into the cockpit (or not). In other words, when they want my two cents, they will let me know.

I can't tell you how many women I speak to who are grieved over their unsaved husbands. They desperately want him to know Jesus. And equally there are women whose husbands are Christian but they struggle with making Jesus Lord over every aspect of their lives. For us women, it's hard to respect and even follow a man who won't submit to and follow Christ.

1 Peter 3:1 says that wives must accept their husband's authority, even when they refuse to live according to the Bible because your godly life or example will show them Jesus and they will desire to know Him.

Ladies, your nagging, controlling, demeaning, and unappreciative ways are not going to speed up the process of your husband becoming the man you wish he would be or the man God created him to be. In fact, if you are not careful, your behavior may push him away, giving him a one-way ticket to Hell.

THE NEW CONSECRATED COCOON

You cannot control your kids, either. You can't control whether someone purposes in their heart to hurt you or not. The bottom line is – people find a way to do what they want to do. You can't manage every aspect of other people's lives and you should not want to. That's more than a full-time job. Besides, don't you realize that God is fully capable of getting a person's attention far better than you?

1 Peter 3:1 speaks of something far better than control. It speaks of influence. God gave Eve influence in the Garden and she misused it for personal gain rather than God's glory. Influence is the ability to persuade without using words. The best sales people in the world are the ones who cause you to believe what they are offering will radically change your life. We are Jesus' saleswomen, and the best way to win others to Christ is for them to look at our lives and desire what we have. And when they ask what we have, we can tell them who we have.

Ladies, God isn't calling you to be worriers. He's looking for Warriors! He's looking for women who will rise up with weapons of prayer. If you are going to worry, why pray? If you are going to pray, why worry? It's one or the other.

God is calling forth bold and courageous women this hour. He's looking for those of us who aren't conducting ourselves from a place of fear, but rather a place of faith in Him. A person who walks in fear doesn't fully grasp or receive God's unconditional love. When we receive God's perfect love for us, it casts out all fear (1 John 4:18). God loves you so much that He orchestrates everything in your life to benefit you and to lead others to Himself (Romans 8:28).

For God's sake, lose all control! Give it up. Give the control over to God. He wants to do much more than you can ask, imagine, or even think (Ephesians 3:20). Imagine big. Ask big. Expect big. And in doing so, you will be amazed at how much God can actually accomplish without your help.

There is one thing that you do have control over and that is you. God is desperately seeking women who strive to live a life of self-control and self-discipline. He's seeking omen who pray before they speak, act, and respond. When we master the art of self-control, we release God to move mountains on our behalf.

"Rather he must be hospitable, one who loves what is good, who is self-controlled, upright, holy and disciplined." Titus 1:8 (New International Version)

Reflection ----------------------------------

1. Reflect upon your decisions over the la r or two. Have you created any "Ishmael type" situations due to being impatient with God?
2. Are you pursuing an INTIMATE relationship with Jesus? A relationship that desires HIM to meet all of your needs?
3. Are you trying to meet your needs in other ways (men, food, shopping, hanging out, over working etc.)?
4. Unforgiveness is disobedience. Is there a person you are not willing to forgive?
5. If you answered yes to the previous question, what is stopping you from extending forgiveness?
6. Is there someone whom you've hurt and you need to ask for their forgiveness?
7. Feelings of condemnation, shame, and guilt might be an indicator that you need to forgive yourself. Do you need to release yourself from a past you can't change?
8. Would you or others describe you as controlling?

Calling the crowd to join his disciples, he said, "Anyone who intends to come with me has to let me lead. You're not in the driver's seat; I am. Don't run from suffering; embrace it. Follow me and I'll show you how. Self-help is no help at all. Self-sacrifice is the way, my way, to saving yourself, your true self." Mark 8: 34-36 (Message)

THE NEW CONSECRATED COCOON

God's Power Versus Ours

As we desperately attempt to embrace our time of consecration, we must acknowledge our need to yield to God's power. We must submit to His authority. In doing so, we are able to release what isn't of Him, and receive what He has for us. Glory be to God!

The more we become like Christ, we learn the right time and way to exercise the power God gives us. And on the flip side we also learn when to stand back and allow God to fight for us.

Our thoughts, words, and emotions have power.

Our thoughts become our words, and our words influence our behavior. When our thoughts and words are submitted to God, our actions can then be pleasing to God. But when they are not, well…it's quite opposite.

During your time of consecration, the goal is to emerge from this experience with a better understanding of the mind and heart of God. When we are on one accord with God, His power can freely flow through us to best accomplish His will in us.

Word Power

If I asked you to share a time in your life when someone spoke hurtful words to or about you, you could probably recall at least one incident. For some, you can probably recall more than one. And regardless to the number of times, the result was the same – crushed feelings and an altered self-image.

Releasing destructive words into the atmosphere is equivalent to sneezing without covering your mouth. Once those germs are airborne, there's no reeling them back in. Once painful things are said, there's no undoing the damage. Sure we can apologize for what was said, but those words have already found a permanent home in the recipient's mind and on their heart.

Words have tremendous power. Once spoken, they produce an outcome. What's the outcome? Ultimately what they were intended to do. God Himself says when His word is sent out, it always accomplishes what He desires and will not return without achieving the purpose for which it was sent (Isaiah 55:11).

We are created in God's image and God's words have power; therefore our words have power too. What kind of power? The power to call things that do not exist (yet) into existence. Remember, God spoke all of creation into being in Genesis chapter one. He said let there be light, and there was. He said let the earth produce every animal, and it did. Every word He spoke did exactly what it was released to do. And so it is with our words – they too can and will accomplish the desired end.

Our words can be used for both good and evil. They can be used to bless or curse, encourage or discourage, build up or berate, complain or accept, praise or pout, and agree with or doubt. It's our choice.

When I was in my early twenties, a young man with whom I was sexually intimate with made a comment about a certain part of my body. And that stuck with me for a very long time. I developed such a complex that each time I looked in the mirror, I heard his words played over and over again. I don't think he understood just how hurtful his words were to me; after all he was a guy. And sometimes, guys can be a little insensitive to just how sensitive we women can be.

For each of us, there is something that someone spoke over us that changed the way we view ourselves, our talents, our passion, desires, and even our dreams. In most cases, people don't realize the life-altering power their words carry.

Both negative and positive words have staying power, but negative words also have "stinging" power, which makes them more difficult to forget. Proverbs 18:21 says, our tongue (words) have the ability to bring life or death and those who love to talk will reap the consequences of their words. Like many of you, I heard this Scripture quoted so many times in church, but had very little understanding and reverence for the truth it holds.

Whether we bless or curse someone with our words, rest assured we will reap the benefits or negative repercussions of what we say. I've said it more than once in this book. As God's daughters, we hold kingdom power and authority. And God expects us to use them to draw others to Him, not push them away. Unfortunately, there are times we misuse, abuse, or underuse this authority.

Our tongue is a powerful weapon that's used for both good and evil. Destructive words can be used to emotionally cut a person into tiny pieces. Words of faith can call things that don't yet exist into existence. Gossiping words can assassinate a person's character. Authoritative words can tell a mountain to be removed. Triumphant words can declare a victory over any situation. Words of praise can usher in blessings, and loving words can heal a broken heart.

Rather than using our words to wage war at people, we are to use our words to wage war against Satan. Instead of using our words to agree with what the devil says about us, we must use our words to agree with what God says about us. Our words are to be used to speak words of victory and not defeat. We must use our words to declare that we have a hope. We have a hope in Jesus. Our words must be used to unlock kingdom authority over our difficult situations.

Mark 11:23 says if you speak to your mountain, or seemingly impossible circumstance and tell it to be lifted up and thrown into the sea (in other words get out of your way), it will happen if you don't doubt in your heart. So that mountain you've been going around for years and feel you can't overcome, tell it to be gone!

Our tongue literally has a mind of its own. The Bible says the tongue is frightening because it cannot be tamed. No man can bring it under submission. Check out James 3:7-10 in the Message translation:

"This is scary: You can tame a tiger, but you can't tame a tongue – It's never been done. The tongue runs wild, a wanton killer. With our tongues we bless God our Father; with the same tongues we curse the very men and women he made in his image. Curses and blessings out of the same mouth! My friends, this can't go on. A spring doesn't gush fresh water one day and brackish the next, does it? Apple trees don't bear strawberries, do they? Raspberry bushes don't bear apples, do they? You're not going to dip into a polluted mud hole and get a cup of clear, cool water, are you?"

Oh my! I love, love, love this translation. Can it be any more plain? I'm amazed by those who call themselves Christians yet have such potty mouths. Seriously! I hear parents cussing (not cursing) in front of their kids and sometimes at them. And then they wonder where their kids get it from.

On Sunday mornings, many kids witness hypocrisy at its finest as their parents use the same lips to worship God that were speaking profanity during the week. Really?

Parents wake up! You can't possibly believe this is okay, do you? In fact, anyone who has the Holy Spirit living in them knows this is not acceptable. If this type of behavior describes you it's time to clean up your mouth. In Jesus' name. It's not that you can't stop speaking that way; it's that you choose not to!

I cussed a lot when I was in high school. But I will be honest and say I totally did it so others would view me as being cool. It became a part of my everyday vocabulary at school. Of course I was cunning enough to make sure I didn't cuss at home or around adults; which is more than I can say for teens today.

One day while attending a track meet at my younger son's middle school, I stood next to a few teens that had the total "potty mouth" thing going on. I wasn't really shocked to

THE NEW CONSECRATED COCOON

hear their language. But I was blown away that my presence didn't seem to have any influence whatsoever.

When I was in high school, we at least had enough sense and respect for adults who were in earshot of our conversations. And back then, we didn't even have to know who the adults were, just the fact that they were grown-ups was enough for us. I miss those days [sigh].

Thank God that the more I matured and when I truly began walking with Christ, I realized that the English language is not at a loss for words to adequately describe how I felt on any given day. In other words, we can express anger, disappointment, or excitement using words that do not require bleeping. When I first started cussing, I did it for the shock value. Do you know what I mean when I say shock value? I did it to invoke a response. I wanted friends to say, "Wow, she's not the angel I thought. Wow, she's a bad girl or a tough girl." And it's no different with a lot of our kids today. Their use of foul language is often done in so they can be accepted.

Currently, my younger son is in his freshman year of high school. And due to playing basketball and his personality, he has become fairly popular. We often have conversations about the friends he hangs around. We discuss their attitudes, language, and beliefs. It is said, "One can tell what lies in a person's future by the people they hang around." Therefore, I am very involved with and am familiar with his close friends.

Unfortunately, many of his friends, even those professing Christianity not only cuss, but make inappropriate remarks and jokes. My son assures me that he doesn't use inappropriate words, but I still caution him about who he spends most of his time with during school hours. I've had coaches and some of his peers attest to the fact that he's a young man of character who doesn't use foul language, etc., and I do not take this for granted.

I don't take it for granted because based on who I was in high school; it's by God's grace that he is such an outstanding young man. I pray over both of my sons daily and I do cover both of them in the area of pressure to conform to the world's way of doing things.

We live in this sinful world, but we are not to conduct ourselves like the world does. We are not to talk, act, and respond the way non-Christians do (Romans 12:2). You can hang around friends that are not saved and don't believe in Jesus without sounding and acting like them. In fact, you might be the only Jesus they encounter and so you can't blend in with the rest of the crowd. Something should set you apart from those who don't have Jesus in their hearts.

Ephesians 4:29 says we are not to allow any corrupt or destructive words to come from our lips. The words we speak should build people up and encourage them. Our words should be appropriate for the occasion and also for the ones who hear them.

Often times, people are listening to us even when we don't realize it.

Some of us wives wonder why our husbands don't want to be around us. Or our kids don't respect us. Or why certain people don't like to hang out with us. Have you checked your words lately? It's not just about cuss words; it's also about curse words. It's about whether the things you say introduce life or death into conversations.

Are your words positive or negative? Do you take pride in being a pessimist? Do you enjoy putting others down? Do people see you coming and run the other way? When you open your mouth, do people realize just how ignorant or foolish you are? Proverbs 17:28 says even a fool is believed to be wise if he can just keep quiet.

Rest assured, precious sister, that on the day that you stand before God, you will be required to give an account or explanation for the careless words you spoke (Matthew 12:36). I don't' know about you, but I want God to be proud of his daughter when I stand before Him on that day.

THE NEW CONSECRATED COCOON

People should desire to be around you because your words encourage them. Did you know that your words can bring healing? Proverbs 12:18 says, harsh words are equivalent to cutting or wounding someone, whereas kind and wise words bring healing. Loving words of encouragement not only bring spiritual healing, but physical healing as well (Proverbs 16:24). Loving words bring healing to the one who hears them, as well as the one who speaks it.

Knowing that your words have healing power, why would you want to declare or speak spiritual or physical sickness over anyone? Your answer might be, "Because they've hurt me." The Bible says that you are to bless those who curse you (Romans 12:14). What does that mean to bless them? It means rather than speaking ill-will over them, you ask God to open their eyes. Ask God to heal their pain. Ask God to forgive their sins even if they are not smart enough to ask for themselves. Ask God to reveal His wonderful love to them. Ask God to prosper their life.

"But Ann, I don't feel like blessing them." Romans 12:14 is not a suggestion. It's a commandment. And when you obey God's commands and serve Him, He blesses and honors your obedience (John 12:26b).

If you haven't fully grasped it yet – your words hold power. Your words can declare blessings or curses over people. Your words can move mountains by faith and belief in God. Your words can build others up or tear them down. Releasing hurtful words is like ringing a bell that can't be un-rung. You can say you are sorry, but the words have already been etched on that person's heart – forever with them.

Many of us have had words spoken over us that cut us to the core. That person may have apologized, or maybe not. Either way, we have not forgotten the words no matter how long it's been.

For many of us, the words reshaped your self-perception, reduced our self-worth, or discouraged our purpose and destiny. If someone did this to you, then why in the world would you want to inflict that type of pain on others? Ask God to give you wisdom and discernment regarding your words – what to say, how to say it, and when to say it.

Let me add a caveat to this section regarding words. Sometimes, God doesn't want us to say anything. He wants us to seal our lips and open our ears. Among the many organs and tissues that become useless when the caterpillar undergoes her change is her mouth. During her cocoon time, her mouth becomes functionless. Don't be surprised if during your time of consecration you find yourself at a loss for words. Sometimes God wants us to simply be quiet so we can hear what He is saying. And for some of us, this requires the grace of God. When we spend alone time with God it's a time to commune with Him. We don't just dominate the conversation with what we want to say; we also position ourselves to hear what God wants to say back. Sometimes, based on the situation He wants us to quietly watch Him give us the victory. There is a time to declare war with our words and there is a time to be silent. Seek God to know the difference.

Praying words have power! Want to see God's plans and purposes fulfilled in your life and the lives of those you love? Begin declaring blessings over your family and friends. When you grab a firm hold of God's promises and refuse to let go – God will surely bring them to pass on your behalf. And He will do it right before your very eyes.

At some point in your Christian walk, your prayers must move from a position of "begging" to "believing." You must move from being under a circumstance to being an overcomer! You must speak by faith. You must talk about those victories that have not yet happened as though they have – that's faith (Hebrews 11:1). Faith is an overwhelming confidence in what God will do, not what your circumstance looks like today.

Revelation 12:11 says you overcome adversity and trials by your words or by your testimony and the power of Jesus Christ. Your testimony is what you say about your circumstance. In other words, Jesus can't make you believe and confess the victory. However, when you believe deep in your heart that you have it and you say you have it, Jesus can then join forces with you and turn your mountain into a footstool. Amen? Amen!

Do you have a situation you are facing that seems impossible? I dare you to begin speaking to it. Speak over it. Declare it a thing of the past. When you pray about it, don't ask God to do anything for you concerning it anymore. Instead, thank Him that He has already taken care of the situation. Praise God before you even see the situation changed or the problem fixed. Praise is the outward expression of an inward appreciation.

Jesus spoke the shortest and most powerful words of declaration right before he died on the cross. He said, "It is finished" (John 19:30). Declare those words over your life right now. Declare it over your family, your circumstances, and over your purpose and destiny!

"Let the words of my mouth and the meditation of my heart be pleasing to you O Lord, my rock and my redeemer." Psalm 19:14 (New Living Translation).

Battlefield of the Mind

Prayerfully, from our previous section you've come into a deeper understanding of just how powerful your words are, and when released into the atmosphere they have either a positive or negative impact. Therefore, we must choose our words wisely. But even more powerful than our words, is the place where our words originate – our heart.

Our words are simply an outward indicator of the inward condition of our heart.

Matthew 12:34b says, "For whatever is in your heart deter- mines what you say" (New Living Translation). This Scripture is not referring to your physical heart that pumps blood throughout your body. It refers to your spiritual heart; the place where your thoughts, feelings, and decisions reside.

Your heart is the command center for your mind, will, and emotions. What you think you believe. What you believe you say. What you say you do.

It really trips me out when I hear people say things like, "Oh, I didn't mean to say that." Chances are they absolutely did. Or they say, "Sorry...that just slipped out." Yeah – doubt it. Your lips do not release words that haven't been authorized by your mind. It's not possible to say something that you didn't already think about.

Now, I will agree that there are some people who have mastered the art of impulsiveness or insensitivity by saying the first thing that pops into their mind without the consideration of others. But that's not because of an inability to control their words; it's about an unwillingness to consider more than just their own feelings.

Can we keep it real?

Let's face it, we're all capable of and are guilty of what I like to call stinking thinking. Stinking thinking are those thoughts we have that are not pleasing to God – thoughts that are critical, lustful, manipulative, condemning, envious, hopeless, etc. This type of thinking extends an open invitation for Satan to lure us into sinful behavior.

Remember, we are daughters of Adam and Eve; which means we all have the tendency to have thoughts that do not please God. Don't think for one second that the first time Eve noticed the fruit was when the serpent brought it up. She had already eye-balled it and thought about the power she could gain if she were to eat it.

The enemy simply took advantage of an opportunity that was already there.

When our adversary tempts us toward sin, God promises a way of escape. 1 Corinthians 10:13 says, there is no temptation that man could ever face that God has not already provided a way out of it. However, we must want to turn away from the temptation and not surrender to the strong emotions and desires. We all struggle with unhealthy thoughts, but it's what we do with them that matters. Jesus was tempted on every front, but we know he did not sin. The fact that no temptation can come your way that is new or different from what Jesus experienced means you can overcome it as well.

The mind is a very secret and private place. That's both a positive and a negative. The positive side of this privacy is the ability to keep some thoughts strictly between me and God. Like everyone else, I have moments when I am not proud of my thoughts and realize my need for God's help to change them. During these times, without embarrassing exposure, I am able to repent before God and submit my thoughts to Him. My surrender in cooperation with God's power changes my thoughts to what pleases Him.

The not so positive side of private thoughts is our unwillingness to submit them to God. We know we are in a bad place, yet we refuse to invite God into our thought process. And therefore, by default we give Satan permission to influence our thoughts. And when he does, he comes in with the big guns. He comes in with a plan that is designed to take us down. He uses our thoughts against us and attacks areas of vulnerability and emotional instability. He belittles our self-worth, raises doubts, introduces scenarios of fear, highlights our inadequacies, feeds feelings of entitlement, encourages a victim mindset, conjures up confusion, fans the flames of worry, promotes division, and ultimately tries to steal your purpose and destiny.

The Bible says Satan is the "accuser of the brethren" (Revelation 12:10b). He goes before God day and night, night and day pointing out our mess-ups. He has nothing better to do. And when he gets tired of being ignored by God, he comes at you directly through your thoughts and accuses you by way of condemnation. He reminds you of each time you blew it. He says you are beyond God's forgiveness and have exhausted God's grace.

He wages war! And in every war there are casualties and captives. In the war of your mind, you can avoid casualties by taking your thoughts captive. 2 Corinthians 10:5 says you have the authority and power to do just that. You can grab a hold of your thoughts and force them to submit to the knowledge and truth of God's word. When you find that your thoughts are out of control, be a spiritual cowgirl and lasso them right back in. Tell those thoughts that they do not rule you – inform them that they are ruled by God almighty.

Under God's authority and by His supernatural power, you can change your stinking thinking to thoughts that please God.

What pleases God? Thinking about things that are true, right, pure, lovely, admirable, excellent, or worthy of praise (Philippians 4:8).

I've learned that it is literally impossible to focus on contradicting thoughts at the same time. In other words, I can't focus on things that are true, while dwelling on things that are false. I can't concentrate on things that are lovely, while meditating on things that are ugly.

I've also learned that our thoughts are even more effective when verbal reinforcement is used. In other words, I'm not just thinking about things that are pure and lovely, I am also speaking it.

If you are like me, there have been times when I am quietly praying in my mind and all of a sudden, a thought pops into the middle of my prayer time that has absolutely nothing to do with what I'm talking to God about. It might be a thought about the dishes that need to be washed or that doctor's appointment I need to make. These distractions are subtle and are designed to lead our thoughts away from God.

Whenever I realize that for whatever reason I am vulnerable to distractions, I pray out loud. I read my Bible out loud. My mind has a difficult time going in the opposite direction of my words. Although our words are influenced by our thoughts, we sometimes have to initially force our thoughts to follow our words. There are times when we must verbalize a truth over and over to allow our minds to finally embrace it.

However, once we align our thoughts with God's thoughts, true change occurs.

Ann, are you saying that when I change my way of thinking God can make me into a different woman? Bingo! Romans 12:2 says, God will transform you into a new woman when you change the way you think. And then there's a promise that goes with that. God promises that when you align your thinking with His, you will get to know His good, pleasing, and perfect will for your life. Come on! It does not get any better than that! Do you want to know what God desires to do in and through you? Then marry your thoughts with His.

For every negative or discouraging thought the enemy wants to use against you, there is a Scripture available to refute the lie and reveal God's truth.

Comparison

If you struggle with thoughts of comparison, 2 Corinthians 10:12 says that comparing yourself with others is foolish. Why? Because comparison leads to one of two temptations: pride or intimidation. You either elevate yourself above others or down- play the uniqueness in which God crated you (Psalm 139:14). God has unique plans for you (Jeremiah 29:11) and you will not reach your God-given potential using human standards as your point of comparison. You must only compare yourself to God's standards for your life.

Fear

If you struggle with thoughts of fear, these feelings are not of God. God did not give you a spirit of fear; He gave you a spirit of love, power, and a sound mind (2 Timothy 1:7). Fear keeps you from accepting God's perfect love for you (1 John 4:18). Living in fear hinders God's ability to protect and provide for you because you're convinced you must have total control over your situation. Faith is the opposite of fear. Living a life of faith gives God the autonomy and control to do what He knows is best for you.

Insecurity

If you struggle with feelings of insecurity or lack of self-confidence, do not quit doing the things God requires of you. Trust Him, press in, and refuse to give up. When you persevere through hard times, God can mature and complete you so you lack nothing in Him (James 1:4). Rest assured that your self-worth isn't determined by any person, but your identity is founded in Christ. And when you said yes to Jesus, He began a beautiful work in you that He promises to complete (Philippians 1:6).

Decision-Making

If you struggle with making the right decisions, seek wisdom from God. There is a way that seems right to you and I, but that way often leads to disaster (Proverbs 14:12). God's wisdom can only come from Him and includes a strategy – what to do, how to do it, and when. If you lack this type of wisdom, God wants you to ask Him with a sincere heart. And when you ask, the Bible says He freely gives you what you need (James 1:5).

Loneliness

If you struggle with feelings of loneliness, know that no matter what, God is always with you (Matthew 28:20). Being alone and being lonely are two different things. You can be in a room full of people and still feel lonely. And you can be alone and not feel lonely. Feelings of isolation, rejection, and abandonment often accompany feelings of loneliness. You serve a God who loves you and desires to be close to you. No matter what's going on in your life, He will never leave you and He will never desert you (Deuteronomy 31:6).

Health Problems

If you struggle with health issues, know that God is equally as concerned about the things that hinder your ability to be fully available for what He wants to do in and through you. It's our responsibility to exercise, eat right, and treat our body like the holy temple that it is (1 Corinthians 6:19). And if you struggle with health issues that are outside of your control, pray and believe that by Jesus' stripes you are already healed (Isaiah 53:5). Jesus was beaten and crucified for your salvation, forgive- ness, and healing. But you must receive and believe that you will be healed. Healings are gradual and over a period of time, so don't lose hope. Remember, what you believe in your mind and what you say with your mouth has power. Boldly speak words of healing over your situation.

Lack

If you struggle with thoughts of not having enough, God will provide for all of your needs. As a matter of fact, His Word says that He knows what you need even before you ask and has already made provision (Matthew 6:8). The Bible says that God cares for the minuscule details of a bird's needs. Think about that. He cares about where the bird lives, what she eats, her young, etc. If He cares this way for the birds, then imagine how much more He will take care of the needs of His precious princess daughter (Matthew 6:26). God owns it all and promises to take care of your needs and the needs of your loved ones.

Worry or Anxiety

Struggling with thoughts of worry and anxiety is a sure sign of not trusting God. There is a saying, "If you pray, why worry? Or if you worry, why pray?" The two can't co-exist. God commands us to not be anxious about anything. But instead, pray and ask Him for what we need and then thank Him for meeting the need. And when we do this, He will replace our anxiety with a peace that will guard our hearts and mind (Philippians 4:6-7).

There are times that we have a tendency to be anxious about what the future holds and worry about things that haven't even happened yet. Matthew 6:34 tells us not to worry about tomorrow because tomorrow has its own cares. Only be concerned about today – but remember, rather than worry let God know your requests and trust He will take care of you.

Revenge

Struggling with thoughts of revenge? This is one that can absolutely consume our thoughts and will not rest until we do something about it. However, we need to understand that we serve a God who is just. Meaning there is nothing that goes unnoticed before Him. He sees every man and woman's actions and words and we will each be held accountable when we stand before Him. Just because the person who hurt you seems to be living a carefree life doesn't mean they are not on God's radar.

However, God's timing and way of doing things is not like ours (Isaiah 55:8). When a person hurts you, they also sin against God. It's so easy to want to inflict pain in return. God doesn't lie when He says, "Whatever a person sows, she will also reap or receive in return" (Galatians 6:7). When God says enough is enough, His way of handling a situation will be a lot better than you and I could ever imagine. God clearly says that getting revenge is His job, not ours (Romans 12:19).

I can write an entire book on just those things that we women tend to struggle with in our thought life. But instead I will close this section by encouraging you that whether it's physical, emotional, mental, or spiritual, God has an answer and a promise to help you overcome your struggle.

Remember, your thoughts are powerful. If the enemy can convince you that you are already defeated, things are hopeless, and no one cares; then he proceeds to persuade you to take the next step of saying and doing something about it. The power you surrender your thoughts to, God or Satan, determines the words you speak and the actions you take.

On a closing note, there are times that our thoughts are completely past the point of self-encouragement and require intervention from others. Situations such as deep depression and thoughts of suicide must be addressed. They must be exposed. They must be brought out of the hidden places of your mind and placed into the open so God can bring the right persons and resources into your path to begin the healing process.

My precious sister, whatever thoughts you struggle with, you can rest assured that God's power is mightier than what's going on in your mind. God is able to heal your emotions and comfort you even in your thoughts. And remember, a thought is just that. It's what you choose to do with it that matters. Choose to align your thoughts with God's Word.

Pride of Life

It never ceases to amaze me when the topic of pride comes up the amount of women that believe it's a "man thing." We women can be so incredibly prideful, but because we associate pride with masculinity we think it doesn't apply.

Pride is often noticeable when someone displays arrogant behavior. But in essence, pride is simply the opposite of humility. Pride is an unwillingness to be broken and repentant. Pride is man-centered, whereas humility is God-centered.

By the end of this section, some of you may look at pride very differently. Prideful behavior is not always what you think or what it appears to be. And truth be told, we ladies are just as challenged in the area of humility as men are. Humility requires vulnerability and being vulnerable isn't easy for someone who has experienced past hurts and disappointments.

A woman who is unwilling to admit she is wrong is being prideful. A woman who refuses to say she is sorry is being prideful. A woman who thinks she is too important to serve others is overwhelmingly prideful.

The interesting thing I've learned about pride is…it's a mask. It's a façade. It's a front. It's used to cover up a fear of exposure – exposure of an area of lack in our life. Pride is a diversion from a major insecurity, lack of self-confidence, or feelings of inadequacy. And when people try too hard to overcompensate in an area where they fall short; it can easily come off as overconfidence or pride. But in reality, it's a total cover up. When I learned this truth I no longer looked at people who displayed arrogant tendencies the same.

I can recall several occasions in my own life when I allowed pride to get the best of me and to rule the outcome of a situation. I wanted to be right. So I refused to apologize even when I knew my apology would greatly impact the hostile atmosphere. My need or desire to be right had deeper feelings of inadequacy attached to it.

Growing up, my dad was a pretty opinionated and strong-willed person. Praise God he is not like that anymore.

But back then it was kind of like his way or the highway. So as a teenager, I didn't feel a freedom to express my true feelings. And I interpreted this inability to express myself as a devaluing of my thoughts and feelings. I felt like what I had to say was not important. As an adult I learned that my grandfather was the type of man who believed kids should be seen and not heard. So it was difficult for my dad to express himself as well. As an adult, my dad became a passionate communicator with a desire to be heard and affirmed. And this apple didn't roll far from the tree because I too became an adult who needed that affirmation and easily felt devalued if my opinion wasn't celebrated. I thought if I spoke the loudest, the longest, or with the most fervor, my self- worth was somehow validated.

I said all of that to say, that by the grace of God I finally understood that my argumentative, prideful, and overly passionate way of communicating, along with my unwillingness to be told what to do; was really my attempts to feel valued in the eyes of others.

I have a dear friend whose pride is displayed in her inability to ask others for help. She is used to doing everything for herself and others and everyone else has gotten used to her doing it all. Growing up, her mom was an alcoholic who dumped all parental responsibilities in her lap. As the oldest of her siblings, she literally raised her brothers and sister while her mom was out gallivanting around town or just too drunk to peel herself out of bed. Soon everyone expected my friend to do everything, fix it all, and rescue everyone. And eventually, she answered the unrealistic call and began to expect this of herself.

So fast forward to today, she has gotten used to doing everything herself and to some degree believes that no one else can do it as well as she can. She has a hard time asking for and receiving help. She does have her moments of private vulnerability that only few like myself are privy to. There are times when she is completely overwhelmed to tears. When this happens she disappears from the public eye for a day or two. There are times when she absolutely wants to say no to someone's request but feels totally obligated to say yes.

She has moments where she secretly wants to fail, mess up, and drop the ball so people would realize she is only human. There are times when she just wants to be left alone and not be expected to be there for everyone and their problems. But this façade she has kept up for all these years always takes precedence over her moments of vulnerability and despair. Yet beneath it all is a fear that people will one day discover she isn't as strong as they believe her to be.

Do you want to know the biggest problem my friend has? It's not meeting the expectation of others. She can handle that. It's not putting her life on hold for everyone else. She has mastered that quite well. Her biggest challenge is going before God in a state of weakness because she believes God, like everyone else expects her to be strong. She has a difficult time being totally transparent even before God. She has a hard time allowing God to be in control of her life. She has become her own god; and might I add a god to others. She feels she has to perform for God's approval and acceptance.

She doesn't realize that her true strength lies in God and that she needs Him more than she could ever imagine.

So what can God do with a woman like this? Nothing. Unfortunately, He has to patiently and painfully watch her get to the end of herself, where He will be ready and willing to pick her up, love on her, comfort her, and give her what she truly needs. Coming to the end of ourselves is never a pleasant experience; but an often needed one.

When I finally got to the end of my prideful journey, it was an ugly crash. But through it all, God helped me understand that my value wasn't rooted in whether I could yell the loudest, have the last word, or hold a grudge the longest. I learned that my value was rooted in who He said I was and that His ability to entrust kingdom riches into my care was equivalent to the degree in which I humbled myself. God isn't able to trust the things that matters most to Him into the care of those who are prideful because pride takes God's credit and hoards it for self.

When it comes down to it, pride is about control. It's about our desire to be our own god. In the Garden of Eden, Eve's issues were bigger than lust. She had a pride problem. She wanted to be like God. She wanted power. She wanted control. And she saw the fruit as the avenue by which she could obtain it. Like Eve, many of us want control and power and are willing to go to great lengths to get it.

Another friend of mine leaves her day job and goes home to another full-time job – monitoring her husband's affairs. Each night she goes through his wallet, rummages through his briefcase, looks through his cell phone records, and checks the Internet history on his laptop. Oh my! When does she even have time to enjoy life?

Newsflash, she doesn't!

I have told her repeatedly that this is extremely unhealthy and unproductive behavior. She uncovered stuff that was inappropriate. She learned he was having an affair. And what does she plan on doing with the information she found? Your guess is as good as mine, as she has not yet confronted him. Instead she continues to monitor his activities. It's been several months now.

Let's face it. Even when she tells him what she found, if her husband purposes in his heart to continue this dishonoring relationship (which by the way is not the first time he's cheated) she will not be able to control his actions. The only person she can control is herself. She has to decide whether she will continue to subject herself to his sin.

Of course his behavior has heightened her insecurities and chips away at her self-esteem. And if she doesn't deal with the hurts appropriately, she will enter into and try to control other relationships in an effort to avoid being wounded again.

Now here is the thing about my friend – she refuses to dis- play any signs of sorrow or grief regarding the condition of her marriage. In the years I've known her I can't recall seeing her shed one tear. In fact, she puts on a façade stating she is used to his behavior and she will make him pay one way or the other. I've talked to her about establishing a relationship with God and seeking Him to help her through this. But she sees humility as a weakness and she refuses to allow herself to be vulnerable to anyone – including God. She treats this situation with her husband like a game or competition as she shared "I intend to win."

On the surface, her words might appear to be to be self-righteous, strong, lacking emotion, or even prideful; but beneath it all is extreme hurt, disappointment, weariness, and years of suppressed pain. I truly feel for her. However, until she is willing to humble herself and ask God to step into her situation, she will continue to fight this losing battle. This makes me very sad.

Do you still view the word pride the same as you did when you began reading this chapter? Is the Lord revealing any areas of pride in your life? Are there areas that you have been unwilling to surrender to God? Are there situations in which you have refused to humble yourself?

So what does the Bible say about the issue of pride? Several things. First and foremost, God absolutely detests pride and arrogance. Proverbs 16:5 says God will punish those who engage in prideful behavior. Remember, Satan and his fallen angels were cast out of Heaven because Satan (then named Lucifer) became prideful. He desired to take God's place.

Psalm 138:6 says although God sits on high, He still pays attention to and draws near to those who humble themselves. However, He keeps his distance from those who are proud.

Humility welcomes God into our situation, while Pride tells God "No thank you."

I mentioned in a previous section that God freely gives wisdom to those who ask. Proverbs 11:2 says a person who is prideful can only expect dishonor and disgrace, whereas one who humbles herself will receive the wisdom of God.

Finally, one of the most eye-opening and life-altering truths about pride is the inevitable fall that accompanies a heart that repeatedly ignores God's invitation to be Lord over her life. God desires that we voluntarily submit our will to His. I've heard it said, "Every knee will bow before Christ. Whether it's voluntarily or because we've bumped our head." Everyone will at one time or another humble themselves before almighty God. Sadly, women who have not humbled themselves before God don't realize the incredible love, support, strength, and Godly character that come with humility. They are missing out!

For those who refuse to surrender to God, inevitable destruction is in their future. Proverbs 16:18 says a mighty crash or fall follows prideful behavior. And the bigger the ego, the harder the fall.

Unfortunately, we've seen (and will continue to see) the falling away of many great men and women (Christian and non-Christian) who got a little too big for their britches. They either believed they were above the law or that everyone would turn a blind eye to their sin. But whether human beings hold us accountable or not, rest assured that God will not tolerate pride and allow it to go unpunished.

One of the areas where I seek to humble myself on a regular basis is forgiveness. Not only am I quick to ask my family and friends, but even more so with my sons. It is my desire to model the gift of humility before them.

I have not always been this way, but by God's grace and recognizing my need for His forgiveness daily, I have no problem asking for my son's forgiveness when I'm wrong. And there are times I don't believe I am wrong, but if my inappropriate response caused further hurt or confusion, I apologize so we can invite the Holy Spirit to enter into the situation. Many of us have a difficult time apologizing if we feel like we are right and the other person is wrong. But God doesn't call us to be right. He calls us to be righteous (right with Him). Being right is an act of pride. Being righteous requires humility.

If there is active pride in your life, I encourage you to repent before God and ask Him to cover you with His grace and mercy. Do you want God's protection, favor, and wisdom – be a woman who isn't afraid to humble herself.

"The LORD Almighty has a day in store for all the proud and lofty, for all that is exalted (and they will be humbled)." Isaiah 2:12 (New International Version)

Reflection

1. If people were to describe your personality or character according to the words you speak, what would they say?
2. Did anyone speak words over you at some point in your life that still affect, bother, or hurt you today?
3. Are your words filled with faith or fear when facing a difficult situation?

4. Can you recall a time when you used your words to build up someone? How about to tear them down?
5. What do you do to overcome stinking thinking?
6. Recognizing that pride is rooted in a fear of exposure, have you displayed an attitude of pride in the past or recently?
7. Do you have a difficult time asking for help? If yes, why?
8. Do you struggle with saying you are sorry?

"The Spirit searches all things, even the deep things of God. For who knows a person's thoughts except their own spirit within them? In the same way no one knows the thoughts of God except the Spirit of God. What we have received is not the spirit of the world, but the Spirit who is from God, so that we may understand what God has freely given us. This is what we speak, not in words taught us by human wisdom but in words taught by the Spirit, explaining spiritual realities with Spirit-taught words. The person without the Spirit does not accept the things that come from the Spirit of God but considers them foolishness, and cannot understand them because they are discerned only through the Spirit. The person with the Spirit makes judgments about all things, but such a person is not subject to merely human judgments, for, "Who has known the mind of the Lord so as to instruct him?" But we have the mind of Christ." 1 Corinthians 2:10-16 (NIV)

THE NEW CONSECRATED COCOON

Intimacy with God – It's Personal

In my time of isolation, my cocoon time, I experienced three seasons: A time of Pruning (stripping away and refining), Presence (intimacy and worship), and Power (preparing to be released).

At first we all go into the cocoon kicking and screaming. You didn't? Okay, maybe it was just me. But if you're like me, we want God to make the necessary changes; but on our terms and in our timing. I often said, "God can you please transform me with less pain and tears, less correction, and less refining. Oh, and can we finish this by the end of next week. Thank you very much."

If I knew ahead of time that things were going to get as intense and lonely as they did, I would have at least requested to have a few friends join me for my initial pity party. Unfortunately, it doesn't work that way. God needed me all to Himself. He had to isolate me. To isolate means to separate or detach from. And that's exactly what God does when He is ready to do a major work in our lives. He separates us from any and everything that has become more of a priority than Him and that we've become more dependent upon than Him. He does this to make sure we focus on Him and Him alone.

To some of you this might sound scary or even cruel, but quite frankly, it is the total opposite. This dedicated time with God becomes the place where you are least scared and most protected, greatly loved and, uniquely empowered!

Pruning

We often hear the word pruning associated with plants or trees. The process of pruning includes cutting back or shaping for the purpose of improving or maintaining healthy growth.

John chapter 15 speaks of the Vine (Jesus), the branches (us) and the Gardener (God). Verse 2 says the branches that don't bear fruit are cut off and the ones that do bear fruit are pruned to bear even more fruit.

When we enter into our isolation process with God (our gardener) He does just that. He cuts off or removes any and everything in our life that is non-productive and prepares or prunes us to be even more productive for His kingdom. Those non-productive areas can be anything from an unhealthy relationship to a sinful behavior. In His stripping or cutting away, He targets anything that has become more of a priority than our relationship with Him. We all say God is first and may very well mean it. But each day, there are people and things that compete for our attention, affection, and allegiance; and if we are not careful, we can inadvertently place God on the back burner.

God stripped away many things. Some I was willing to let go of, and others He had to pry from my fingers. Many times we're not ignorant of the things in our lives that are counterproductive and potentially harmful to our destiny. It's different for each of us. For some it's a destructive habit, sinful behavior, or an unhealthy relationship. Most times we are fully aware when something or someone needs to be cut out of our life, but we struggle to let go due to familiarity. But in His great love, there are times when God steps in and makes the decision for us. He did that for me on more than one occasion and looking back I am so grateful.

I am led by the Holy Spirit to add this side note. This will apply to someone specific, not everyone.

That friend that you have not been in contact with for quite some time and you are contemplating contacting him/her; God says it's time to let that relationship go. I know you thought you would be friends forever. You have struggled with whether to contact him/her because deep in your heart you know the season for that relationship has come to an end. Has your life not been better and less complicated without them? I want to affirm that God in His grace and mercy has closed that door on your behalf.

Do not attempt to re-open it!

Doing so will only invite pain and heartache into your life. Recognize that people come in and out of our lives all the time. Few remain friends for life, and most are friends for a particular season. When that season is over, God will bring new people into your life for the new season you are about to enter. The mindset of the old season cannot understand the mindset of the new; and therefore friends from previous seasons are not equipped to propel you to where God is taking you. Receive the closed door as a blessing from God. Thank Him for his loving protection. Be grateful for the previous season but fix your eyes on what's to come. She who puts her hand to the plow and looks back is not fit for the kingdom of God (Luke 9:62).

In the first stage of my isolation process, God removed anything that competed for my attention and anything I depended heavily upon. These things could not go where God was taking me. In the stripping away process, bondages were broken, my emotions were being healed, and I experienced first-hand the incredible power of forgiveness and grace.

When God removed everything that stood between Him and me, I was able to focus on Him alone. He had my undivided attention. And there were times when it felt like He even turned out the lights so I couldn't see anything but His loving, compassionate eyes staring deep into my soul.

Presence

Once God had my undivided attention, it was time for me to transition to the next phase of my isolation process – His presence. I was about to experience God like never before. He didn't force Himself on me. He wanted me to desire more of Him. And so He waited. And I waited. And I waited. I learned how to be still. I wasn't waiting without hope; I waited with great expectancy that the wait would be worth it. In my time of being still, I learned how to call on the name of Jesus. Jesus, the most beautiful name I know. His name brings comfort, healing, and reassurance. After all, He had been beaten, whipped, rejected, abandoned, abused, and betrayed; so He knew exactly what I was experiencing and He knew exactly how to console me.

In waiting, I learned how to worship. I don't mean worship as it pertains to just music. I mean worship as it pertains to developing an increasingly thankful heart for who God is – His character. While waiting, I reflected on His faithfulness and unconditional love and was daily moved to tears. I remember sharing with my mentor that I found myself crying on a daily basis. If I wasn't crying from a broken heart, I was crying from a grateful heart. I am positive there is an ocean somewhere in Heaven that was created by my tears.

The more I cried, the more Jesus wiped my tears. The more He wiped my tears the more I fell in love with Him. The intimacy I experienced in my time of isolation was at a level I never knew existed.

Sadly, it often takes a trial for us to draw close to God only to find that He wants to be close to us every single day.

The intimacy I am describing can only be understood by those who have experienced it. Now that I've experienced this closeness, I don't ever want to be without it again. And might I add, this level of intimacy is for everyone – everyone who is hungry enough to go after it. Jesus is a gentleman. He doesn't force Himself on us – but He has so much to give us once we invite Him in.

There is a saying, "If you've never had something, then you don't know what you are missing." Years ago, I had no clue the type of intimacy I was missing in my relationship with Christ. I had a very shallow and misinformed understanding of what it meant to spend time with God. A couple of times a week I grabbed my Bible, a devotional book, prayed, answered questions, and considered that my time with God.

THE NEW CONSECRATED COCOON

Now don't get me wrong. A part of our time spent with God should be to read, study, and grow in a deeper understanding of His written word. But that's just one part of it. There are other components to developing a relationship with Jesus that include two-way communication, sharing, receiving, thanking, requesting, and adoring.

When we meet and fall in love with a man, we can't stop thinking about him and count the waking hours until the next time we see him. That's how I now feel about Jesus. I can't wait to be in His presence. I look forward to cuddling up next to Him and looking deep into His eyes. I want to be so close to Him that I feel His heart beat and He feels mine. I want to dance with Him and feel His loving and comforting arms around me. His grip is stronger and more reassuring than any other's.

I love sharing my day with Him and hearing about the things that concern Him and make Him happy. I share my deepest desires with Him so that He knows me like no other. Sometimes I simply weep when we are together and He gently dries my tears. I love that He knows me inside and out and yet loves me unconditionally. When I get alone with Jesus I never know what to expect, but I go expecting that He has something special for me.

Each encounter with Jesus differs. There are some days I get with Him and I do read my Bible, pray, talk to Him, and He speaks so clearly through His written word. And from our time together, I receive the answer to questions I have. Other times, I might not crack open my Bible because all I want to do is lie flat on the floor, quiet myself and listen for what He wants to say to me. Sometimes, I play music and He asks me to dance and if you were to peek through my bedroom window you would see me literally dancing with Him.

Have you ever danced with Jesus? It's one of the most freeing and beautiful experiences. I often dance before Him and with Him.

At other times you might find me singing and praising at the top of my lungs, or weeping and worshipping as He is tenderly loving on me. Like I said, each time is incredibly different. Many a days, I show up with no agenda in mind and He never disappoints me.

My time with God is spent in my secret place. Where is that place? It's where I close myself off from the world to spend time with God. For each of us, that place is different. I have friends who have an entire prayer room devoted to just that. Some women have a special location in their home, such as a walk-in closet or the bathroom. Wherever that special spot happens to be is not as important as what occurs once you get there. Your secret place is basically where you go to give God your undivided attention. A place that is away from all distractions.

During my intimate time with God, I often play music. And I am amazed at how I can listen to the same song five days in a row and on day six, it speaks to my heart in a way it never did before. I'm also amazed at those still, quiet times when there is no music, but I can sense that God Himself is singing over me.

His presence is tangible and His peace floods my heart.

God greatly desires to have a deep and intimate relationship with His children. However, the more time you spend with Him you will quickly realize that you yearn for that intimacy with Him almost as much as He wants it with you. You and I were created for intimacy with God.

This deep intimacy with the Lord prepared me for the final stage of my isolation process - Power. Once God knew He had all of me, He could then begin to prepare my release papers.

Power

So there I was...stripped of all that hindered my ability to go to the next level with God. I both wept and celebrated over some things that were removed. I waited and I worshipped. I

THE NEW CONSECRATED COCOON

drew closer to Jesus and He drew even closer to me. And eventually I was able to sense that my time of release was drawing near. I didn't know when, but I knew in my heart I was getting closer. I knew my morning would come, my cocoon would crack, and I would eventually emerge a new woman. Finally...a light at the end of the tunnel.

That light was Jesus saying, "Follow me, and I will lead you to the exit sign." I can't describe the incredible feeling of knowing that my day of freedom was finally coming and that I would soon be on the other side of the refining process. I was excited to trade in my battle wounds for battle scars. I looked forward to stepping into a new journey that would allow me to help others through their consecration process.

God gave me the title and inspiration for this book toward the end of 2010. My goal was to complete it by the end of 2011. I wrote a rough outline around March, 2011. Then I started writing around June. But then I began to struggle. I was crushed and unable to express myself. I tried to write but couldn't find the words. I talked to God and asked Him to give me the words. I needed inspiration. And then He lovingly revealed to me that I was trying to write about a process He had not yet completed in me. I couldn't take my reader where I had not yet gone. With this revelation, I stopped writing – for months. During that time I literally felt like I went underground or into hiding. I guess in a sense I did. I went deeper in God.

As I deepened my relationship with God during the Presence phase, I sensed that God was possibly preparing me to begin writing again, but I waited. I worshipped, and I waited. And then one day He told me it was time. It was time to return to writing and He assured me that He would continue the work He began in me simultaneous to my writing.

As I transitioned from Presence to Power, I felt a shift in my spirit. I knew I was being prepared for something even greater than I could imagine. The devil sensed it too. And as I picked up my laptop, he sent a trial my way. And then another, and then another. He attacked me physically, emotionally, and spiritually.

However, he had the wrong girl!

Who I was when I entered the cocoon and who I had become as I prepared to emerge were two different people. In my secret place with God He not only strengthened me and empowered me to overcome the enemy's schemes, but He gave me wisdom and strategies to douse the fiery darts coming my way.

You see, the devil didn't want me to continue writing because he knew I would expose him for the liar he is. He knew I would inform you that he had no new tricks up his sleeves. He's been doing the same old stuff he tried in the garden. He knew I would tell you don't be afraid when God pursues you because He has a plan for you. He knew I would encourage you that the victory is already yours. He knew I would equip you with Scriptures and truths that would disarm his devices. He knew that I would encourage you to draw even closer to Jesus during your time of struggle, rather than pull away. He didn't want me to encourage you toward your finish line, because a beautiful prize awaits.

Luke 12:48b says, to whom God gives much, even more is required from them. God had given me much and I understood that He expected more. My answer to God – a resounding yes.

When I saw the devil's reaction to God's releasing me to write again, I surrendered all the more. I had nothing to lose and everything to gain. As I waited for my cocoon to crack, God gave me glimpses of His faithfulness every step of the way. He showed me my finish line and whispered in my ear, "Keep going, girl, it's not long now." Some days He stood in front of me and led the way. Other days He stood behind me, giving me the extra nudge I needed. Some days He held my hand and walked right beside me, allowing me to lay my head on His shoulder when needed. But even more important – there were days where He simply picked me up and carried me because I wanted to quit. He refused to let me quit.

THE NEW CONSECRATED COCOON

My cocoon, the place I initially despised because I perceived it as a punishment. But I soon understood and embraced it as my place of pruning, protection, and preparation. It was the place where I was strengthened and sharpened. I was revived and renewed. It was my hiding place and my fortress. It was my place of rest, refuge, and rejuvenation. I experienced God's pleasure, presence, and power. I learned how to endure and persevere. I learned how to praise through my pain, and I learned how to thank God even before I could see my wings forming.

If you are in the midst of a difficult time and feel all alone, I encourage you to turn your time of isolation into a time of deeper intimacy with God. And if you aren't in the midst of a trial, don't wait until one arises to draw closer to God. He has so much He wants to do in and through you during your time with Him. There is strength he wants to give you before, during, and after a trial.

It's impossible to pour more water into a cup that is already full and overflowing. To add to the cup you must first empty it or pour out some of the water. How can God fill you with the things He wants to give you if you refuse to let go of the things He doesn't want for you?

Are you ready to receive what He has for you?

Reflection

1. God prunes us to prepare us to be more productive. Is there anything or anyone in your life that is hindering your ability to be fully devoted to God?
2. Is there someone or something that's preventing you from reading your Bible or praying like you want/need to?
3. Is there a person or thing in your life that influences you to do things that do not please God?
4. Has God allowed a door to close on a relationship that you are still trying to keep open?

5. Do you spend regular time in God's presence without interruptions?
6. When last have you cried in God's presence (tears of joy or sorrow)?
7. Do you have a designated "secret place" where you meet with God?
8. In what area of your life do you need more of God's power (to do what you can't do for yourself)?

"O God, you are my God; I earnestly search for you. My soul thirsts for you; my whole body longs for you in this parched and weary land where there is no water. I have seen you in your sanctuary and gazed upon your power and glory. Your unfailing love is better than life itself; how I praise you! I will praise you as long as I live, lifting up my hands to you in prayer. You satisfy me more than the richest feast. I will praise you with songs of joy. I lie awake thinking of you, meditating on you through the night. Because you are my helper, I sing for joy in the shadow of your wings. I cling to you; your strong right hand holds me securely." Psalm 63:1-8 (New Living Translation).

THE NEW CONSECRATED COCOON

TRANSFORMATION

The final stage of the caterpillar's life cycle is called the Adult Butterfly. This is the stage where the evidence of all of the hard work reveals itself. The butterfly emerges from the cocoon. It is said that her emergence usually happens after dark, in the morning. She is beautiful. Her wings burst with stunning colors.

As glorious as the release is, she doesn't immediately take flight, though.

At first her wings are soft and wet due to a fluid called hemolymph that's pumped into her body to enlarge her wings. When she breaks out of the cocoon she must immediately find a place to stretch and allow her wings to dry.

This stretching strengthens her wings.

Once dried, she soars into her purpose and destiny. What's next? Reproducing and raising up the next generation of butterflies.

Like the butterfly, we too emerge after our darkness and step into a new season. We are not the same woman who entered in; we are a new creation in Christ. The old is gone and the new is here to stay (2 Corinthians 5:17). The changes that occurred in the secret place become publicly visible and will be used to point others toward God.

When you look at the life span of a butterfly in the natural, it's very short. I believe the message we should receive from this truth is...time is short! We can't afford to waste any time. We must emerge ready to be about our Father's business.

The Bible says life is like a vapor, here one day and then it vanishes (James 4:14b). It's not the amount of time we have in this life; it's what we do with it. This transformation is not just about us. Like the butterfly we are called to reproduce ourselves. Ladies, there is a generation of struggling caterpillars and even butterflies who may have lost their way, who are waiting for a strong, renewed, and mature butterfly to take them under her wing and help launch them toward their purpose and destiny in Christ.

They are waiting for you!

THE NEW CONSECRATED COCOON

I'm Coming Out

How many of you remember that song by Diana Ross that was released in 1980 titled, "I'm Coming Out"? For some of you, that song may take you back to an era in your life you would rather forget. However, this song became somewhat of an anthem for anyone who received a new lease on life and wanted the world to know about it.

In this song, Diana talks about breaking out of a shell, being positive, spreading love, and exercising all of her abilities. But most importantly, she wants the world to know about her transformation and has to let it show. In other words, this new thing that has happened can't be kept a secret. She must broadcast it to others so they can have a hope!

Ladies, when God transforms you, this new thing cannot be contained. It must be released. There is great power in sharing and declaring God's goodness. Each time you proclaim your victory, the enemy is defeated yet again. God is not going to allow you to go through a trial to be defeated. He has already equipped you with everything you need to beat up on the enemy and you must boldly proclaim the victory even before you see it.

We live in a world that is lost and spiritually dying. Many are living in darkness and seek someone to give them a ray of hope. Someone who's personally experienced God's redemptive power. That's you and me. Remember, we've been set apart for such a time as this. Being set apart means we stand out. There should be something different about us.

The Bible says Christians are the light of the world. What does a light do? Illuminate dark places. Matthew 5:14-15 says you are the light of the world, a city on a hill that can't be hidden. No one lights a lamp and then puts it under a basket. But instead the lamp is placed on a stand where it gives light to everyone in the house.

Imagine you and your family are at home during a storm and lightning hits. The power is out. If you live in Florida, this is a regular occurrence. It's pitch black and everyone starts calling out to each other from the different rooms. You're in the kitchen. You find a candle and light it. The area where you are standing is now illuminated. As the one carrying the light, either you take the light to others or they gravitate toward the light. Bottom line, in a dark place everyone wants the light to help them find their way.

You are that light for Jesus.

The darker it is, the brighter your light shines. And when you emerge from your cocoon your light is even brighter than before. That light shines through your smile, personality, genuine love and care for people, your authenticity, your faith, and even the new level of authority you walk in.

God is not going to hide that light. Like the city on the hill, He will divinely position you in places where you will attract those who are hurting, broken, and feeling hopeless, all for the purpose of pointing to Jesus. Pointing to the ONE who comforts, heals, and gives hope.

You didn't spend all that time in your cocoon with God to emerge a beautiful trophy. Trophies are set on a stand to be gawked at and become outdated. A trophy symbolizes what happened in the past.

Your time of consecration and isolation with God was for the purpose of becoming a utensil - worthy and ready to be used and reused by Him (2 Timothy 2:21). God doesn't want to use you one time and then move on. God invented recycling. He has many different ways He wants to utilize your gifts.

When you settle it in your mind and heart you want to be used by God, your daily perspective changes. You wake up each morning anticipating what God has planned for the day. Each morning introduces new opportunities. And so it's quite fitting that the butterfly emerges from the cocoon during the morning hours.

THE NEW CONSECRATED COCOON

The day I emerged from my cocoon and stepped into my new season with God, I was not even aware. Just like no one knows the day or hour Jesus will return, we don't know when God will release us into our new season. That time is appointed by Him and we are simply to be in position and be ready for when it happens.

Interestingly enough, it wasn't until days later while spending time with the Lord that He revealed I was released days earlier.

I didn't realize it, but others around me did. Many recognized something was clearly different that day.

My coming out day was a Sunday morning – the most beautiful day of the week to get a fresh start; at least in my opinion. I absolutely love Sundays. It's the day I fellowship with my brothers and sisters in Christ; love on God through powerful praise and worship; and sit under life-transforming preaching. Did I mention that I love Sundays?

As I reflect back, I did awake with a little extra pep in my step. I'm not a woman who wears a lot of big or flashy jewelry, but I am constantly being recruited in that direction by several women in my life. A few, one in particular just started buying me new jewelry – no more suggesting. That morning I felt like blinging a little bit, so I grabbed a necklace and matching earrings. I chose a colorful blouse, styled my hair slightly different and was off to church.

When I arrived, one after the other, several ladies complimented my overall appearance, and a few stated I had a glow about me. Another said that I looked radiant. I thought to myself, "Wow, is this what happens when I wear bling?

What people were noticing on the outside was purely an out pouring of what was happening on the inside. In my heart. That Sunday morning I jumped higher than usual. I praised louder than most around me; and I called on the name of Jesus repeatedly. The wellspring in my heart was overflowing and being released through my words and actions. That morning I praised and worshipped my Lord like never before. It was evident that my spirit man knew what was occurring.

Although we don't know the exact day God will release us, He does give us glimpses to encourage us we are getting closer. He doesn't want us to lose hope. With each glimpse I received, I held on tighter and pressed in harder, believing that my "morning" was approaching.

Ladies, there is nothing like knowing that God has done a new work in you. He is always doing a work in us, but when it's so radical that He separates us from everyone, we can rest assured we are going to a level we've never been before. A level where we finally embrace our God-given authority and refuse to live a life less than daughters of the most high King.

The weekend after my emergence, I was asked to teach our women's Sunday school class. I leaped for joy as I realized it was a total setup from God. He had released me and He had something He wanted to say and do through me.

That Sunday during the class, I made the first public pronouncement regarding my divorce. Until this time, very few close friends knew all I had being going through. I gave a brief testimony after the message as a way to transition to the entire reason God placed me there. God wanted to encourage and strengthen women who were weary. Many of the women's jaws dropped in surprise as they learned of my divorce. Some could sense I was going through a trial, but most did not realize the depth or intensity. Until that Sunday, I did not have a peace to share this information because I didn't want to dishonor my ex-husband in any way or hinder what God was doing.

I told the ladies that during that difficult time God raised up Aarons and Hurs to come alongside me and lift my wearied arms. And through our unified strength the battle was victoriously won. As I delivered the message that morning, God showed me there were many women who were battling. They hadn't given up yet, but were incredibly worn out. They were tired and on the brink of quitting. He told me to call forth the

THE NEW CONSECRATED COCOON

ones needing encouragement. He wanted them to make themselves known.

At first, only a few stood. But then I encouraged them that coming forward was not a sign of weakness, but an indicator of their resolve to not quit and a request for fellow warriors to stand with them. More stood and came forward. And then I called on the Aarons and Hurs to stand alongside them, encourage, and lift their tired arms.

Ladies, we are always in one of two places: heavily engaged in a battle and in need of encouragement. Or we have come out of a battle and are strong enough to reach back and bring others to where we are. That morning an army arose and encircled the weary, and the power of the Holy Spirit took over. There were tears, declarations, and new resolutions. Many were strengthened and ready to forge forward with new vigor. Thank you, Jesus. All glory to God!

Ladies, when we emerge from our time of consecration, it's not about us. It's about the lives God wants to impact through us.

We are not empowered to do greater things for ourselves. We are empowered to do greater things for others. We are to actively seek out other caterpillars and butterflies. We are to encourage caterpillars to remain in their consecration process and walk with them through it. We're to seek out other butterflies to band together and create a powerful army for God. There is amazing strength in numbers. Don't think as a butterfly you won't ever be weak again. You will. But if you are soaring with an army, the momentum from many wings flapping and soaring will spread to and lift those who are not as strong.

That Sunday morning I saw an army of both caterpillars and butterflies arising and uniting. I watched as God's powerful love engulfed the room. Ladies, Jesus is coming back soon, and Satan knows this. He's intensified his attacks, and therefore we must increase our unity. We must band together. We must strengthen our army. The victory is ours, but the battle must still be fought and we can't do it alone. We need each other. Trials and hard times will come. It's a part of life. But how we step into the battle makes all the difference. You must step in believing with all of your heart that the victory is yours – allowing you to fight like you've already won.

Butterfly, you have been released. You have come out. There are others waiting to hear your testimony. There are others waiting to experience your new power in Christ. There are others waiting to know that God hasn't forgotten them and He has a purpose and destiny for their lives.

Are you ready to step out, butterfly? This is your time to live a life of greater power, to reclaim and possess what God has for you, and to be divinely positioned to be used mightily by God.

Woo-hoo!

THE NEW CONSECRATED COCOON

Wave-Walking Power

"But in that coming day no weapon turned against you will succeed. You will silence every voice raised up to accuse you. These benefits are enjoyed by the servant of the Lord. Their vindication will come from me. I, the Lord, have spoken." Isaiah 54:17 (New Living Translation)

My nephew Blaize is just about as fearless as it gets. He is the epitome of what it means to have childlike faith. When he climbs onto the highest point of the couch and courageously jumps to the floor below, he has faith that the ground will break his fall but not his legs. And his faith is so strong he is willing to do it again and again.

That's the kind of faith God wants from you and me. The kind that doesn't quit and trusts Him with no limitations. He wants the kind of faith that's willing to go or do whatever He says without knowing the end result first. The kind of faith that will speak words of healing over someone, believing they are already healed. The kind of faith that speaks words of blessings over someone even though their behavior and attitude contrasts what you are declaring. The kind of faith that says, "Yes, Lord," before you know the question.

Butterfly, once transformed you begin to operate in a new realm of power. Your power is fueled by your unwavering faith in God's word and promises. By faith, you tap into the power of Isaiah 54:17. You can silence every voice that rises up against you. The word "voice" symbolizes anything that erects or presents itself in a way that is contrary to God's word and His promises. Remember, through your preparation and isolation you experienced His promises. God didn't leave you and everything He allowed was for your good, not to harm you. Therefore anything or anyone that rises up and tells you God's promises are not true you can confidently shut down because you know the truth. Anything or anyone that rises up against your identity in Christ or your inheritance as God's daughter – call it out and expose it for the lie it is.

When you consistently operate in the realm of faith, God's going to ask you to do things others around you are not willing or able to do. He's going to ask you to step into places where others around you can't or won't go. Is faith something that comes easy in the natural? No. We need the grace of God to walk by faith. What's grace? It's God's strength that enables you beyond your own ability.

Having faith is beyond our natural ability – it's supernatural. Faith is like a muscle. The more you build it, the stronger it gets and the more you use it. And eventually you look forward to God tapping on you to do nothing less than heavy lifting for His kingdom. The light-weight stuff becomes boring because you understand that God is always bigger and more powerful than we give Him credit for. And you get excited about God showing up and showing out each and every time.

Faith separates ordinary Christians from the ones who God is working through mightily. Your transformation positions you to be anything but an ordinary Christian. Your expectancy in God is hinged upon your faith in Him.

A practical definition of faith is believing and speaking God's promises into existence while there is absolutely no tangible evidence to support what you are believing and speaking.

I can't begin to tell you the amount of testimonies I hear time and time again of men and women of God who believe God for a healing, miracle, or provision and He shows up in ways that are undeniably Him. A dear friend of mine, who travels regularly sharing the gospel, told me about one time in particular where God waited until the last minute to show up. Beloved, may it never be said that God is ever too early or too late. We serve an on time God. His timing is always perfect.

God told him to return to his home country, where he hadn't been in over five years. He gave my friend the dates he was to travel and told him to check the flight times and prices. He did so. Then he checked his bank account and in the natural, even if he wanted to obey God, he couldn't afford to

THE NEW CONSECRATED COCOON

purchase the ticket. But God assured him He would make a way for him to get to his home country.

The day the Lord told him to leave arrived and still, no miracle money showed up in his account. No unexpected check showed up in the mail. But believing God, he packed his suitcase and went to the airport. He sat and waited, believing that God was going to provide. About one hour before the flight was to take off, he began talking to God. "Did I miss you, Lord? Did I hear you incorrectly?" I love his spirit. He didn't begin to doubt whether God would or could provide for the need. He questioned whether he was in tune with God regarding the trip.

About thirty minutes before the flight was to depart, he grabbed his carry on suitcase and considered leaving, but heard God's voice telling him to wait. So he did. A few minutes later, a former co-worker walked past him, headed toward security when he looked back and recognized him. They hugged and talked for a few minutes. He asked my friend where he was going and he explained he was there in obedience to what God told him to do. The former co-worker was so moved by his faith in God that he walked him to the counter and purchased a ticket for him to go. And the only thing he wanted in return from my friend was to hear the praise report when he returned. By the way, the former co-worker was not a Christian.

He definitely had a praise report. He preached at a couple of churches and there were many who gave their lives to the Lord at each service. However, the biggest miracle of all was his reconnecting with his father, whom he had not spoken to or seen in many years. They wept, talked, and reconciled. But even more so, his father gave his life to the Lord. Although my friend's actions may have seemed foolish to many, it was exactly what God was seeking – an obedient heart. And as a result, God blessed him above and beyond.

The opposite of faith is doubt and disbelief. Doubt ties God's hands and limits Him to display only those things the human brain can explain and rationalize. Whereas faith allows God to unleash His powers in a way that surpass human understanding, thereby allowing Heaven and earth to shake hands in agreement with God's promises.

Faith is so important to God that He's willing to accept the smallest measure of faith we give to Him. He says in Luke 17:6 that if we would simply have faith the size of a mustard seed, He will do great and powerful things through us.

A mustard seed is about one-sixteenth of an inch in diameter. That's small. And in my opinion, God is being quite generous when He makes provision for this tiny measure of faith.

I believe that "mustard seed faith" should be the starting point for our faith. As we grow in our relationship with God and He proves Himself time and time again, at some point the size of our faith should grow in proportion to our level of intimacy with God. So if your faith in God isn't increasing, you should assess the amount of time you are spending one-on-one with Him. I'm just giving you something to think about.

Faith is so important to God that He dedicated an entire chapter in the book of Hebrews (chapter 11) to the men and women who exercised great faith. By the way, there is only one woman whose name is specifically mentioned in this chapter. Her name is Rahab and she was a prostitute (verse 31). Ha! Go figure! That's the God we serve. He didn't mention a pure, valiant, or upstanding woman. He chose a woman who in the world's eyes would not be worthy of honorable mention. But in God's eyes she became a woman worthy of recognition because she walked in obedience and exercised her faith in God.

I sense there are some of you with tainted pasts who might feel disqualified from "honorable mention" by God. But I have great news for you. God doesn't consult your past failures to determine your level of faith. God is interested in your willingness to obey Him today. And when you ask Jesus into your heart, your name is written in the most important book of all. Your name is entered into the Lamb's Book of Life. Hallelujah!

THE NEW CONSECRATED COCOON

Of all the faith stories written in the Bible, I really like and can relate to one that didn't make it into the "Hall of Faith" chapter in Hebrews – Peter walking on water.

Mark chapter 14 tells of Peter exercising what some might view as "mustard seed faith" when he stepped out of the boat and walked toward Jesus on water. But as minuscule as his faith appeared to be, I won't knock Peter because he was the only one willing to get out of the boat.

The waves were crashing all around the boat. And then when Peter stepped onto the water, the waves were crashing all around him. As long as Peter kept his gaze fixed on Jesus he actually walked on water. But the minute he paid attention to the feisty waves around him and took his eyes off Jesus, he began to sink.

Now again, I've got to give it to Peter. He was no fool. Realizing he didn't have time for a lengthy, long-winded prayer, he simply cried out, "Jesus save me." And Jesus reached out and grabbed a hold of him. I'm willing to bet everything I have that Peter never walked on water before. Therefore it did take a measure of faith to step out of a perfectly good boat into the crashing waves. But Peter understood what many of us are learning today. It's better to be in the storm with Jesus than to be in the boat without Him. Amen?

Although Jesus did express disappointment in Peter's lack of faith, Jesus knew Peter's heart and He knows yours. Jesus is still looking for those who are willing to walk on water with Him. He's looking for those who will lock eyes with Him in faith rather than fix their gaze upon their circumstance in fear.

Butterfly, God is calling you to be a "wave-walker" not a "wave-watcher." Now that you've matured in Christ, now that your confidence in His love for you is sealed, He will call you to step out into the water with Him. And when He does, don't go looking around at the other ones still in the boat. He didn't call them. He called you. He empowered you!

Don't focus on your perceived limitations. If He tells you to take a step, He has already equipped you with all you need.

Listen...there will always be waves of chaos, distraction, confusion, and conflict crashing around you, vying to shift your attention from Jesus to the fear of sinking. But you need to stand with confidence, knowing that the one who calmed the raging seas with His voice (Luke 8:24b) is standing with you. Jesus will not allow you to drown nor to be consumed by the waves of life.

As you emerge from your cocoon, your new and improved faith empowers you to walk in the same authority that Jesus did. Don't slip that authority into your back pocket with the intent of pulling it out when things are going really bad. Wake up each morning and by faith speak blessings over your day. By faith speak healing over sickness. Use the most powerful words you have – Scriptures. Call on the most powerful name you know – Jesus.

Having faith means when you don't know what tomorrow holds, you are confident that Jesus holds not just tomorrow, but all the days in your life. Faith doesn't look for earthly solutions; it's stands on Heavenly promises. God promises to take every trial, hardship, and disappointment and make it turn out good for those who love Him and are called according to His purpose (Romans 8:28). Are you called by God? Do you love Him? Then He will work it out for your good.

Sister, you are now empowered to go boldly before God's throne with consecrated confidence to receive God's grace, strength, and power for whatever you need (Hebrews 4:16). You are set apart from those who know God's promises versus those who stand on them. When you speak His promises watch and expect them to come to pass.

What are you empowered to do? Step into your purpose and destiny. Serve others. Bless others. Lead others to Christ. By faith you possess resurrection power and therefore can do all things through Christ (Philippians 4:13). You are empowered to take authority over your home, over your marriage, and over your children.

THE NEW CONSECRATED COCOON

With your new power you can look the enemy square in the eyes and tell him to give it his best shot. Why? Because overwhelming victory is yours through Christ (Romans 8:37).

I will close this section with a powerful Scripture that declares the authority you have in Jesus Christ. I've worded these verses so you can speak and boldly declare them over yourself.

"I will trample upon lions and cobras. I will crush fierce lions and serpents under my feet. The Lord will rescue me because I love Him and he will protect me because I trust in his name. When I call upon Him, he will answer. The Lord will be with me in trouble. He will rescue and honor me. He will reward me with a long life and salvation." Psalm 91:13-16 (New Living Translation).

ANN THOMAS

Possessing the Promise

"**S**ee, the LORD your God has given you the land. Go up and take possession of it as the LORD, the God of your fathers, told you. Do not be afraid; do not be discouraged." Deuteronomy 1:21 (New International Version)

Each year during my younger son's basketball season, we travel to unfamiliar locations for some of his tournaments. When we jump into the SUV, we enter the destination in our trusted GPS and watch as it calculates the distance and estimated time of arrival in seconds. I love my GPS. I don't know what I'd do without it. Obviously, I would have to find an alternative, but would prefer not to.

Back in Biblical days, they probably would have appreciated having a GPS, especially for some of those longer journeys. There is one journey in particular where the GPS would have been useless though – the journey from Egypt to the Promised Land.

Moses and the Israelites set out on a trip that was to last only days, but ended up taking forty years. I can see it now, Moses enters the start and end destination into the GPS, it estimates the amount of days and everyone cheers. This should be a breeze. And then after about two years of going around in circles and passing the same landmarks, someone finally taps Moses on the shoulder and says, "Hey, I think we might be lost."

How in the world does a trip that should have lasted days take forty years? Did they make too many stops along the way? Did they miscalculate the directions? No. They were a totally disobedient and rebellious people. The Promised Land was for those who loved God with all of their hearts. And until they got their hearts right, God didn't allow them to enter into the Promised Land. So they wandered around in the desert for forty long, hot, and dry years. Everybody's trip was delayed, even those who were being obedient.

THE NEW CONSECRATED COCOON

They literally walked around in circles, sinning over and over again, while moaning and groaning about what they didn't have. Philippians 2:14-15 says to do everything without complaining or arguing so that we may become blameless and pure children of God. Why, so we can reflect God's love, goodness, and faithfulness.

God wanted the Israelites to get an attitude adjustment so He could be glorified through them, but instead they insisted on murmuring.

"If you complain, you remain." And remain they did – for forty long and difficult years. Sadly enough, many only heard of the Promised Land because they died before they could possess it.

The Promised Land is described as the land flowing with milk and honey (Exodus 3:8) and represents the fulfillment of God's promises to Abraham and his descendants through Isaac and Jacob. Overall, God's promises included abundant blessings, land or territory that would be theirs, innumerable descendants, the ability to conquer all enemies, and a rich generational inheritance.

I have wonderful news for you today. These blessings were not just for Abraham, they were also for his descendants. Guess who qualifies as a descendant? You and I, and these promises aren't just for Biblical days; they are still alive and well today. Amen?

As you emerge from your time of consecration with greater power, you must grab a hold of these promises. To fulfill your God-given purpose and destiny and to help your loved ones fulfill theirs, you must claim and even fight to regain these promises.

John 10:10 says Satan, the thief invades our lives for the purpose of stealing, killing, and destroying what God intends for us to have. But in Joel 2:25a, God says He will restore or give us back the years the locusts have eaten. Locusts are insects that cause major devastation to vegetation. They appear like a mighty army and destroy everything in their path. And in this passage the locusts are symbolic of an enemy army coming in and stealing years of joy, peace, blessings, etc.

Don't think for a second that Satan will quietly sit by and watch you reclaim what's yours. He will try to tempt you to complain about the hardships of your journey or try to convince you that you are not worthy to possess it. But you must fight for your blessings. You must take what is yours by force. And, sister, you already possess the God-given power and authority to wage war on the enemy's camp and get back what was rightfully yours to begin with.

You are armed with Christ's restorative power and you also have the keys to God's kingdom. These keys give you free and clear access to everything God owns. These keys remove all barriers between Heaven and earth so that whatever you accept or say yes to here on earth will also be done in Heaven. And likewise whatever you say no to or reject on earth will also be rejected in Heaven (Matthew 16:19).

Let's pause here for a moment. Do you understand the power you possess, beloved? God has given you keys to unlock what is purposeful in your life and to lock those things that aren't. You can unlock blessings that have been held up. And lock curses that were released. Lock them up once and for all!

Your keys allow you to secure your rich inheritance. It's yours for the taking! The territory or Promised Land God gave to Abraham thousands of years ago is yours today. You have a Promised Land whether you possess it or not.

Your Promised Land is the place where you stand firm and watch God do what He says He will do. It's the place where miracles happen, petitions are granted, and giants are defeated. Don't be like some of the Israelites and die before you experience the promises God has already set aside for you.

When I emerged from my time of consecration, I faced a giant that had to be put to bed once and for all. It was one thing to say I'm moving forward, but how would I know unless my resolve was tested?

THE NEW CONSECRATED COCOON

I believed in my heart that I had truly forgiven my ex and released him. I regularly spoke blessings over him and lifted him in prayer. However, I knew that one day we would end up at an event (more than likely a basketball game) where we would both need to support our son. And, honestly, I wasn't looking forward to the first time as I knew it would be quite awkward. But this bridge would need to be crossed at some inevitable point.

Seeing him was going to be more than just crossing a bridge; it was going to test my trust in God, my ability to receive and walk in His grace, and selflessly put my own feelings aside for the sake of our son. The giant I had to face was not my ex; it was feelings of fear, inadequacy, and rejection.

It was time to seal my transformation by reclaiming and firmly establishing my territory of faith and confidence in the Lord and standing on the promise of God's unconditional love and my unshakable identity in Him. Like I said, it's one thing to say it to yourself and others; but it's another to walk it out in a real life situation. In the deepest and most secret places of my heart I wanted to please God. I wanted to make Him proud. And I am positive He knew that.

So here I am, a transformed beautiful, powerful, and soaring butterfly who had a caterpillar moment. Ladies, I'm going to let my hair down for a minute. Is that okay? Of course it is. You wouldn't want me to be anything but honest.

One day I did learn my ex was coming to town for one of our son's games. I immediately worried about my appearance. I had not exercised in a while as I was healing from a surgery. I hadn't seen my hair stylists in weeks. I received 24-hour's notice so I couldn't even run and get a decent manicure and pedicure.

Keeping it real...I wanted to look so stunning that he might have looked at me and realized he made a mistake. There, I said it.

But, what have I been talking about throughout this book? Jesus' unconditional love and acceptance, right? My worth is not measured by what my ex thinks of me, or even what my sons think, or anyone else for that matter. My worth was established when Jesus died on the cross for me.

It was time to slay a giant and reclaim my God-given territory – my Promised Land. I was to finally meet, greet, and defeat the giant of inferiority, lack of self-worth, and uncertainty. It was time to reclaim my territory as the daughter of the Most High King. It was time to reclaim my promise of being joint heirs with Christ. It was time to reclaim my inheritance as a descendant of Abraham, Isaac, and Jacob.

That night I began bathing the undesired moment in much prayer. My heart desired a more than cordial relationship with him for the sake of our son. I didn't want to waste years unpacking unhealthy and unproductive feelings that were counterproductive to raising our son in unity.

Ladies, can I tell you that God not only answered my prayers, but He exceeded my expectations that evening. The meeting was very cordial. We had good conversation, but most importantly we enjoyed watching our son play basketball together for the first time in almost two years. And my son was able to look into the bleachers and see his mom and dad at the same game.

That evening I went home and wept at God's goodness. God truly answers prayers. Ladies, God doesn't have favorites. That night He showed me that He loves me, my ex, and my sons all the same. Jesus died for all of us.

That afternoon I stared my supernatural giant in the face, eyeball to eyeball and I won! Ladies, especially those of you who have kids, when war is waged you must confidently step forward and engage the enemy.

Beloved, the battles we don't fight or fail to win today are the wars our kids will have to face tomorrow. I'm setting my sons up to kick the enemy's behind. I'm teaching my sons by example that in Christ we have the victory. Satan tried to come

THE NEW CONSECRATED COCOON

on my turf and rule, but I stepped forward with God's all sufficient grace (empowerment) and claimed my territory.

When you emerge with new power in your wings, butterfly, you too will need to reclaim territory the enemy has taken from you. What territory has he stolen? Has he robbed you of peace, finances, meaningful relationships, or purpose? To reclaim what's yours, you might need to do several things. You might need to break family curses and speak blessings over yourself and your loved ones. You might need to get financial counseling to get your house in order and get out of debt. You might need to establish rules and boundaries in your home that didn't exist before. You might need to break off an ungodly relationship. You might need to take a firm stand on something that might cause you to lose popularity and friends. You might need to rearrange your days so you can get up early in the morning to spend time with God in your secret place. Regardless of what God shows you, it's time!

Reclaiming what the enemy has stolen from you is imperative to moving toward your purpose and destiny. It's time to grab a hold of, possess, step into, reestablish, and reclaim what is rightfully yours and serve notice on Satan that he will not steal from you anymore!

Claim your promises in your Promised Land. God promised He has great plans for you. Plans to prosper you and give you the future you hope for (Jeremiah 29:11). God promises that when you are worn out and are carrying heavy burdens, He will give you rest if you come to Him (Matthew 11:28). He promises that you will always have His peace and that His peace is not like the false peace this world tries to give you (John 14:27). He promises that He will give you power and strength when you are weak and that you will soar high like an eagle (Isaiah 40:29-31).

He promises that nothing or no one can separate you from His unconditional and unyielding love (Romans 8:37-39). He promises that you are more than a conqueror (Romans 8:37). He promises that you can do all things with Christ (Philippians 4:13). He promises that as His child He will always take care of your needs even before you ask (Matthew 6:31-33). He promises that no weapon formed against you shall prosper (Isaiah 54:17). This promise about the weapon forming requires God's grace and faith.

The promise doesn't say the weapon will not form, in fact it will form. But God promises the weapon will not prosper. Trust God when weapons form against you that they will not have the victory. He promises salvation (Romans 10:9) and that you will live with Him in eternity in Heaven (Romans 6:23).

The above doesn't even begin to cover all the promises God makes in the Bible. But I also want to encourage you that there are promises He makes to us individually and uniquely. These are intimate promises we receive when we spend time with Him in our secret place. These promises align with Scripture and often include distinctive strategies that are just for you. When God gives you a promise, receive it and tuck it deep in your heart of faith. Then stand back and watch Him be a God of His word!

I will close this section with a great Scripture that speaks to God's restorative power in our lives. It declares those loved ones will return with hearts ready to serve God and that the wealth and inheritance that is rightfully yours will be brought back to you, all for God's glory. I've worded these verses so you can speak and boldly declare them over yourself.

"I will arise and let my light shine for all to see. For God's glory rises and shines on me. Darkness as black as night covers all the nations of the earth, but the glory of the Lord rises and appears over me. All nations will come to my light; mighty kings will come to see my radiance. I will look and see everyone is coming home. My sons are coming from distant lands and my daughters will be carried home. My eyes will shine and my heart will thrill with joy. For merchants from around the world will come to me. Vast caravans of camels will converge upon me. The people of Sheba will bring gold and frankincense and will come worshiping the Lord. I will accept their offerings and I will make my Temple glorious." Isaiah 60:1-7 (New Living Translation)

THE NEW CONSECRATED COCOON

Divine Positioning

So here we are at the close of our time together, and I am impressed to encourage you to stand firm in the place where God has planted and established you. To soar with power and to possess what God has for you – you must position yourself.

Position yourself to be a woman He can trust and use greatly – a woman after His heart. Remember, a woman after His heart is not one who does a bunch of things. He's looking for obedience. He's looking for a heart that's willing to say "Yes" even before He asks the question. God consistently shows Himself faithful, now He's looking for our faithfulness.

How do you position yourself to be a mighty vessel in God's hands? First, through fervent prayer and intimacy. Beloved, there is nothing you can or should want to do apart from God. Now that you've emerged with new vision, new or renewed purpose, and a grateful heart, spending one-on-one time with God should be the highlight of each day. You should anticipate that time with Him. You should look forward to it with a smile on your face and expectancy in your heart. And if you miss it, there should be a noticeable and nagging void in your day.

Positioning has to do with being in the right place or location to obtain what's needed or intended.

Each day you need strength. You need counsel. You need mercy and grace. You need a reminder of how much God loves you. You need comfort. You need reassurance. If necessary, you need to be warned. You need to be given a battle plan or strategy. With all of this, how can you miss spending time with God? Although He enjoys spending time with you; this time is more for you than it is for Him. Position yourself daily to spend time with the one who loves you beyond what you can imagine.

Reflection

1. Has God done anything wonderful in your life lately?
2. Who have you told about it?
3. When you pray over people, do you really expect God to answer your prayers?
4. What are you doing to exercise your faith muscle?
5. Is your faith in God evident in how you conduct yourself daily (actions, conversations, prayers)?
6. Are there any areas in your life where faith is taking a backseat to doubt or disbelief?
7. God has called you to be a wave-walker, not a wave-watcher. Is there an area of your life where God is calling you to step out of your boat by faith?
8. Do you find yourself murmuring or complaining when things don't go your way?
9. What promise(s) are you waiting for God to fulfill in your life?
10. You have the keys to heaven in your possession. What things are you using your key to lock and unlock?
11. What are you doing to intentionally position yourself as a powerful vessel in God's hands?

"See what I've given you? Safe passage as you walk on snakes and scorpions, and protection from every assault of the Enemy. No one can put a hand on you. All the same, the great triumph is not in your authority over evil, but in God's authority over you and presence with you. Not what you do for God but what God does for you—that's the agenda for rejoicing." Luke 10:19-20 (Message)

THE NEW CONSECRATED COCOON

Going All the Way

If you've trusted me to come this far in the book, it proves you have a hunger and desire to have and be more than you are today. It tells me that you want to live a life of more blessings and you want to walk in your God-given authority and power. It tells me that you seek a deeper intimacy than your husband, kids, parents, and friends can give you. It tells me that you want to impact more lives in a positive way. It tells me you believe you have a purpose that is bigger than what you've seen so far.

I wish I could tell you that you can have all of the above apart from a relationship with Jesus, but I would be lying. Regardless to where you are in your faith walk, God has divinely positioned you for this moment in the book.

Many of you reading this book have not given your heart to Jesus. And there are numerous reasons why. Your view of God and Jesus has been one of religion – be a good person. You feel like having this relationship with Jesus means you must stop being a fun person. You are worried that becoming a Christian means you will lose certain relationships. You are concerned your husband or boyfriend won't understand. You feel like you've done too much bad and so this is only for those who have done good most of their lives. You feel unworthy for the type of love I described that Jesus has for you.

There are so many other reasons I can list, but it all comes down to the following realization. Without Jesus in our heart, we lack power, peace, blessings, protection, and the Godly inheritance He has for us. There isn't a do it yourself book that exists that can give you what I just described. And I will let you in on a secret. Most of the principles quoted and suggested in these types of books are scriptural anyway. They simply conveniently leave out the Bible as their source.

Ladies, happiness comes from God. Peace comes from God. Peace is an inner joy that is not contingent upon your circumstance. There is nothing or no one that can give you that in the midst of a hard trial other than Jesus.

I know you are thinking that becoming a Christian means you lose your freedom. You want your freedom to cuss, have sex with who you want, do whatever you wish to your body, and not have to answer to anyone. However, the most freedom I've experienced is when I said yes to Jesus. Why? Because the closer I get to Him, I realize how much He loves me and then His love is contagious and I'm able to love myself for real. I can truly love myself. And when I love myself I am free to be who I am, not who or what others want me to be. I don't care to cuss. I don't care to sleep around. I don't care to get high. I don't care to be in relationships where people use, abuse, and disrespect me. Now that's freedom!

"Well Ann, I hear what you are saying. But when I say yes to Jesus I will have to give up a lot of things I enjoy and act holy and better than other people." Can I tell you something? That's religion. Jesus didn't die on the cross for religion. I hate to hear people say they are religious. Religion is about rules and punishment.

I'm inviting you to have a relationship with Jesus; a relationship with Jesus. There is a difference. And whatever you think you don't want to give up, you won't miss once you experience His love. It's a TRUE love!

Please don't feel like if you smoke, drink, etc., you can't come to Jesus. One of the most beautiful things about Him is He will meet you right where you are. He doesn't want you to clean up before coming to Him. He wants you to come just as you are. And if you trust Him, He will help you make the changes your heart desires.

When we die, there is only one of two places we will go – Heaven or Hell. There is no in between, and we don't come back as another person or animal (reincarnation). And there is only one way to get to Heaven and that's through Jesus. Some people have a hard time with Jesus being the only way. John 14:6 says that Jesus is the way and the truth. No one can get to his father (God in Heaven) except through Him. Beloved, hasn't He paid enough of a price to earn that right? Hasn't He sacrificed enough to have the privilege of being used by God to populate Heaven?

Consider this. Suppose you get to Heaven and find out that Jesus wasn't the only way – there were other ways? What would you have lost? But what if you get to Hell and find out He was the only way? What will you lose then? You lose the chance to spend eternity in Heaven with Him. You have nothing to lose when you accept Jesus and everything to gain. If you don't accept Jesus you have everything to lose and nothing to gain.

Are you ready to live a life of purpose and destiny? Do you want a blessed marriage? Do you want your kids to have a rich heritage? Do you want to experience a love like you've never experienced before? I invite you to enter into a relationship with Jesus. Below is a prayer that if you say the prayer and believe it in your heart, you will receive salvation. You will begin a relationship with Jesus. Or maybe you asked Jesus into your heart before but you've drifted from Him and back into a life of sin – but you want to re-establish your relationship with him. This prayer is for you too.

Sister, I bless you as you say the prayer on the following page with me.

May God's love and the power of the Holy Spirit come in and flood your heart.

ANN THOMAS

Please Pray With Me

Dear God. Thank you for loving me. Thank you for the chance to have a personal and intimate relationship with you.

Lord, please forgive me for my sins. I know I have hurt you. I confess my need for you. I acknowledge that you died for my sins and I thank you. I realize I am a sinner and that I need your forgiveness. Thank you for forgiving me. And in the same way that you forgive me, right now I forgive all those who have hurt me, used me, or abused me [call out those names right now]. Help me also to forgive myself.

Lord lead me to a church where I can learn more about the Bible and meet authentic people who are trying to grow like I am. Help me to read my Bible and spend time with you daily. Thank you for loving me. I will do my best to serve you in the best way I know how – trusting that you will teach me.

In Jesus name. Amen!

Wow! I'm so excited for you. You've just prayed the most powerful prayer ever! Have you ever had a party thrown in your honor? Well there's one happening right now. Luke 15:7 says Heaven rejoices when one person repents and turns to God. Jesus and the angels are dancing and shouting over the decision you just made.

If you prayed with me, I want to hear from you. Please let me know. Send an email to me so I can rejoice with you. Email address: email@annthomasministry.com

Now, let's take baby steps. Find a Christian at school, work, or in your neighborhood and tell them about your decision. And I pray they rejoice with you like I am rejoicing now in my heart. This is the beginning of the rest of your life. Thank you, Jesus!

THE NEW CONSECRATED COCOON

Thank you for taking this journey with me and I speak blessings of God's grace and favor over your journey. If I don't have a chance to meet you on this side of Heaven, I look forward to seeing your precious face when we hug each other in eternity!

Until then...soar butterfly.

Spread your bold, big, and beautiful wings.

Take flight. Don't look back.

Let the winds of God's grace take you higher than you've ever been.

You were created to soar!

About the Author

Ann Thomas, a powerful and spirit-filled minister, author, speaker, and mentor is the founder of Ann Thomas Ministry – a ministry dedicated to **ENCOURAGING**, **EQUIPPING**, and **EMPOWERING** individuals to boldly pursue their purpose in Christ.

A proud mom of two sons, Ann serves in her local church, ministers in the prisons weekly, and speaks at various events and churches around the world.

Known for her compassion, boldness, and transparency, Ann captures the hearts of men and women of all ages.

Using the Word of God, wisdom, humor and personal experiences, Ann shares Biblical Truth in a way that's easy to understand and is applicable.

Her life-changing book, "The New Consecrated Cocoon – Emerging from Intimate Isolation with Power and Purpose" is a birthing place for revelation, healing, truth, and freedom for those who struggle with issues such as: rejection, disappointment, anger, shame, and loss. Her book is a compelling read that provides powerful insight as to why separation and preparation are required for elevation.

Visit Ann's website to learn more, watch inspirational videos, and invite her to speak at your next event.

www.annthomasministry.com
email@annthomasministry.com

THE NEW CONSECRATED COCOON

A Message from Ann to You

Hi. I would like to thank you so very much for taking this journey with me and allowing the voice of God to speak to your heart.

I originally wrote this book shortly after my divorce was final and here I am almost four years later publishing a new version that is packed with reflective questions and more Scriptures to stir your heart. It is my sincere prayer that you have discovered or re-discovered God's amazing plan for your life.

I have grown sooooooo much in the last number of years. My faith has been challenged in ways I didn't know possible. I've endured challenges and celebrated victories. And I want you to know that the journey with God is STILL more than worth it! Through it all, God has remained faithful!

I had moments when things got tough, but I want to encourage you that you and God has what it takes to overcome. So quitting is never, ever an option!

I would love very much to connect with you and hear how God used this book to provide insight, reveal truth, facilitate healing, and even introduce salvation.

I would like to ask you to please do four things:

1. Leave book review comments on Amazon to let others know why you recommend this book.
2. If this book blessed you, share your copy with others or purchase one and 'gift' it to someone.
3. Send an email to me with a prayer request or testimony (email@annthomasministry.com)
4. Take a moment to connect with me:
   - **Facebook:** AnnThomasMinistry
   - **Twitter:** iamannthomas
   - **Website:** www.annthomasministry.com

Other Books

Paperbacks and eBooks available at www.simplyidealpublishing.com and www.annthomasministry.com

The New Consecrated Cocoon "Reflection Journal" is the perfect companion to this book. The journal includes Scripture inserts, powerful quotes from "The New Consecrated Cocoon," and lined pages, which makes it perfect for expressing your thoughts and prayers. Get your copy today.

Coming soon!
"The Big Push. Birthing Your Spiritual Promise."

Many are spiritually pregnant with a powerful promise from God but are in danger of a spiritual miscarriage due to lack of Godly wisdom, faith, and obedience.

In this 31-day devotional, Ann shows the similarities of a natural and spiritual pregnancy, while providing Godly insight needed to help you deliver a healthy baby (promise).

Powerful 3-Book Prayer Series by Author Willie L. Benton

This Christian fiction series will capture your heart as you experience the power of prayer through the lives of the Jensen family. From the first book, "A Mother's Prayer" to "A Daughter's Prayer" and finally "A Father's Prayer" - you will embark on a journey filled with humor, surprises, powerful messages, and thought-provoking conversations.

Visit **www.simplyidealpublishing.com** to purchase these and other inspirational books.

Simply Ideal Publishing

Mission: Using our combined resources, gifts, talents, education, and experiences, our goal is to Entertain, Edify, Encourage, Enlighten, Equip, and Empower. As a faith-based company, we are committed to building a nation, a people, who are obedient to God by providing distinctive products and unique services. Our hope is to restore unto the rightful owners the rich, godly inheritance that has been stolen, lost, abused, or surrendered.

ANN THOMAS

Made in the USA
Charleston, SC
27 February 2016